# DEER
## A Personal View

# Ian Alcock
### Illustrated by Diana E. Brown

SWAN·HILL
PRESS

First published in the UK in 1996
by Swan Hill Press, an imprint of Airlife Publishing Ltd

**British Library Cataloguing in Publication Data**
  A catalogue record for this book
  is available from the British Library

ISBN 1 85310 575 9

Typeset by Hewer Text Composition Services, Edinburgh
Printed in England by Livesey Ltd, Shrewsbury

# Swan Hill Press
an imprint of Airlife Publishing Ltd
101 Longden Road, Shrewsbury SY3 9EB, England

# Contents

# Chapter 1
# The Enchanted Cottage

The half dozen or so most important decisions affecting my life have been remarkably easy ones for me to make. The three houses that I have bought required no troubled pondering about the possibilities of purchase. I knew instantly that they were what I wanted. Deciding to throw up a good job in the City, at the age of 38, to adopt the precarious living of running a hill farm in the north of Scotland was a decision that I made overnight. The most important decision of all, that of asking Diana to be my wife, was a spontaneous reaction after knowing her for a total of only eight hours, though not consecutively, but over a few weeks. So it was with Meadow Plat Cottage, the first house that I owned, which I purchased shortly before I met Diana.

My parents and I had moved from a house in the country to live in a flat in London when my father was dying of cancer. Shortly after his death my mother developed debilitating arthritis and other problems, and it was not practical to move to the country again from our flat in a large block in a quiet cul-de-sac in west London, much as I hated the claustrophobia of the huge urban environment. My mother's death came shortly before the expiry of the term of the lease on our flat, and I decided that I would move out of London. I looked at a number of houses, learning to translate the glossy terminology of estate agents into more real terms in the process, and becoming depressed at the apparently hopeless prospect of finding somewhere tolerable to live, from which I could commute to my job in the City, yet within my restricted financial limitations. It so happened that I was at home with 'flu on the day that the postman brought the estate agent's brochure for Meadow Plat Cottage. Surrey did not appeal to me, since I regarded it as semi-suburban stockbroker country. I did not know then that it is one of the most wooded of all counties. The particulars and picture of the cottage were not especially inviting, but it had six acres of woodland with the property, and that appealed to me as much as the house.

I did not feel like driving, being ill, but my brother volunteered to take me down to see the place. The lease of the flat was running out and I should soon be under pressure to make a move. The cottage was approached down a rough flint track, really only fit for a Land-Rover, which we negotiated with caution. As we emerged through the edge of the woodland into the little open glade in which the cottage was situated, I knew that this was the place for me. I was not so concerned about the house itself, being a young bachelor, or else I might have been put off by its unusual appearance. It had been a tiny keeper's cottage for a long defunct estate, and the original part was constructed of flint in a style traditional to the area. This had consisted of one reasonable sized room and a small bedroom, and two small rooms in the semi-circular end of the building. Onto this the then present owners had added two bedrooms and a good sized kitchen constructed of cedarwood. There was a very small flowerbed and a small lawn in front of the house, beyond which were some tall conifers and a mixture of hardwoods, beech, ash, oak and sweet chestnut. This was the place for which I had been looking, I decided without hesitation, and in a comparatively short period the place became mine.

Meadow Plat Cottage was situated on the chalk North Downs. From forestry land about half a mile away one could watch with binoculars aeroplanes starting to land at Heathrow Airport to the north. The cottage was surrounded by hundreds of acres of woodland, with an oak wood, containing a scattering of beech trees and hazel at its edges, on one side, and extensive forestry conifer plantations on the other. At that time I did not realise that this area contained a high, and expanding, roe deer population.

The house was situated at one end of a little shallow valley, with the open lawn extending part way along the bottom, whilst in front of the cottage the opposite slope consisted of a mixture of Ponticum rhododendron with some elm and birch scrub, and a few scattered large hardwood trees. Behind the house a path lined by mature maple trees and several huge Corsican pines ran from the back door up a shallow gully in the chalk to a little gate leading out onto what was once the main estate land but now Forestry Commission woodland of varying ages. On the right of the path was scrub of hardwoods and bramble and on the left, extending up the valley, the bank had a clear bottom because of a thick canopy created by a mixture of large yew trees, beech, and a few Scots pines along the edge. The setting of the little cottage, in its clearing in the woods, aptly fitted the name given to it by the owners of the adjacent woodland, as I discovered subsequently, of The Enchanted Cottage, which, in its original entirely flint form,

8

before the wooden additions, must have given a fairy tale impression.

Not long after I moved into the cottage I decided to clear some of the scrub and rhododendron at the front to give more view and make lighter the garden that I proposed to create, and also to clear away some of the tangle at the back to give more view from the main bedroom with its large plate glass windows. This work took some time, but resulted in a clearing of three or four acres in front of the house, dotted with a few mature oak and sweet chestnut trees, and another of about half an acre at the back that was bordered on one side by the maple-lined path and on the other by oak and hazel wood, with a background of several ancient yew trees, behind which stretched a forestry plantation of young beech trees interspersed with conifers.

At that time I was not aware that the surrounding woods were full of roe deer. I knew there were foxes, since I had heard vixens screaming behind the house during the winter, and I had seen badger tracks on the footpaths through the woods below the house on frequent occasions, and had heard noises at night that I presumed were badgers fighting or playing. When spring came the cleared ground began to burst into new life. Large patches of rosebay willowherb appeared and wild raspberries grew in abundance, which I was later to find bore fruit almost as large as cultivated berries, but far tastier. This new growth became an undoubted attraction to deer, apparently roe being especially fond of raspberry leaves and the succulent tops of willowherb plants.

In this woodland setting there was no shortage of wildlife. Indeed the enormous population of grey squirrels, and the large numbers of jays and magpies, were clearly too abundant for the well-being of smaller songbirds. Nevertheless all these creatures had some charm and fascination of their own, and I spent many hours watching them through the windows while they hopped about on the lawn, searched for nuts or beechmast below the trees, or raided the bird table. This latter was situated just outside the large kitchen window, and provided endless amusement, since the kitchen was were I spent much of my time when in the house. As well as four species of tits, the regular visitors to the bird table included nuthatches and both green and greater spotted woodpeckers, amongst a host of other birds.

One day, whilst I was watching the birds feeding on the table, I noticed in the background a roe deer walking slowly down the bank under the yew trees. I was greatly excited. I had seen a few roe previously in different parts of the country but this was my first deer on my own property. I was entranced by its graceful body and delicate movement. I had recently visited East Africa to stay with friends and we had gone on safari around several Game Parks and seen many species of antelope, but even the lovely impala did not compare in gracefulness to this dainty roe doe. It was the start of my interest in deer in earnest.

The doe moved down the bank towards the more open ground at the end of the lawn, and moving into another room I was able to observe her feeding. I watched her for quite some time, before she eventually moved out of sight obscured by thicker undergrowth. This was the first of many roe that we were to watch from the windows of Meadow Plat Cottage, and the enthusiasm fostered by this first sighting subsequently had a marked effect upon my life. Namely, it was this fascination for deer that led to my acquisition of Cashel Dhu, in Sutherland, which itself engendered the notion of abandoning City life, and it was a mutual interest in deer that brought Diana and myself together.

At that time there was a large, and possibly still expanding, roe population and extensive acreages of new tree plantations, mostly conifers but some hardwoods in this area. Many of these young woods were at the ideal age for roe deer habitat, being either reaching the thicket stage for cover, or newly planted and offering plentiful feeding. I often wondered about population estimates, but gave up attempts as hopeless. Even using the impressions of bucks seen in an area, which I felt I could differentiate from one another, and doubling the figures by adding does, suggested a high population. However, I was quite certain that there were many deer that I never saw, simply basing this upon the number of roe bucks that I saw only once and never again. The idea of basing population estimates on counts of droppings or crotties, suggested in desperation by some quasi-scientists these days, would have been laughable. Carrying out such an experiment on the clearings where we watched deer regularly, and so could get some idea of numbers using the area and their habits, would quite clearly have produced absurd results, of little value, from the evidence that we saw on the ground there.

The environment in that part of Surrey seemed to be ideal for roe, except for the absence of water, which did not appear to affect them. I always wondered if the chalk downs perhaps led to improved calcium absorption and therefore better antler growth, but there was no evidence of this really. However, the plantations round the house provided ideal cover; especially since in the early stages these were heavily infested with blackberry in places, and the grassy rides and open patches had a lovely population of downland plants. Bee orchids and fly orchids both grew at the side of rides in a couple of places, and there were large patches of sweetly-scented butterfly orchids, now probably shaded out by the grown up conifers alas. Twayblades and helleborines grew in the young woods too, and a whole collection of other flowers. Dandelions grew luxuriantly, and I recall a splendid picture of a doe standing chewing an enormous leaf that stuck out of her mouth as she chewed her way up it. Adjacent to the large area of conifer plantings were extensive woods of oak and beech, bordered by hazel and elderberry and carpeted with bluebells in the spring. Around and between these were fields of barley, edged by hawthorn and occasional spindle trees. The disturbance from humans then was not great, and most of the locals seemed to be blissfully unaware that there were deer in the area at all. Only when they had problems with gardens being raided did the subject even occur to them. At that time there were almost no rabbits in the area, although before we left the south just a few had started to appear in places here and there, but in sufficiently small numbers to be a subject of comment if we saw them. Young people these days would have difficulty in visualising what the countryside was like in the 1950s when myxomatosis was introduced, and within two years had wiped out over 90 per cent of the rabbit population, removing it completely in some places. The result was that areas then no longer grazed by rabbits produced lush growth, which was ideal for the expanding roe population.

Our little cottage, situated half a mile off the road in a small valley in the midst of these woods, provided superb opportunities for watch-

ing and studying roe deer. More so, too, because of the numbers and variety of the animals. One season we reckoned to have seen fourteen different individuals within a hundred and fifty yards of the house. The regulars must have lived quite close to us, because apparently they became used to our usual activities and noises and seemed to be little disturbed by these. They did little more than look up at the daily arrival of the postman in the mornings and our conversations with him, or with the arrival of visitors in other vehicles, and the accompanying barking of the dogs. If they saw our movements in the house or studio through the large windows they did not seem to be ill at ease as a result.

Whilst many people sit inanely, even addictively, gawping at television, we feel privileged, in a way, to be able to watch real wildlife scenes outside our windows. To many people windows are a source of light and little more, but to us they have always been a means of observing what is happening outside. We almost never draw curtains across the windows, except rarely on particularly foul winter nights in a snowstorm or some such to give an illusion of cosiness. On wakening in daylight we like to see what is going on outside in the countryside around us, and as dawn breaks we enjoy watching the first robin visiting the bird table, or seeing the deer feeding beneath the chestnut tree. We have no near neighbours, and there is nobody to peer into the house from outside, so curtains serve little purpose for us, but indeed somehow function as a symbolic severance with the fascinating life going on outside. We have some friends who live in grand houses, and sometimes we envy their large kitchens, with plenty of room to move about and space to put things; but we do so only briefly. In the days when their houses were built the kitchen was the domain of domestic staff, and the role or amenity of these did not include looking out of the window. The result was that their large kitchens have no nice view; yet in these days without domestic staff such friends spend much time in their kitchens with their gloomy outlook. Our little houses, on the other hand, have had windows that make washing up, or kitchen chores, light work as a result of the entertainment derived from watching the wildlife outside.

The bird table at Meadow Plat was just outside a large window in front of the kitchen sink, and throughout daylight hours there was constant activity there with a stream of bird visitors, and occasional rather unwelcome marauding grey squirrels. Here in the north-east of Scotland we look out from the kitchen immediately onto a hayfield, and throughout the spring and summer there is constant ornithological activity. Early in spring a pair of oystercatchers take up residence, often accompanied by visiting green plovers and curlews, all marching about probing the ground for earthworms. As the young clover leaves start to grow, woodpigeons come to feed on these abundant rich swards. To many garden owners woodpigeons are a pest that destroy their brassica plants, and farmers with vulnerable crops dislike them as a result of their depredations upon these. Yet, when one is able to watch these birds quietly strutting about in a blue-grey flock filling their crops to bulging with young clover leaves, just a few yards outside the window, one is able to appreciate what beautiful clean looking birds they are with their pink glossy breasts and flashes of white on their necks. As the spring progresses into summer dandelions grow in profusion in the unsprayed field, and as these in turn seed, the plant heads provide a great attraction to seed-eating birds. We can stand at the window and watch large flocks of linnets, mixed with a few greenfinches and goldfinches, feeding busily on the dandelion seeds, fluttering from one plant to another, and, as the grass grows tall, disappearing from view temporarily into the crop, and then from time to time in unison the whole flock, or sometimes only part of it, flitting up to sit on the electricity wire stretched overhead as a convenient perch.

In spring, here in north-east Scotland, we often see deer emerging to feed on the fields of new grass; mostly roe deer, but occasionally a red deer makes a brief appearance. One season a young roe buck took up residence in the hay field outside the kitchen window when the grass was tall. A doe frequented an adjacent field, but only once did we glimpse them together. We often saw the little buck, who usually

attracted our attention by shaking his head or flicking his ears, pestered by flies. He was easier to see from an upstairs window, for the long grass hid most of him, and when he lay down he was completely invisible. Often we saw no sign of a deer, but we knew that he was there because when he reappeared it was mostly in the same part of the field, and there was no reason for him to leave it until the time came for it to be cut, of course. Another season a doe took up residence in a tiny shelterbelt behind the house and her kid was born there. We saw them regularly throughout the summer. The first time was when I spotted the doe from our landing window. She was crossing the little hay field outside, and I noticed the clearly very new kid walking rather feebly behind. When the doe came to the fence dividing that field from the adjacent one I was astonished, and rather annoyed at her apparent stupidity, to see her jump the fence, knowing that this was sheep netting and the kid could not get through this. The doe turned and waited for her kid, walking back towards the fence a couple of paces. I thought that she had changed her mind and was going to jump back again, when, to my amazement, I saw the kid through the fence and moving towards her.

The following morning I was walking the dogs outside a paddock containing our own tame red deer hind and her week-old calf. The hind was running alongside the fence, as is her custom, keeping a wary eye on the dogs, which she chases if given the chance. Suddenly one of my vizslas pointed in the long herbage on the other side of the farm road, and to my amazement I saw a red deer calf lying a couple of feet in front of his nose. I quickly noted the large ear tag with which I had marked our hind's calf, as hopeful protection for later should he move off the farm and become a target for a local keeper or stalker. Fortunately I was able to grab the calf as he lay and carry him across the road to the paddock and return him to his mother. I puzzled as to how he could possibly have got out, and concluded that since the fence is only a normal Rylock stock fence he must have jumped this even at that age. The hind has never jumped it, to our knowledge, though obviously she could do so with ease. That evening I was relating these incidences to a friend who had worked on a deer farm, and who coincidentally had telephoned us. He told me that on the deer farm they had much trouble with young red deer calves getting through Rylock netting stock fence and that they had to reinforce this with rabbit netting all the way around to avoid calves getting out. This explained how our calf had escaped and I learned not only that a red deer calf can get through the Rylock stock fence netting but that a roe kid can manage to squeeze through sheep netting.

14

On another occasion I watched a buck running a doe at the time of the rut and then mounting her, in the middle of the day, in a field of turnips behind the farm buildings, which we were just able to see from the back windows of the house. I had not seen these animals there before, nor did so again. I have seen it written that roe have rutting rings that are used regularly and even from season to season, but my personal experience leads me to view this as nonsense. Some herd deer, such as red and fallow, may well favour areas as suitable rutting stands because of the terrain, but rutting rings made by roe deer that I have found both in the south of England and in the north-east of Scotland have not shown any sign of use in a following season. This is doubtless because they have been situated in areas of changing habitat where trees, bushes and grass have grown up since the previous season and altered the immediate environment. So far as I have ascertained, roe rutting rings mostly occur in thickish cover. In more open country, or in mature woods with little undercover, the buck chases the doe round and about, often over quite a distance. I suspect that in thicker cover the buck chases the doe round and round, often around some object such as a tree stump or a bush, and keeps her going in a circle or figure of eight pattern, or maybe she leads him on rather than the buck driving her, to avoid losing contact and to maintain proximity, which is probably an important part of the mechanism of hormonal stimulation associated with mating.

The environment outside Meadow Plat Cottage in Surrey was a quite different one from north-east Scotland, being a clearing in the woods, and although we saw a roe chasing another occasionally in temporary aggression, mostly we were able to watch roe behaving in a more leisurely manner. Sometimes deer, especially does, would spend long periods in the clearing, feeding and resting. Sometimes the deer would lie down quietly to chew the cud, or to snooze in the sun, or lie under the shelter of a yew tree on the bank outside the kitchen window in less clement weather. We have also watched a doe clearly sleeping on her feet, as horses do. Often we watched does suckling and grooming their kids in summer and, although at times it is difficult to bear in mind just how small these animals are, we never failed to be fascinated and entranced at the daintiness and delicate movement of the graceful little roe deer. The roe were more frequent or more obvious visitors to our clearings in the summer than the winter, probably owing to the better food availability then, but perhaps because the deer seem to become rather more crepuscular, or even nocturnal, when the days are shorter and colder.

Identifying, and judging the ages of, roe deer is not a precise art. Some people claim to be able to judge ages by the look of a roe buck's antlers, but this is not a reliable guide. Old bucks tend to have coronets that droop more to the outside perhaps, and may have stockier and more worn looking antlers, if one can use such a description, but the size of antlers may be little guide in itself to the age of the beast. Whilst a young buck may have small antlers, or spikes not even up to its ear length, occasionally one sees a beast with such spikes that appears not to be a yearling animal. Moreover, ear lengths in roe can vary, and judging antler length against these, as inevitably one does, can produce a very different assessment if the ears of the deer happen to be 150 cms (6 inches) long rather than only 125 cms (5 inches). I have always felt that the best assessment of age is from seeing the animal moving about and observing its stance, the way it carries its head, and the way it walks and behaves, as well as its general appearance. One forms an impression as to whether the animal is young, say a yearling or perhaps a two-year old, or middle-aged, which might mean up to four or five years of age, or an old beast of say six or seven. How one arrives at such an impression, often formed quickly, is difficult to define precisely, because it relies upon the judgement of a number of imprecise factors, but it is something that one learns after watching a good many deer. In the same way a stock farmer learns instinctively to recognise lambs, gimmers and old ewes in a flock of sheep, or young and old cattle, whereas to many people a flock of sheep consists of simply sheep that are difficult to distinguish from each other. In the same way one forms an opinion as to the age of fellow humans. The judgement is not always correct, but mostly one can differentiate between a teenager and a pensioner, and probably guess ages in the twenties, thirties, forties and fifties categories with reasonable accuracy. So one forms a comparative opinion of the likely age of deer.

Undoubtedly general behavioural appearance is the most reliable guide to ageing a deer, and with experience one can form a confident impression that even a distant speck is a buck or a doe, or a young or old beast, even before closer examination with a pair of binoculars or telescope. However, I am not really able to explain satisfactorily just how one forms this impression. Very often an older buck is more wary than a young one, and moves more stealthily. Yet he may also move more purposefully and aggressively if he sees another deer. Watching the way the animal emerges into the open out into a clearing or field edge may give a guide to his wary behaviour, and the older buck will remain watchful when feeding, both for other deer and for potential danger. With the experience of seeing and watching roe one soon learns to recognise that the mature animal is more stockily built, and generally gives the appearance of maturity lacking in a young deer, whereas an old buck tends to carry his head and neck lower when he walks, rather like some old humans. One can also form a fairly reliable opinion as to the age of a roe buck by his face. There is a theory that the coloration of his face indicates age, but this is not a reliable factor, though it may well help to form an accurate overall impression. One theory is that a two-year-old buck has a whitish patch just above his nose, which is absent in a yearling, that gradually merges into other coloration and disappears after the beast has passed the age of three. Whilst this may be the case with some roe, I do not accept that it is a reliable guide but merely something that might be borne in mind as a possibility. In the same way that a general greying of the face does not necessarily equate with age. The facial coloration does undoubtedly help to create the expression of the animal however, and this is often a good guide to ageing the beast. A middle-aged, fully mature, in his prime roe buck, especially when disturbed, can look almost aggressive with suspicious concentration upon whatever catches his attention, quite different from the youthful inquisitiveness shown by a young buck.

These points are difficult to illustrate in words, and the surest way of recognising the differences is to be able to see animals of various ages together. These differential factors are less easy to see when the roe are in their winter coats, which gives all the deer a plumper appearance and less contrasting facial markings, though the experienced deer watcher can still note the more aggressive and determined demeanour of a mature buck. With the older bucks shedding their antlers earlier in the winter, the new growth is likely to be at a more advanced stage than that of a younger deer, and consequently he will also shed the velvet from these earlier in the spring. On the other hand, the older animals tend to change their coats last, and an old beast may still have some straggly grey patches in his new summer coat when the younger ones are sleek and red.

The ageing of roe does follows much the same sort of lines, although in this case there are no antlers to guide, or mislead, the observer. Of course there are no antlers either on a buck that has newly shed these and not yet started growing new ones, and so in the early part of winter one may need to check the sex of the deer by looking for the prominent genital tush, or tuft of hairs, on the belly of the buck, or the equally prominent tush of the female, which resembles a readily seen little tail, only placed rather low down on her backside. From a back view this tush accentuates the heart-shaped rump patch of a roe doe, which is readily distinguishable from the kidney-shaped patch of a buck in winter. A yearling doe is quite easy to differentiate from an older one in winter coat by its obviously youthful face, but it is not so easy to age mature does. In summer the difference is more discernible because the deeper body of an old doe is clear as the seasons of carrying kids make their mark. A heavily pregnant doe in spring is easy to spot, and later one can often notice a significant udder in a milking doe and know that she has a kid or kids somewhere, even if they are not with her.

Of course there are always rare exceptions to the guidelines, which present the watcher with a puzzle. Diana spent some time watching and sketching a young roe one morning in summer and was convinced this was a buck, even though looking through binoculars did not reveal any sign of antlers on his head, despite his being quite close. Eventually he confirmed his sex by urinating and it appeared that she was watching a roe hummel (a hummel is the name for an antler-less male deer, perhaps derived from the word humble). I would expect that a roe buck that still had antlers in velvet in late June either had something wrong with it or was a bad doer. Yet the young buck that we watched regularly in the hayfield behind our house in Scotland between 8 July and 28 July one summer appeared to me to be in good condition and of good body size so far as I could tell from observation at quite close range. Nevertheless, he carried on his head only two velvet bumps, which were not easy to discern at some angles. Why he did not have antlers in hard horn, albeit small spikes, I do not know.

19

There are very rare examples of roe does having antlers. This may result from damage to its head and the site where pedicles would have been in a male, or because of an alteration in hormonal balance, as occurs in poultry occasionally, and even rarely in humans. However, it is not unusual to find bony growths like small pedicles on the heads of very old does. I suppose that, again, this is occasioned by hormonal influence, rather in the same way that some elderly female humans develop a degree of hirsuteness upon occasion.

Some people reckon to differentiate not only bucks from does but also animals of different ages by the tone of their bark. It is quite possible that my hearing is defective in some way, but personally I have never been able to draw either distinction, and as far as I am concerned I am quite unable to identify the sex of a deer, nor to estimate its age grouping, by means of listening to its bark despite watching them doing so on many occasions. I believe that the voices of deer vary with individual animals just as with those of sheep or cattle.

Studying deer and trying to learn about them and understand their ways a little better has always interested us, and increasingly one is struck by the behavioural similarities between all animals in many aspects. Although roe deer have very small tails, which the casual observer might not notice, this becomes obvious when the animal raises it. This it does when it defecates of course, as do all animals with tails, and it also may do so when aroused by either concern or anger, or sometimes when stretching after rising from a session of sleeping or lying chewing the cud. If someone walks through a field of cattle or sheep, very often animals disturbed by the proximity of the person, especially a stranger, but not alarmed, urinate or defecate. They also do so noticeably if driven, and one sees this particularly where the animals are herded along a road for instance. Deer exhibit precisely the same proclivity. Watching a roe deer that is mildly disturbed or disquieted, but not alarmed, one can see that very often the animal will walk a few steps rather stiffly and then pee, or sometimes defecate. If a little more worried the animal may flare up its rump patch by erecting the white or paler hairs. Sometimes it does so temporarily, if its moment of disquiet passes, and resumes normality, but if the deer is really alarmed it will flare up its white or buff coloured backside and bounce off with the bobbing white bottom acting as a warning for other deer that might see this.

# Chapter 2
# The Greening Beeches

Spring is an exciting time of the year. The new growth of plants and fresh life emerging everywhere inspire enthusiasm and expectation of better things to come, a new clean start and fresh opportunities. The renewed vigour of the countryside, and the promise of warm sunshine and longer days, provoke the feeling of waking well rested after the long winter. The birds in the garden and woods are busy about the important task of nesting, and the bird table no longer attracts many of them, for there is an increasing abundance of natural food available. Only the audacious squirrels still visit regularly in search of peanuts or scraps of food.

It has always intrigued me how certain trees sprout green shoots and leaves long before others of the same species, even those growing beside them. Moreover, certain branches on some of these trees show green before the remainder of the tree. I suppose that a combination of factors help to make these precocious branches show forward growth. Perhaps shelter, or better exposure to sunlight, or a root system nearer water, or some mineral more available in the ground, or some other factor stimulates the tree into earlier growth. Whatever it is, I was always intrigued by the way that certain lower branches of one large mature beech tree, lining the bank outside the kitchen window, always showed green leaves some days before the rest of the tree or the other beeches adjacent to it. In the spring I watched eagerly each day for this sign of growth and the indication that soon the bank would be covered in the pale green of spring.

Some years ago I visited Australia on a business trip. In the middle of the trip I took a break for a few days to camp in the bush, a large area of eucalyptus forest with a few odd patches of tea trees and others in damp hollows, but mostly just gums. We were hoping to see Sambar deer, originally imported to that country and now living wild in the forests. I asked the companions that took me there about the seasons and the growth of the trees, and it seemed strange to me to have only wet and dry seasons without spring and autumn. On the return journey the plane stopped briefly in Germany and we disembarked temporarily. I vividly recall standing in the doorway of the airport on a crisp sunny morning in early spring, admiring blossom on a tree and thinking that I could not live happily anywhere that did not experience the invigorating spring of the northern hemisphere and the beautiful, if somewhat melancholy autumnal passing of the season, with the gathering of the harvest ready for winter.

The large area of ground that we cleared on the bank in front of the Surrey cottage, relieved from the canopy and heavy shade of rhododendron and scrub, sprouted new plant life all over, and willowherb, raspberry and bramble sprang up. This new succulent growth was an attraction to the deer from the neighbouring woods, and I did my best to encourage this. I purchased an ancient tractor and a forage harvester on its last legs from an agricultural dealer, and I used these to top the herbage in the clearing each year. This effectively kept it mown at about ankle or calf height, but left patches of raspberry and blackberry dotted about, partly as food and shelter for the deer and partly so that we could benefit from the fruit in due course. When Diana's studio at the back of the house was built, overlooking the small clearing but not obscuring the view from our bedroom window, I planted a few conifer seedlings at the end of this in the knowledge that these were likely to be frayed by roe bucks. I chose Lodgepole pine, Thuya and others which I felt would attract the deer! At the end of the lawn in front of the house I planted shrub roses, which I hoped would grow vigorously enough not to be destroyed by the roe but would be attractive to the deer, knowing that they liked to eat the flowers and buds of roses! In fact these were not very successful for their main objective, since the deer seemed to prefer other plants.

In the spring most of the deer we watched seemed to be does. There were bucks in evidence, and we often saw these, for, unlike the area of north-east Scotland where we now live, the sexes in that part of

England seemed to be evenly matched, with apparently as many bucks in the area as does. However, at this time of year, there is pressure on the does to optimise their food intake, with embryos growing and lactation soon to make demands upon the female. Most does there seemed to have twin kids. Singles were comparatively unusual, and triplets more so, although not especially uncommon. We would see does heavy in kid in early spring eagerly feeding upon the new growth to replenish their condition after the winter and respond to the demands made upon their bodies by their rapidly growing foetuses. In early spring the roe does we saw in the clearing were generally accompanied by their kids of the previous year, now almost yearlings. Whether the doe actually chased these away before her time came to have her new kids, or whether they drifted away spontaneously, as young at that stage of life are wont to do, I am not sure. Certainly occasionally one saw a doe chase off a younger beast for a short distance, but roe are basically solitary and not herd animals in summer, and doubtless the tendency was to part company from the parent and siblings, especially in the case of the yearling bucks. We often saw young bucks, probably siblings, wandering about feeding together for a few days in spring after they had parted company with the doe, but soon they disappeared, presumably shortly to split up and go their own ways. Most yearling bucks in that area of good feeding and amenable climate carried six point antlers, and those with less we regarded as of poor quality. In that part of Surrey the roe antlers tended to conform to a general type of appearance, being rather narrow in shape and quite heavily pearled, though there were exceptions.

In years of watching deer, and dealing with livestock generally, I have learned that it is dangerous to be dogmatic. Animals are almost as varied and idiosyncratic as humans in many respects. One of the great problems of watching wild deer is the difficulty, and indeed impossibility in almost all cases, of positive identification. Even Diana, who, with an artist's eye and perception is able to recognise facial characteristics in animals that I am unable to discern, found distinction between roe does unreliable, and often impossible. Because of this we could never be sure in most cases whether the deer we were watching were regulars or not. Occasional individuals had specific marks that ensured identification, however. A doe that we saw on occasion one season had a scar on her side at the back, caused by an aggressive buck perhaps, or maybe a barbed wire fence, and we were able to distinguish her by this mark. Another doe, whom we also saw for only one season, appeared to be blind in one eye. Neither of these

animals were particularly regular in appearance, and we saw them only for a brief period, which once again raised doubts about the regularity of deer behaviour over any significant length of time.

One of the great differences between watching deer from the windows of one's home and going deer watching in the woods, or sitting up high seats, is that from the house one is constantly watching the same area. Even were one to visit a high seat or vantage point in a wood with great regularity, it is highly unlikely that one could ever do so with the frequency and consistency of looking out of the window of one's house. Thus a house situated in a clearing of a wood provides a unique vantage point for studying deer in that particular place over a long period and in varying conditions. One of the things that we have learned about roe, and woodland red deer too, is that they are not consistent in behaviour. Some people say that deer always follow the same paths and even the same pattern of behaviour, such that one can almost know where a roe buck will be at a certain time. That is not our experience. Without doubt, deer have certain paths which they follow through a wood. In a similar way sheep have definite paths, even in open grass fields, when moving from one part of the field to another, to the extent that these paths become not only visible to the human eye, but actually quite worn tracks. What determines the specific route of these paths is difficult to perceive, but they may simply result from one animal walking somewhat haphazardly in a general direction, and later beasts scenting and thus following the route. When one is walking in the vicinity of such deer or sheep paths one often finds oneself following them instinctively. Perhaps they follow the optimum route, even if not straight. Deer certainly have well formed paths in the woods, often following man-made tracks, and they tend to use the same crossing points when negotiating fences or other obstacles.

There can be little doubt that two factors governing the movements and feeding places of undisturbed deer are weather and food supply. If some particular food source attracts deer they will frequent this whilst

24

it is at the appropriate stage of attraction or whatever. However, their approach to feed, times of feeding and place of feeding may well be dictated by the weather to a great degree. Moreover, habitat undoubtedly has a definite bearing on roe behaviour, and animals living in a large area of dense woodland clearly differ in habit from beasts living in smaller areas of cover in open country or those living out on the open hill. My observations in the clearings around our Surrey cottage relate to roe deer living in a large area of woodland, and in the particular habitat in which I observed them. The behaviour, and indeed appearance, of roe deer in north-east Scotland differs noticeably from those in the south. For instance, most roe in north-east Scotland have white rump patches even in unflared summer coat, whereas in many areas in the south their backsides are not similarly white in summer but often more of a pale buff colour that is much less readily detectable, and barely noticeable unless the rump is flared in alarm. Nevertheless, in both places, our impression is that their behaviour is not routine or conforming to any consistent or detectable pattern. Where deer have a plentiful supply of food, little disturbance and favourable weather conditions, they are able to feed and rest as they choose, and their movements may be comparatively haphazard, or even eclectic. Where the deer are subjected to disturbance their feeding patterns may necessarily be restricted to times when they can feed quietly and they may tend to more crepuscular activity or even become nocturnal.

Without being able to identify an individual roe deer positively, by means of identification marks or whatever, it is difficult to form an opinion as to whether one is viewing the same deer regularly or not. Bucks are easier to identify, of course, by reason of the pattern of their antlers. These often give a good guide, but one has always to bear in mind the possibility of there being another buck, perhaps a sibling, in the same locality with similar antlers. Even bucks with apparently unusual or deformed antlers can have doubles, as has been proved on occasions. However, it is a reasonable supposition that the same deer seen in the same area on consecutive days is the same beast. In the spring we used to see does that we assumed to be regular visitors, identified by the accompaniment of their yearling offspring. A doe with twin young bucks with well formed antlers, or a doe with perhaps only a single last year's doe kid were likely to be the same deer if seen successively over a period, especially if these fed in view of each other in different parts of the clearing without any apparent unease at the presence of the other, and therefore presumably used to one another. Roe, and indeed all deer, are very conscious of the presence of strange deer, and one can watch them eyeing approaching animals warily. Sometimes they apparently recognise the new arrival and tolerate it and resume feeding. At other times, depending upon their own standing with regard to dominance or age, they will nervously start to retreat and vanish from the clearing, or else advance aggressively towards the newcomer. Almost always these behavioural postures have the desired effect and actual confrontation is avoided, with the apparently subordinate beast either retiring from view or remaining at a distance from the dominant animal.

In spring there tends to be a movement of deer in most areas. This is partly as a result of the availability of food supplies, such as in the clearings around our house, where the openness to sunlight encouraged earlier growth of many plants than in the surrounding woods and so attracted deer from the woodland to feed and not simply those that might live in or adjacent to the clearings. Spring movement is also caused by the drifting away, or the chasing away, of yearling animals from groups, with roe once again becoming solitary creatures; the does settling to establish new home ground in which to have their kids and raise these through the summer, and the bucks to establish their so-called territories and space themselves out to avoid close proximity with one another. This movement, and almost a resettling of the deer population, was apparent to us watching the roe from our house; though, as happens when one enquires closely into these subjects, each facet of behaviour observed raised many more questions to which the obtaining of the answers seemed impossible. I remember one year when we had a doe that fed regularly just beyond the end of the lawn accompanied by two young bucks, which were her kids of the previous year. Both of these yearling bucks had particularly attractive six point antlers, such as would have been classified as good heads in the part of Scotland where we now live. The young bucks were difficult to tell apart and their antlers were quite similar, having a nice shape with a pretty curve to the main beam, unlike most of the Surrey bucks that tended to have rather straight, narrow antlers. As spring progressed these bucks disappeared, though the doe, or rather a doe that we presumed to be the same animal, continued to visit the clearing at various times of the day. Although I spent a good deal of time walking in the adjoining woods and watching deer, I never saw these young bucks again, and I often wondered where they went. One simply had no idea whether they took up residence in thick conifer plantations in the neighbourhood and remained unseen, or whether they wandered, perhaps considerable distances, in search of quiet quarters where they could spend the summer undisturbed by humans or other deer.

This lack of certain identification of deer is frustrating. A study has been carried out on an estate at Kalø in Denmark, where deer have been trapped and numbered collars put on them and the roe subsequently studied over a long period of years. A few roe have also been caught and collared on an estate in the south of England. A good deal has been learned from this research, often confounding previously held ideas. However, anybody who has studied deer in different areas becomes aware of the differences between them in various habitats and parts of the country, and is therefore reluctant to apply dogmatically the results recorded in one area to another, without some questioning. The movement and dispersal of young deer may well depend upon not only habitat and population levels of resident animals, and human disturbance, but also be affected by the idiosyncratic behaviour of the deer themselves. Just as some red deer stags have been recorded as wandering considerable distances, especially at rutting time, so roe bucks may sometimes travel equally long distances for all we know.

On many occasions we saw roe bucks, especially in spring time, that we never saw again. Sometimes we might see a buck for a day or two and then no more. At other times we might see a buck only once as he passed through. Whilst one cannot be sure that a beast with recognisable antlers does not have a double with similar antlers nearby, nor can one expect to see that buck with similar antlers the following season, one can ascertain whether or not one sees again that season any buck with antlers of similar shape. There is no such guide to identification with does, and one can only seek to identify beasts of differing age groups. In spring the does will not have settled in their chosen summer areas until near the time for giving birth to their kids.

In early spring, when the new leaves and flower buds begin to appear and the deer are eager to feed on the fresh young growth, the roe are more tolerant of the presence of other deer. In some areas, particularly in more open country, roe often join up into mixed family groups during the winter, and a number of beasts of different ages and sex can be seen feeding together in fields. Solitary proclivities seem to be forgotten during the winter, and in early spring this may still be apparent to some extent, with priority clearly given to availing themselves of the newly emerged supply of nutritious spring food. As the urge to feed lessens somewhat as life in that respect becomes easier for the deer, and doubtless hormonal activity changes behaviour and priorities, so, as spring progresses into summer, the roe become less tolerant of the presence of others of their kind. Although some people interpret this as entirely as what is described as territorial behaviour, there is doubtless a mutual feeling of discomfort when roe are aware of the presence of others in close proximity, as is the case with most solitary creatures, and so they endeavour to avoid close contact.

Roe of both sexes certainly mark out territories in spring, with the buck behaviour in this respect being more obvious by the fraying of trees and saplings with their antlers, and both sexes making scrapes at the base of small trees or bushes. However, just how much of this behaviour is specifically indicating or delineating defended territory and how much is anthropomorphically interpreted as such is open to debate. If one watches the behaviour of other male animals one appreciates that in one way or another they all tend to demonstrate their maleness in differing ways, whether provoked by the presence of other males or not. A bull, or even a cow, put into a field with a sandy bank or large rabbit burrows, often seems to enjoy butting and scraping the earth with its head in a sort of trial of strength or flexing of its neck muscles, and will scrape and paw loose soil with its hooves, completely without provocation from any possible competitor. Male

cattle and sheep, especially young adults or adolescents, regularly spar with one another, particularly in the evenings around dusk, in a form of horseplay. Indeed such is far from uncommon in humans. I have often watched roe bucks fraying young trees and saplings, and also stags of varying ages fraying trees and bushes. If one sees a roe buck walking apparently purposefully around an area, wiping his facial glands on a twig from time to time or stopping to fray briefly a couple of times before walking on in a determined manner, the animals behaviour certainly suggests the deliberate patrolling and marking out of a territory. However, when one sees a buck or stag, especially a young beast, fraying hard a sapling or tree branch almost as if fighting it, occasionally jumping round to the opposite side, and virtually destroying the object of its attack, one certainly gets the impression that this fraying is a type of horseplay, demonstrating its male aggressiveness and putting it to mock use, without any competitor necessarily in mind. When a buck has gone down a small row of trees fraying each one, even over a matter of a few days, this would seem to me to be more likely to be motivated by such tendencies, perhaps precipitated or accentuated by the sappy smell of freshly frayed tree rather than by territorial marking.

The spring growth of foliage has a high water constituent, and the early flush of new herbage tends to have a lower mineral or trace element content as a result of the rapid growth than that growing later. In agriculture this situation can lead to problems, and, where grass is heavily fertilised to produce a flush of early growth, deficiencies of minerals in the metabolisms of cattle and sheep can occur. One of the more common of such problems is hypomagnesaemia or magnesium deficiency, which causes a significant number of deaths in cattle each year. Some trace elements, including magnesium, are not stored in the animal's body, and so it needs to ingest its requirement daily, which presents no problem with normal feeding. However, in the spring with the lush growth, the intake of herbage may be high, but the actual amount of nutrients, as opposed to water, may be low. This can be seen readily in the scouring of cattle and sheep on new spring grass. The same applies to deer, and observation can show roe droppings to be considerably looser and lighter coloured than normal, and on occasion of almost cow-like consistency. I rarely found evidence of dead roe in Surrey, but with abundant thick cover, and a high scavenging fox population, this does not necessarily mean that there were no spring deaths among roe, although the generally more amenable environment leads one to think that the occurrence was not significant. In the north-east of Scotland, and in many other areas, it is normal to find one or two roe carcasses in spring, particularly those of yearlings, and in hill country it is in May that many deaths occur amongst red deer. I suspect that a good many of these deaths result from gorging upon lush spring growth at a time when their body conditions are low after a hard winter, and mineral deficiencies in the succulent food supply may well be the specific cause, although other problems such as liver fluke are probably important.

The water content of foliage must have a significant influence upon roe generally. Meadow Plat Cottage is situated on the top of the North Downs, and the higher ground on which our property lay was basically entirely chalk. There was a small disused well behind the house, but this was a brick constructed one, that may have relied to a large extent on the collection of rainwater from the roof of the cottage or to the collection of seepage. However, I never fully investigated this, and kept the beautifully made, quite large diameter construction carefully sealed to avoid animals, including my dogs, falling into it. The area of woodland that I frequented in my deer watching around the house extended to perhaps two thousand acres, and to my knowledge the only water supply throughout this area was a small, rather overgrown dew pond in the centre of it. This pond was quite ancient, being marked on old maps, and always contained water. I presume that it was a dew pond, since it was on the top rather than the bottom of the hill, and had no visible water source. Its construction and efficacy always intrigued me, and being circular I presume that it was man-made. However, I was not prepared to investigate by digging, or whatever, for fear of spoiling it. Though I might see occasional roe tracks around this pond, I never saw evidence of deer actually using it as a source from which to drink, nor indeed regular tracks of other animals such as the many foxes and badgers that inhabited the vicinity. I have always wondered about the drinking habits of these animals, particularly those of foxes and badgers, although the latter could undoubtedly obtain a good deal of moisture from food such as wild hyacinth or bluebell bulbs, and probably earthworms offered a reasonably succulent supply too. Cattle drink quite large quantities of water and drink regularly. They therefore require access to a good water supply, although in years past it was the custom in some parts of the country to feed cattle tied up for the winter in standings in byres with turnips as their only moisture source. This is now illegal and a proper water supply is correctly required by law. However, most of the farm buildings in the area where we now live, in which cattle were housed for the winter, and in which many bullocks were fattened to a high level over that period, had no running water at all, and the moisture for the requirement of the animals was apparently entirely derived from root crops fed to them for the purpose.

Sheep drink quite regularly from water sources, but not to the same degree as cattle, and this can be demonstrated both by the lack of sheep tracks to streams or other water supplies in sheep country, and the drier consistency of their droppings. The probability of the water intake by drinking being significantly lower in deer is indicated by the quite hard consistency of their droppings, especially that of roe pellets. Although we used to see roe from our windows at all times of the day upon occasions, there was definitely a tendency for the deer to become more active and feed in the early mornings and evenings. It was also noticeable that deer were frequently more obvious out feeding in clearings in evenings after rain. Presumably the bulk of the moisture intake of roe deer in such areas is therefore derived from herbage with a high water content, and undoubtedly foliage covered in dew or wet from rain would meet this requirement best. Since there was no other water supply in the area of our cottage, this could be the only explanation for the survival, and indeed excellent body condition, of the roe in the area; moreover, it would also explain the definite proclivity for the roe to prefer feeding late in the evenings and early in the mornings, especially in summer, despite the apparent lack of disturbance during the daytime in large parts of the area. In contrast, in this part of the country with plentiful water supplies and damp food, deer can be seen to be moving and feeding at all times of the day throughout the summer.

These differences between deer in diverse environments become more noticeable when one studies animals for some time in one area and then moves one's attention to beasts in a quite different situation. In the south roe lose their winter coats quite early in spring, and by late April in most seasons any that have not donned the sleek foxy red summer colouring could be suspected of suffering from some ailment. Similarly by then the antlers of the bucks will be clean of velvet, and older bucks will have cast their velvet long before then. In the north, with colder temperatures and perhaps with less abundant and nutritious food supplies during winter, the deer seem not only to take much longer over the actual period of shedding the grey hollow winter hairs that give them insulation from wet and cold, but also do so significantly later in the year. It is unusual to see roe in their red summer coats before early June in some areas, and one can see rather moth-eaten looking beasts with their grey coats half shed over a period of quite a few days, particularly if the weather stays or turns cold. To what degree coat change is dictated by day length and by temperature, and in what combination, I do not know, but by the time that winter coats are shed in the north the daylight hours are considerably longer than in the south, even if perhaps the intensity of light might be less, although temperatures are generally lower, which suggests this as a factor as well as light.

Although we used to observe deer from all the windows in our house, many of the best views and times spent watching were from our bedroom and the studio, both of which had large plate glass windows, extending for most of that wall, looking onto the clearing at the back of the house. The windows at the front were smaller, but, with the ones in the end room, enabled us to view almost the entire clearings. Even the loo had a good view! This was situated next to the window in the small bathroom and one was able to sit looking out at the open hollow in front of the kitchen window and a bank opposite upon which grew several large yew trees. There was always something of interest to see from this viewpoint, be it birds visiting the feed table that was also visible, or a jay or squirrel hopping about searching for beechmast or acorns, and often we saw roe. On a number of occasions we watched them browsing the yew trees within twenty yards of the window. Although they did not feed avidly upon it, in winter they certainly nibbled yew from time to time. In the area of Sussex where Diana frequented before we were married, and where she spent a good deal of time observing fallow deer, there was also a lot of yew, and most of these trees showed a definite browse line to where the deer could reach. Whether yew is poisonous only when cut and wilted, or deer living its vicinity acquire some immunity, or the metabolism of deer differs significantly from that of cattle in this respect I do not know. Certainly yew has a reputation for being poisonous to cattle and horses. However, ragwort is also well known to be poisonous to both cattle and horses, and though these usually avoid eating it when it is growing, they can ingest it accidentally in hay and silage, especially the latter, with unfortunate consequences. On the other hand, sheep and deer can eat ragwort without apparent harm, and indeed do so quite avidly. One winter, when snow lay for some weeks, we watched roe feeding at all times of day in a neighbour's field. Sometimes there was one roe, often three, and on occasion five of them. Knowing how that particular field had the worst ragwort infestation I had seen anywhere, and that it had been heavily grazed by cattle in the autumn, leaving untouched bushy ragwort plants everywhere, I suspected this was what attracted the roe. The ragwort plants stuck up almost out of the snow and so were easily located and reached. One day I went deliberately to check on this and confirm my suspicion, or otherwise. There was no doubt at all. The ragwort plants were eaten down to the ground level, the remaining stump of stem, dead flower stalks and a few bits of discarded leaf were obvious in the scrapes in the snow.

I was aware that sheep are able to eat ragwort without coming to harm, and had read of farmers using them to keep the weed down in the past, but it was actually the example of deer that really brought this lesson home to me. We had gone on a visit to one of the earliest deer farms. This was on a very large estate in the central highlands and the owner was using some rough hill pasture that he had surrounded with a deer fence to contain a herd of wild caught deer. I noticed a thick infestation of ragwort outside the deer pens, but not a plant to be seen inside where the deer were. I commented upon this and was told that the deer had eaten all the ragwort. Knowing that deer of all species have a penchant for eating flowers I was not surprised at this, but, nevertheless, I was impressed by the bare deer pens and resolved to investigate further, since ragwort is a major problem in permanent grassland in this part of the world. Since then I have satisfactorily used sheep to control ragwort in my grassland with gratifying success. It is not known why sheep and deer are able to eat this poisonous weed without noticeable harm, when it will cause a build up of toxic substances in the livers of cattle and horses with fatal results. It is thought that either the livers of the former operate in a different way or various other chemicals are formed somehow in the rumen that neutralise the toxic effects. Perhaps similar situations occur in the consumption of yew by deer.

When watching roe it is often difficult to appreciate just how small these deer actually are unless one can have some yardstick by which to measure them. An adult roe stands only two feet high to the top of its back. Standing on flat hard ground beside me the top of the back of a roe buck would be level with the top of my knee. It is when one sees a roe in close proximity to a rabbit or a pheasant, and one gets the impression that the pheasant looks very large, that one can fully appreciate just how small and dainty roe deer are. In early spring before the grass and various forbs grow tall one is able to have good views of roe, but as summer proceeds and the height of the foliage rises the roe disappear. One would imagine that the orange red colour of a summer roe would stand out vividly against bright green leaves, and sometimes it does. Mostly, though, it merges astonishingly well with the background, and it is quite surprising how easy it is to confuse the colour with distant purple fox gloves, that seem to bear no comparability in colour when examined close up through binoculars, and in the woods are many patches of flowers, mosses or tree trunks with which the coat of the roe blends perfectly to marvellously camouflage the red that might seem so obvious when out in the open. When a roe is standing partly or largely obscured by foliage, aided by the darker shade and grey on its face and ears and white patches on either side of its nose, it can be difficult to see, and it is the movement, such as twitching of ears, for which the observer must look. In this respect the patient deer watcher, waiting for the deer, has an advantage over the person wandering through the woods hoping to see the animals, for deer have the advantage of acute hearing and smell as well as sensitivity to movement, and a beast standing browsing but ever watchful is likely to spot the movement of a human walking through the woods, however slowly, before the person sees the deer. Evenings in early spring are often a good time to see roe deer, with less cover to hide them, and the animals eager to feed on the new growth.

# Chapter 3
# The Living is Easy

We have a lovely small oil painting of the view from Diana's studio over our back clearing at Meadow Plat Cottage by the late Leif Ragn Jensen, the leading Danish wildlife and sporting artist, under whom she studied many years ago. It shows a roe buck standing in the clearing, with patches of bluebells and a broom bush just starting to show yellow buds. A drawing of exactly the same view, except showing a roe doe looking at a fox, appears in the superb book *The Ark* by the internationally known Dutch wildlife artist the late Rien Poortvliet. Both pictures were painted and drawn the same weekend in Diana's studio, and seeing them brings back to us happy memories of the very many fascinating views of roe deer and other wildlife that we had on that clearing, so close to the windows, over the years we lived there. This was the splendid weekend when we arranged for the visits of these superb wildlife artists to overlap, so they could meet each other, and we were also delighted that our young friend Rodger McPhail played truant from art college to come and stay a night with us in order to meet them both.

The clearing was not fenced, so animals were able to pass to and from the neighbouring woodland without hindrance. In summer we were able to lie in bed in the mornings and look straight out through the large window onto the open area, scarcely needing binoculars to observe the wildlife there. To us lying in bed, the near end of the clearing was at eye level and gently sloped up away from us so that the whole area was in view.

One year I tried putting salt licks of different types on several tree stumps in the clearing to see if these were of any interest to the deer. However, the only creatures that appeared to take any notice of them were woodpigeons, which seemed to be attracted by the salt. I put out salt licks here on the farm for the cattle and sheep, and very often as I appear through the gate or over the dyke a woodpigeon, or sometimes a pair of them, will fly off from any salt lick that is lying in the field, which is clearly an attraction to them. In fact, over a number of years during summer, I have watched pigeons come daily to a salt lick in the field in front of the house particularly in the early mornings. Sometimes there are two or three there, walking round the salt block or standing on it, pecking at it. Occasionally there are as many as five. I presume that somehow they must smell the salt to distinguish the lump on the ground from a rock, but I often wonder how they locate it. In the same way I puzzle how, in quite thick grass, these birds can locate plants like mouse-eared chickweed, the seed heads of which also seem to attract them in significant numbers. Birds clearly have a sharp sense of smell that enables them to find food in thick cover. Presumably the deer could have located the salt licks too, and indeed they often passed close to them, but I never observed a roe to take the slightest notice of them, let alone to try licking one. In continental Europe salt licks and feed blocks, and other feed, are often put out for deer, and these are apparently well used. So it is probable that in the area in which I tried them, the deer are sufficiently well fed and not lacking in minerals so they have no interest in the licks. Perhaps salt is unattractive to them in an area where there is a lack of water sources. Certainly it seems clear that where animals are not suffering from a shortage of required minerals they show no interest in the artificially supplied ones put out for them. Salesmen and advisory experts have long referred to mineral deficiencies leading to supplemental supply requirements for cattle in this area, and in the earlier years I succumbed to such advice and put out all types of mineral licks and ad lib supplies, but invariably these were ignored by the beasts, which clearly did not need them, obtaining sufficient from the wild plants on the rough hill grazing in winter. I would imagine that the same applies to deer, where the food supply is adequate for all their nutritional requirements.

However, a friend of ours, who lives a few miles further west from us in north-east Scotland and on higher ground that has rather colder winter weather, feeds her roe deer in winter. The habitat in which they live is birch wood with some hazel and some big pines and firs in an adjoining area of what was once a sort of small arboretum. The roe are quite wild, but remarkably tame with her as a result of almost daily contact. We have seen the doe lying thirty yards from her door completely undisturbed by our talking and looking at her, with her well grown kids only marginally more concerned. The bucks are apparently less tame. Possibly because this is the territory of the doe. Our friend feeds the roe in winter with root vegetables, putting out carrots, turnips and swedes for them quite close to the house, and tells us that they come regularly for this in winter and even look for these titbits. Apparently the doe and her kids feed without inhibitions, but the buck tends to circle warily at first. Whether this is because he is not so tame and suspicious of the human connection or because he is wary of the possessive doe, she is not certain. It did not occur to me to try putting out root vegetables in the clearings at Meadow Plat, but I doubt that it would have resulted in such attraction there, with abundant bramble leaves and other food plants readily available for the deer, nor, had it done so, that I would have been prepared to buy expensive vegetables from the greengrocer for the experiment. We did not grow these vegetables ourselves in our garden there, and I would have been dubious about the prospect of feeding well cleaned and almost sterile shop bought vegetables as opposed to those freshly plucked from the ground. Certainly in this area turnip and swede crops, which are grown on many farms for winter feed for cattle and sheep, are clearly a considerable attraction to both roe and red deer in harder weather. On many fields of these roe can be seen feeding at all times of the day in winter, occasionally in some numbers, whilst on farms on higher ground these crops, grown for sheep, have to be protected from red deer by electric wires or high deer fences.

One summer we had a litter of fox cubs apparently born in our back clearing in a clump of brambles at the far end, perhaps a hundred and fifty yards from the house. These gave us a great deal of pleasure and entertainment, and I confess that they caused me to miss my normal train to London on more than one occasion because of my dallying in bed to watch their antics. It was a lovely experience to wake up on an early summer morning and look straight out of the window at several fox cubs playing. I tried tying a couple of bones to tree stumps to see whether these would attract their attention, but, to my surprise, they appeared to show no interest in these at all. One of the more memorable mornings was when we were lying watching the cubs and to our delight a badger appeared and sauntered across the clearing, sniffing and investigating as he went. There were two cubs playing in the open at the time when the badger appeared from the exit in the bramble clump used by the foxes, and was followed by a cub for a short distance before this ran off. The other cub followed the badger with curiosity for a little while, and then they all disappeared into the brambles. After a while the badger reappeared and wandered about, and we had a superb view of him as he stood on an old tree stump at the near end of the clearing.

We often saw roe deer in the same clearing as the fox cubs, sometimes quite close to them. The cubs were mildly curious, but the roe, usually does, took no apparent notice of the foxes at all. Sometimes roe are apprehensive of foxes, and even aggressive towards them. Diana was sitting in a high seat up a tree one evening watching and sketching a young roe buck in an open patch of a bracken-covered clearing at the edge of woodland. She watched a fox approach through the wood and make as if to pass through the fence on the edge of the clearing, quite close to her seat. The buck saw the fox and advanced purposefully towards it, whereupon the latter retreated, waited until the buck recommenced feeding and then tried again. Once more the fox was chased by the buck, and this was repeated three times. The fox then sat down on the opposite side of the fence and had a scratch, and once again walked determinedly towards the buck. This time, when the roe looked up the fox jinked into the bracken out of sight and reappeared thirty yards beyond the buck, out of his view.

One evening I watched a fox playing similarly with some red deer hinds in our top fields. The fox would trot purposefully towards a hind to investigate something, and when he got too close the hind would make a little run at him or her; whereupon the fox would run off for twenty or thirty yards and pretend to sniff interestedly at something.

When the hind settled to feed again the fox would trot towards her, or another hind, and again get chased a few yards. This happened seven or eight times and it appeared the fox rather enjoyed the game.

One morning we woke to find a roe doe lying in the clearing outside, towards the far end and quite close to the area where the cubs usually played. We watched with amusement as a couple of the cubs spent some time circling a few yards from the doe and peering at her inquisitively on tiptoe over the grass, and then retreating a little. The snoozing doe took absolutely no notice of them. Finally she rose to resume feeding, before eventually moving off out of sight, and the cubs retired to their bramble patch.

As summer progressed, so the does that we saw seemed to be more obviously regulars and tended to visit one clearing or the other, or one end rather than the other of the larger clearing in front of the house, and they appeared with their kids. When we were able to identify the sexes of the kids this assisted our attempt at identification, since a doe with two buck kids or two doe kids, or one of each, could be differentiated from one with different young. Occasionally a doe that we saw from the house might have a single kid, but most of them had twins. We never saw a doe with triplets from the house, but I knew of at least two sets of such families in areas not far away one summer, and reckoned to see at least one lot of triplets in the area each year. Single kids were not very common in that area of mild winters and plentiful feed, although this might have changed in the intervening years as the population reached saturation point. In the several years between my first moving to Meadow Plat Cottage and leaving there to move north, the size, body weights and the general antler quality of the roe had deteriorated noticeably. This could have been due to a gradual change in habitat as large areas of young plantation grew up and the lush undergrowth diminished when the overhead canopy of the trees increased, perhaps reducing the quality of the environment for roe somewhat, or it could have resulted from the increase in population of the deer in the area. There can be little doubt that

40

food and stress are major factors in the condition of deer, and the largest specimens are often found in outlying or newly colonised areas. The presence of other deer undoubtedly is a source of disturbance to roe, and I would speculate that this depends quite a lot on habitat. In large areas of continuous woodland there may well be more movement of deer and more confrontation, especially where the population is high. This disturbance factor clearly applies more to roe deer that are not herding animals and are inclined to be solitary in summer, even if forming family parties in some areas in winter, than to other species such as red deer, fallow and sika that normally exist in groups together. The forming of winter parties by roe seems to occur in open country rather than in areas with heavy cover or extensive woodland. We have seen large parties of roe in winter and late spring in open country in northern Germany and Denmark, and occasionally small groups, which might appear to be little more than a couple of family units, in open agricultural parts of this country, but we never saw large groups in the thickly wooded part of Surrey where we lived, nor in this part of Scotland.

In the woods in southern England the living in summer is easy for roe deer. They have plenty of thick cover and abundant food, especially in the more open areas or in deciduous woodland. I often wondered just how many acres per deer there were in such a highly deer populated woodland habitat. In places where there was not a dense conifer canopy, the growth of bramble or blackberry was lush and almost impenetrable, and the edges of the woodland rides had abundant growth of forbs of many kinds, including large stands of rosebay willowherb and wild raspberry, all of which were readily browsed. Thick patches of conifer, though providing less food for the deer, offered not only shelter from adverse weather and somewhere undisturbed in which the beasts could rest, but also a dark haven away from the torment of summer flies. Such a mixture of habitat seems ideal for roe deer, and it is little wonder that the quality of the animals, as well as their fecundity, was high. In order to maintain our ability to see deer clearly from the house I kept the undergrowth on the back clearing low with the aid of a motor-powered Allen scythe, and it is likely that the fresh younger growth regenerating from the cut herbage may well have served as an added attraction to the roe. The larger area in the front of the house was a laborious struggle in which to maintain open areas, even though I left large patches of wild raspberries uncut, and when finally I purchased an ancient tractor fit for little else and a forage harvester that was no longer useful in fields, I was able to slash the herbage along cut rides and larger cleared areas in order to maintain our views. I was never sure how much these open feeding areas, with perhaps more attractive young growth than the surrounding woodland, drew deer or acted as a sort of focal feeding point for deer with adjoining territories. In parts of the country with open fields interspersed with small blocks of woodland, or even in larger planted acreages with well defined plantations of widely differing ages, particularly with newly cleared spaces or patches of recently planted trees, it may be possible to determine the territories frequented by does and bucks as a result of seeing them with regularity, assuming some degree of possible positive identification. In large blocks of thick woodland, where deer are seen only momentarily when emerged onto rides or feeding in isolated open spaces, it is difficult to form any idea of the likely home patch of deer, let alone judge the extent of numbers. So we never knew whether the deer that we saw from the house inhabited specific territories that bordered, or converged, upon the open area in which we saw them feeding, or whether they shared the same adjoining woodland, even if avoiding close proximity to each other. Had certain deer, so far as we could judge or identify, emerged onto the cleared areas from apparently regular directions we might have assumed the former and decided that that doe and her kids must have a territory in this area of woodland or that, but in practice we were never able to detect such regularity and concluded that the latter was more likely. In other words, although the deer that we saw were deemed to be regulars or locals, all inhabiting the adjoining woodland acreage surrounding the house, they did not do so in a very locally specific territorial manner by jealously defending their chosen patch from all intruders.

Our impression was that the does, if we identified these correctly as the same familiar animals, were more regular than the bucks. From much of what is written about roe one would perhaps have expected that bucks seen in our clearings would emerge onto these from regular directions and show some sign of patrolling or defending these places. In areas of open agricultural land with small areas of cover, copses, and so on, roe are likely to be of more regular habit than in large areas of often dense woodland. We had permission to study deer in adjoining woodland and there were several open areas that had just been planted when we started to frequent these. Two of these new plantations were large, perhaps extending to twenty or thirty acres, and we had high seats overlooking them, either large easily climbed trees with a couple of branches removed to increase visibility and a small plank for a seat, or in one case a portable metal high seat. We spent many evenings in these vantage points with binoculars watching for roe deer. The time spent there was full of fascination, and there was always something to see or hear. One clearing was a haunt of grasshopper warblers, whose churring song was a regular feature in early summer. The other was the territory of a pair of nightjars, and at dusk they would be flitting about like huge moths, catching these insects, and their presence was obvious from afar by their distant, quite different churring, which always reminded me of somebody trying to tune an old-fashioned crystal set radio. Sometimes there would be a loud, angry squeaking from below as shrews squabbled in the long grass, and as the evening drew on and one started to think about the light fading before long the woodcock would appear on its regular circuit with its repetitive but fascinating croaking call. The appearance of the woodcock often seemed to be the signal for the emergence of the roe deer, eager for their evening feed after lying up for much of the day. Sometimes we would see a roe moving through the wood below, to stop briefly at the cover edge to listen and observe, before stepping out into the clearing, but more often than not we would suddenly be aware of a roe out in the open and already feeding, and be astonished that the animal could have got there, as if by magic, without our spotting it earlier.

We saw a lot of roe in these clearings each season over a number of years, and although the deer of both sexes favoured some parts of the areas more than others, and tended to enter into view from fairly regular directions, it was difficult to conclude ideas of consistent regularity shown by the deer, or territorial behaviour of a permanent or semi-permanent nature. We might see a particular buck in a certain part of the clearing on several occasions, but there was no certainty that we would see him again, or that we would not see another buck happily feeding in the same spot on another morning or evening. Fraying of young trees appeared to be somewhat haphazard, and not necessarily indicative of the presence of another deer, though ob-

viously it was demonstrating the presence of the buck carrying out the marking. When one watched bucks fraying, or indeed when one discovered frayed trees when walking in the area, the impression was usually of sporadic attacks upon the young trees when the deer were of such a mood. Fraying often appears to be at the edge of plantations, but where this occurs seems to be influenced by the suitability of fraying stocks, and open areas in the midst of plantings are just as likely to show fraying damage as trees along the edges. Many people suggest that roe bucks form territories, which they regularly patrol and guard jealously, hence the master buck theory whereby fraying damage in woodland is kept to a minimum by preserving the adjudged master buck of that area and removing all the opposition that might annoy or challenge him, especially young bucks. I see no reason to doubt that in an aggressive mood, occasioned by the presence of another buck, one, or both, may resort to the furious fraying of a tree, or several trees. However, if the master buck regularly patrolled his patch, and frayed and left his scent on trees and saplings as a warning for other bucks to keep out, then one would expect to find fraying showing some regularity of ageing. That is to say, that if one visited the area constantly throughout the season one would expect to find fresh fraying on most visits as the patrolling buck had re-marked his territory, or come across evidence of other deer trespassing. My experience has been that when one finds signs of roe buck fraying, even in areas with a good deal of damage, mostly it is old signs, and often appears to have been carried out at a similar period, looking to be of much the same age of wilting or whatever, or if new damage, then one may not find further fresh damage for a while. If there was regular territory marking I would expect to see new fraying quite frequently in certain appropriate sites.

I often wonder whether the ideas put forward on roe behaviour by people unfamiliar with that of other animal species are formed as a result of experience that is too narrowly based, or whether my interpretation is misguided by my attributing to deer the likelihood of behaviour shown by many other species. If one observes a group of antlered stags, especially young beasts, it is quite common to see them have a sparring match with a willow bush or young tree, not as an indication of hostility to others in the group but simply out of play or masculine behaviour or whatever. If one lets cattle into a field containing a rabbit warren with a lot of large holes and loose earth, or a high burn bank with exposed soil, it is usual to see one or two beasts go to these and start to paw the soil and throw up clouds of it with their hooves, especially in dusty weather, or to get down on their knees and butt the ground and bore into the soil with their heads. This applies to both cows and bulls, and if they have horns they may tear up lumps of turf with these. The behaviour seems to both give them pleasure, satisfaction, or relief, or simply be a display of excitement. Horned sheep have much trouble from head flies (*Hydrotaea irritans*), which open skin around the base of the horns and cause sores and great irritation. These sheep often bury their heads in rabbit holes or undergrowth to give relief or scratch their heads on branches or twigs of bushes. People out walking with a stick, especially youngsters, often hit at thistle or flower heads to knock these off the stem. Hang a punch bag in the corridor of a boys school and it is likely that many of the boys passing this will give it a playful punch. Take a dog to the decaying remains of a rabbit or a kelt on a river bank or a pile of evil-smelling fox faeces, and the brute may well delight to roll in this if given the opportunity. Often when one watches a roe buck fraying a tree, particularly a whippy one, it will attack this almost dancing round it. Frequently one finds that bad fraying damage has actually stripped the bark from all round a tree, which will result in the death of that tree. Sometimes this happens to a whole row or clump of trees together, clearly all done on the same day.

We have a small shelter-belt at the bottom of a field by the march burn. I planted a large number of well-grown alder trees in this, without rabbit protection, risking this because of observation that self-sown alder seedlings rarely are attacked by rabbits. I planted a number of larch trees also, these were protected by rabbit wire netting in a small enclosure, and various more ornamental trees were protected by plastic sleeves. The first summer, when the trees had taken well, a roe buck went down the lines of alder trees, some four feet high, and frayed and smashed almost all of them. That buck lived in a wood on the other side of a grass field over the march burn. With only the narrow strip of shelter-belt for cover, it being on the edge of a grass field on my side, I cannot think that this was a display of territorial claim, since I doubt that another buck could have approached, certainly from my side. The following winter rabbits took advantage of a heavy snowfall to chew those trees protected by plastic sleeves above that level, and subsequently ripped off the sleeves when the snow went and killed the plants altogether. They also learned to climb over the wire netting and chewed the bark from some of the larch trees. A few of the trees survived and grew well. Last summer, when the larches were about eight feet high and looking well a roe buck jumped into the small enclosure and wrecked almost every tree in it. The trunks of the trees were stripped white all the way round. This was not an aggressive territorial display, in my opinion, but a frenzied excited attack, and it took place in mid-summer long after the buck would have cleaned the velvet from his antlers or established his chosen summer quarters. My guess is that this fraying damage was a boisterous excited attack, exacerbated by the splendid smell of the stripped larches, and the sticky slippery texture of the tree stems and branches with the bark knocked off. I do not believe that the initial extensive damage, nor the completed destruction of the shelter-belt later was merely the result of territorial marking or aggression towards another buck. Had it been so, I believe that the logical expectation would have been the fraying of a single tree or perhaps a couple of them, followed by a chase of the other beast. Indeed, my impression gained from watching roe bucks chasing other bucks, especially younger or smaller animals, is that there would not be any display of fraying but that the dominant buck would simply launch an attack immediately and chase off the intruder, if the latter was so imprudent as to remain in the vicinity. Depending upon the length and effort of the chase the dominant buck might then vent some of his aggression upon a nearby tree.

Certainly I have often watched bucks walking through a wood, or along a path or hedgerow, and seen them stop to fray briefly, and this may well be leaving their sign. However, in clearings where I have seen several different bucks, of different ages, sometimes at the same time, I have not seen any evidence of aggressive fraying display, although this by no means indicates that it does not occur. Generally when a dominant buck is aware of the presence of a lesser beast he merely has to advance purposefully for the latter to retire. I have only witnessed roe bucks actually fighting quite seriously, as opposed to young bucks sparring, on one occasion. I was sitting in our metal high seat overlooking one of the large newly planted areas, on which there was excellent visibility. A youngish buck with nice antlers emerged a short distance away on to the open area from the wood behind me. He was followed shortly afterwards by an older buck, though not apparently noticeably bigger. They ran well out into the open area, not especially energetically, and then the front buck turned and squared up to the chasing beast and advanced and locked horns briefly. He did this a couple of times, but I did not feel that the fight was particularly aggressive, and finally they parted and the younger buck went off to the far side of the clearing whilst the older one returned to the wood behind me. It seemed to me that having chased the younger animal away from his patch, and out onto neutral territory, he was satisfied. However, I have been told by a friend that he watched a pair of roe fighting late one evening until the light went, and the following morning he visited the site and found one buck lying dead with several noticeable wounds. Our friend near here who feeds her tame roe in winter tells me that she has watched bucks fighting twice. On one occasion an older buck attacked a younger beast, which she thought was his yearling son, as she watched from her window. She thought that the big buck had gored the young one in the face from his reaction, and it retired, clearly badly hurt. The following morning when walking her dog she found the young buck lying dead, gored through its eye. On the second occasion she was in her garden and saw two bucks fighting on the slope in the woodland area outside her fence above her garden. The dominant buck bashed the other beast and knocked him over so that he rolled down the slope and crashed into the wire netting fence. The loser then got up and limped off hurriedly.

I have watched a buck chasing another aggressively on a number of occasions, and last year in the early part of the summer I saw an older buck, still with signs of his winter grey coat on his flanks, chasing a younger buck with pale antlers on several days successively. I was able to lie in bed and see these roe on the slope of our hill opposite the

window. On two mornings I could see the younger buck amongst some scattered birch trees at the top of the slope and a doe feeding in the open lower down. The older buck appeared from the wood opposite the doe and she moved off back into the wood, followed in due course by the older buck. A little later the younger buck moved down and then the older buck appeared out of the wood, chased him and they disappeared out of sight into trees on the other side of the open ground. On the other two mornings I merely saw both bucks run across the slope, the older one in pursuit of the younger.

At the same time of year, in early June, a few days prior to seeing these bucks, I had a very close view of a prolonged chase. On this occasion I was at the far side of our farm, across the one road through the end of the farm in one of a group of small fields next to a wood and opposite some of our hill ground. I was among my cattle, perhaps fifty yards from the road, talking to and scratching a particularly tame and friendly cow. I noticed that she was not paying attention to what I was saying but staring at something over the stone dyke and across the road. I followed her gaze and saw something run into a clump of birches. I first thought it was dogs, since I had been bothered with these hunting rabbits on a number of occasions in previous weeks, despite appeals to neighbours to keep them shut in because of the sheep, but quickly I realised that the hindmost beast was a roe. As I watched, they came running out of the trees and into an open rushy area opposite, and round and back into the trees again. I could see then that it was a big buck chasing a smaller one. I moved over to the dyke beside the road and, as I reached it, back came the bucks in a steady fast lope, mouths open panting, round the open area thirty yards opposite me and returned to the trees again. They repeated this six or seven times, and finally the smaller buck came right up to the fence opposite me. I thought he was going to come through, since it is only four wires with a few scattered gorse bushes along it and he could easily have pushed through or jumped it. I was quite concerned for had he done so he would clearly have crossed the road and jumped the stone wall virtually on top of me. However, he hesitated, barely a yard from the fence, no more than the width of the road opposite me, and turned as he did. The big buck accelerated and clearly meant to spike him. The younger beast managed to just keep ahead and they raced off once again up to the trees a hundred yards away.

By this time all the cows had spotted them, and the herd ran up the field in front of me mooing loudly parallel to the roe. Again the bucks turned and came down to opposite where I stood, followed on my side of the road by the excited cattle. However, these did not follow up the field this time when the bucks turned back to the birches and, as I watched, the smaller buck appeared in the road above me and with a great jump leaped the stone wall and the fence behind it into my field. I imagined that now the object of bigger buck's displeasure had left his territory he would leave off the chase, but I was wrong, and he too appeared in the road and then leaped into the field in hot pursuit. Meanwhile the cows had spotted the first buck and with tails in the air set off in pursuit. The result of this was that they got between the two roe. The pursuer thus stopped, decided that this was too much and fled back whence he had come with a huge leap up the bank clearing the fence and dyke and landing on the road. I watched him cross back panting hard. The young buck funked jumping the fence in the far corner of the field, ran down the side and back along the end straight towards me. As he got close he saw me, and jinked round flat out, skirting the cows, and fled to the far corner again, where he cleared the fence easily and disappeared into the wood. The victor, if one could call him that, stood panting in the birches for a minute or two, and through my monocular, which I always carry, I watched him walk slowly back across to thicker cover on the hill, still panting hard, and little tail stuck out horizontally.

The longest antlers that I have seen on any live roe buck belonged to what we called our big house buck, whom we saw at intervals throughout one summer at Meadow Plat, mostly in the back clearing. I tried taking photographs of him, but my skill with a camera, as in other things, is greatly limited. Even then, but more so now, when I look at those pictures of him I find it difficult to believe that his antlers could be so large. If ever there was a master buck it surely must have been him! Yet we saw other bucks in the clearing on occasion that summer, and we saw no sign of aggressive territorial behaviour, frantic fraying or scraping to mark out the ground claimed by him, or activity suggesting challenges by other beasts. I remember one morning when we watched him saunter across the back clearing, nibbling here and there as he went, and then a little later in the day we watched a much smaller buck cross along apparently the same route. Presumably both would have left some scent. Therefore, from my own observations and experiences I have to conclude that, as a generalised theory, the answer to roe damage of leaving a master buck in charge and removing his challengers, or indeed that a roe buck takes over and defends a specific territory as a generalised rule, is unsubstantiated. I am not prepared to dispute that the idea may apply to certain areas, perhaps especially in isolated pockets of woodland, but I cannot understand how it is judged to apply to large areas of woodland. One of the problems in understanding the behaviour of roe deer is that there is not a great deal of history attached to interest in these deer in this country, such interest being comparatively recent, and much of the lore and preaching quoted has been gleaned from continental sources. Not only are circumstances, environment, and climate very different there, but a number of the theories promulgated are not borne out by results, especially concerning selectivity, control and improvement of the deer.

Given the caveat that the positive identification of roe does is very difficult under normal circumstances, but assuming that our guess at this based upon doe behaviour and attempted identification of her kids was reasonably acceptable, it appears to us that the doe is more territorial in summer than the buck. Bearing in mind that researches have shown how red deer hinds become hefted to an area very close to where they were born, and that certain breeds of hill sheep also become hefted to quite small areas on their ground where they have lambed or been born, it seems logical that roe does should become hefted to the area where they have produced their kids, particularly whilst these are still young. So far as I can judge, the roe doe seeks out an area where she proposes to raise her kids and stays there throughout the summer, defending this territory quite aggressively from other does. Sometimes one has the opportunity to identify individual does by some characteristic. My dentist tells me that she has seen the same doe in her garden for three years running. I asked her how she was certain and she told me that the doe had a lump on her right leg above the hock, so they were able to check that it was the same animal. She told me that her feelings towards the doe and her offspring were ambivalent, since she liked to watch them but they had destroyed all her vegetables. Several wires placed above the rabbit netting, to a height of six feet, were of no avail, since she had watched the roe jump between these strands.

One occasionally sees a doe chasing another doe, especially in spring and early summer. Often this may be the mother chasing off a yearling that has accompanied her through winter, but we have frequently watched a doe approach another from a different direction, both apparently feeding contentedly, until the dominant doe spots the other and gives chase. Merely the awareness of the presence of the dominant doe, and perhaps her posture, may be sufficient to warn off the lesser animal. I was watching a doe feeding in woodland on a slope about eighty yards below me in early summer. Gradually she fed closer, until she was only twenty yards from where I stood partly concealed by a birch tree and downwind of her. Suddenly I was aware of another doe that had appeared in the centre of a long narrow clearing to my left, and which was standing staring fixedly at the first beast. The latter saw her, looked briefly but continued to feed. However, she continued to glance towards the new arrival between every few mouthfuls, giving the impression of unease. The second doe crossed the clearing into bracken on the lower side, and I could see her start to move in our direction, slowly but deliberately. The doe close to me, which had been feeding steadily and unconcernedly until the appearance of the second animal, clearly became increasingly nervous and started to move away, which meant she passed within about ten yards of me. I was unable to move round the tree to endeavour to hide, for she would surely have spotted my movement, but she saw me anyway and departed barking. I did not see the second doe again. Perhaps she was disturbed by the barking.

I am hopeless at imitating things, and so I have never been able to bark back at roe with any effect. However, I know some people can do so, and I have been with a companion who has successfully attracted a disturbed barking beast and drawn him to within sight of us by barking back at the animal. The barking of roe has nevertheless fascinated me. It seems to be very much a summer noise. Often from the house we hear roe barking in the woods or on the hill in the distance during summer and I wonder at the cause. Generally, when I first hear a roe barking in spring, I am aware of it being the first bark of the year, and in autumn I realise that the barks have ceased. Where we lived in Surrey, with thicker and more extensive woodland, we did not hear this distant barking very often, such noise being largely restricted to when we ourselves were the cause. I have watched roe through binoculars whilst they barked on numerous occasions when out in the woods. Sometimes one has the opportunity of seeing several roe at a time feeding in different parts of a clearing or open woodland, and it has always surprised me that when one deer is disturbed and barks the others do not invariably assume instant alertness from the warning noise. Sometimes one can watch a beast barking and see another, further away, through the glass at the same time, continue feeding without any sign of having heard, or it may look up briefly and then resume feeding. At other times one can watch a deer that is only slightly disturbed give a couple of barks, and then continue to feed, looking up in an alert manner between bites and giving low barks with its mouth full.

The barking of roe deer appears to be a reaction of uncertainty rather than specifically a danger signal. If a roe hears a noise or sees a strange object, which it views with suspicion as a possible source of danger, then it will bark. If the animal is properly alarmed it will simply turn tail and run, or vanish into cover, clearly not wishing to draw attention to itself, as barking so plainly does. It seems that if a roe hears a noise that it cannot identify, or perhaps is unsure about it, or maybe just catches a faint whiff of an unattractive scent, such as that from a human, but without seeing the source, it is likely to bark. Sometimes the deer will stand its ground in thick cover, barking loudly, almost challenging the source of its uncertainty to reveal itself. Mostly it will decide that discretion is better and move away, barking from time to time as it does so, until it falls silent when it feels secure again having put sufficient distance between itself and the cause of its disquiet. At other times the roe bounds away barking as it does so, its voice receding into the distance. I have not seen a roe bark at another deer specifically, nor at a fox, but I feel that most of the occasional barking that I hear in the woods from the house is unlikely to be the result of human disturbance, and therefore must originate as a result of the intrusion of other animals. A twig cracked, and heard by another unseen beast, or perhaps a pigeon clattering out of a tree, may be the cause.

Sometimes when one calls a roe deer and the animal, having come close, is suspicious because it cannot find another deer, or perhaps does not like the sound of the noise at close range, it will retire barking in a puzzled and wary manner. This is perhaps less frequent with roe does, whose maternal instinct, when aroused, seems stronger than the sexual urge of a buck. I have kept does quite close for some time when I have been calling from a tree or high seat with a kid noise. Maybe this is because the kid sound is more realistic than the attempt to imitate a doe in season. One can call bucks quite close, but often they are rather suspicious, frequently circling the site from which the call emanates to get down wind of this. They may be suspicious of the noise not sounding quite correct, or wonder why the fieping noise from the supposed doe remains in the same place when in reality she utters this when running in front of a buck, or perhaps he is wary of there being a rival already in attendance. Usually, having come to the call and not finding a doe waiting for him, the buck realises that all is not as expected and he retreats, barking as he does so. Undoubtedly my most unusual roe calling experience was when I lured a buck right up to within about fifteen or twenty yards of my window. I was in a small room at the end of Meadow Plat Cottage, and it being the beginning of August the roe deer rut was in full swing in the Surrey woods. Spotting a buck in our front clearing, just at the end of the small lawn, I wondered whether he was in a responsive mood. I had a Buttolo rubber roe call handy, and so I carefully opened the window slowly and noiselessly and put my hand out holding the call and squeezed this three or four times. Instantly the buck put up his head and stared hard in my direction. I never expected him to do more, but to my surprise he advanced on to the end of the narrow lawn about seventy yards away. I squeezed the call again, giving four fieps, and the buck advanced cautiously but purposefully straight towards the house. Astonished that he should be attracted by a call from such an unlikely source, and intrigued as to just how close he would come or what he would do, I called again. He came steadily forward, and the thought actually went through my head that he might attack my hand outstretched through the window! However, at about fifteen or twenty yards from the house he stopped and would come no nearer. Three times he turned away and trotted a couple of yards, and each time I squeaked and he came back again, but finally it was too much for him and he pranced off, barking as he bounded away, and I could hear him disappear into the wood.

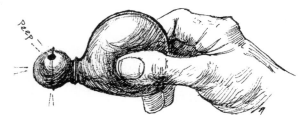

The fieping or peeping call made by these artificial devices can attract other creatures on occasion. I have had a fox come apparently to investigate the sound, but perhaps the most interesting experience of inadvertently attracting an unsuspecting dupe was an occasion some years ago, I think in 1972. It was at the end of July in Surrey, in warm muggy weather, and the roe rutting season was in progress. I had seen plenty of signs of activity when out in the woods, with bucks chasing does. I was sitting up a tree, which had been left when the area was cleared, in the centre of a small new plantation of conifers. With me was our artist friend, Rodger McPhail, to whom I hoped to demonstrate calling a roe buck. My procedure is to wait twenty minutes or so to allow time for the area to settle after I arrive at the place from which I intend calling, and then to peep four or five times every five minutes or so. This procedure I adopted many years ago, having seen it successfully used by someone of mid-European origin; but it does not accord entirely with my experience of watching does making the noise, since when one sees a doe pursued by a buck she appears to peep every couple of steps continuously. There is a variation to the observer, or listener, since when the deer run around, and in and out of woodland, one is not able to hear the sound continuously because of the acoustics. Nevertheless, having found that my procedure works I have maintained it. I had only called a few times when a sparrowhawk suddenly flew out of the trees opposite and landed in our tree above our heads, calling as it did so. It stayed a few moments before deciding that we were not desirable company and flew off. With the similarity of the noise there was no doubt in our minds that the bird had come to our call. Wandering in the woods in mid-summer I have heard noises from time to time that I have been quite unable to decide if they were attributable to young kestrels or hawks, or to roe deer.

Ever since she was very young Diana has been a compulsive, and rapid, sketcher of things that interested her, and she has filled many sketch books with drawings, always carrying one with her. Long before most of those currently interested in deer in this country knew anything about them, these animals became her main interest amongst wildlife subjects. Sketch books and pencils or pens have always been kept strategically close to windows in our house. These quick sketches, as well as any notes appended, convey admirably many of the deer sightings that we were delighted to experience over the years. Many drawings and paintings have the ability to be so much more evocative than photographs, since the former capture an experience, whereas a photograph captures an instance in time. I always describe a good painting or drawing as telling a little story, which a photograph can rarely do. An example of this is demonstrated if one stops a film to show a single frame, and then advances it frame by frame. This does not convey the same impression as the film should despite being composed of the actual same frames. Thus most competent artists and those interested in pictures are able to tell the majority of paintings and drawings copied from photographs, and may well remember the photographs too, if they have seen them before. In some way that I cannot explain, animals in photographs appear different from those in reality or in paintings, and very few photographs convey the impression desired by those deeply interested in, and familiar with, the animals. In the same way, equally difficult to describe in words, captive deer and tame deer have a different look and appearance to the perceptive observer from truly wild deer.

Diana's sketches and notes confirm the view that I formed over the years of watching deer from our windows in the same areas, that roe does have been the more regular visitors to the clearings than the bucks. Bearing in mind always that we cannot substantiate the identification of does without positive identifying marks or characteristics of some kind, it appeared to be the same does with their kids that we saw feeding in the clearings around the house in summer, and also they spent more time there, often lying and resting in these same places. Clearly the doe with kids has a greater need to feed, for she has not only to sustain herself and rebuild after carrying growing kids in spring, but she has to provide milk for these as well. The growing kids with her also have an increasing food requirement. The bucks, on the other hand, especially mature beasts, have only to maintain themselves. We certainly saw familiar bucks quite often, but we also saw bucks that we could not recall seeing before and perhaps never saw again, and there seemed to be far less regularity in their behaviour. The beast that we called our big house buck, with such spectacularly large antlers that we were astonished whenever we saw him, was one we were always especially delighted to see and note his visits. As well as long antlers, they were also thick and heavy, though rather straighter than I care to see, as was the case with most roe from that part of Surrey. I find the more conventional curved antlers more attractive than the typically straight and narrow ones that seemed to be most common in that part of the country.

For the one season we saw our big house buck quite often. Whether we ever saw him before with a lesser head, or indeed subsequently, we shall not know, but for just one spring and summer we saw him from time to time, mostly on the smaller back clearing. That season I believe we counted what we believe to have been fourteen different roe individuals, including kids, from our windows on both clearings. These included several different bucks. Mostly these appeared singly, and there was no sign of competition or aggression. They stayed feeding for a while and then wandered off. Sometimes in spring a buck might seem to chase off a doe, but I suspect that this was more a result of the roe preferring a solitary existence and not wishing for the company of either sex than anything else. However, one can see activity in spring that seems to have more to it than this, and I have certainly observed roe behaviour that seemed to be attributable to what has been described as a false rut both in north-east Scotland and in Surrey. In the south of England, with earlier seasons, I have seen this in early May, at a time when does are heavily pregnant. In the north I have watched this in June, when the timing might be similar. I recall watching a pair of roe under such circumstances in early summer here on the farm, and I not only observed them for quite some time but I was able to see them for a considerable distance. In this case it was not a question of the buck chasing the doe, but rather he seemed to wish to stay near her. If he got too close she moved off, but they fed in close proximity for quite some time, and then gradually the doe moved off, and he followed after her at a distance, both feeding as they went, until eventually I lost sight of them both perhaps half a mile from where I was first looking at them. Although I could not describe this buck as rutting in any way, nevertheless he appeared to me to have an undue interest in the doe not shown at other times by other deer except for the brief mating period. We have noted a buck chasing a doe on our Surrey clearing on 9 May, having also noted a doe as being heavily pregnant three days earlier, and we have seen bucks chasing does in north-east Scotland at the end of that month and in early June.

Occasionally in literature, or in talking to stalkers and deerwatchers, one comes across a reference to the false roe deer rut in autumn. How did this idea arise, and what basis might there be for it? The answer to the first part of this question is easy. Before the last century the little roe deer were hardly considered, and when one spoke of deer it undoubtedly meant red or fallow. These herd species, often kept in parks, have an obvious mating season in autumn. Consequently it was assumed that all deer rutted in autumn. The phenomenon of delayed implantation was unknown. However, in the second part of the last century, researchers on the continent discovered that roe does experienced that marvellous condition known as delayed implantation, whereby growth of the fertilised egg, and thus the foetus, did not start until some long time after mating. It is now well known that roe, as with a number of animals (for instance stoats but not weasels), experience delayed implantation and that their mating season is actually in mid-summer and not in the autumn.

There is little doubt that the old idea of an autumn rut of roe deer influenced thinking and writing, and to the extent that some writers have suggested that the activities of some roe bucks in autumn, where they have noticed apparent aggressive territorial behaviour or bucks following doe scent lines, indicates erotic behaviour. It seems to me that this is an unlikely interpretation of the behaviour of roe bucks in October or later. On the other hand there are definite signs of what one might regard as a false rut in spring, especially at the end of May and the beginning of June in this part of north-eastern Scotland and possibly earlier in the south. At one time it occurred to me that this behaviour, which may well be regarded as erotic on the part of the buck, might have a similarity to the apparent sexual interest shown on occasion by other cattle, including males, to a cow close to parturition, when the roe doe is near to giving birth. However, research in recent years has provided the clear confirmation of this behaviour by the buck and evidence of the reason for it.

Until perhaps twenty years ago, or less, the mechanism and chemistry of antler growth of deer was not well known. Indeed this is still not well understood by many stalkers and deer enthusiasts. The process of annual antler growth is governed principally by photoperiod, or changes in daylight length, which in turn influences hormone production. The rate or size of antler growth is largely influenced by food quality and quantity and stress factors, with presumably some genetic influence in shape pattern, but the period of growth is governed by hormone levels. Growth of the antlers takes place whilst testosterone levels are low, but a rise in the level of this hormone causes the antlers to ossify, blood supply to these to cease and the velvet to dry and be shed. In the case of red deer this precedes the rut by a short time, and the rise in testosterone level in the stag also causes the growth of the neck muscles and the mane, the testicles and other male characteristics emphasised at the mating season, and generally precipitates the onset of the rut so far as stags are concerned. Of course for mating to take place the hind also has to come into oestrus.

In the case of roe deer the cycle is different, since antler growth takes place at a different time of year, with the antlers ossifying and cleaning in May in this part of the country, but of course much earlier in southern England. The roe rut and genuine mating season takes place generally in the second half of July and the first half of August. It has been shown that roe bucks demonstrate two periods of rise in testosterone levels. The first is in spring, when this signals hardening and cleaning of the antlers, and the second in July, precipitating the sexual behaviour to promote mating. The difference between these two periods is that during the first time of high testosterone levels in the buck the doe does not have similar levels of hormone activity, with the pregnant does being about to give birth to their kids. Does only come into oestrus during the second period in the middle of summer. In other words the high hormone levels in spring stimulate the bucks, but the does are quite unreceptive.

I have seen several clear examples of this behaviour during the latter part of May and the beginning of June. The most obvious example of an unmistakably rutting buck running an unreceptive doe occurred one morning when I was checking my cattle. As I approached a field of heifers I could see one of these, and then another, watching something in rough ground at the edge of a wood just beyond their field. As I got close to this a roe doe, closely followed by a buck, leaped across the farm track and up onto the hill above me and stood thirty yards from me in full view but apparently oblivious of my presence. The buck was a mature beast with a fine pair of antlers as good as I have seen in this area. Both animals were panting, with their mouths open, and had clearly been running for some time. After pausing for a minute or so they continued their run for another fifty yards and paused again. This pattern was repeated a number of times, the running being rather more of a lolloping movement than any evidence of the buck straining to catch up with the doe or attempt on her part to flee at full speed. It was the sort of action that I expect to see in early August. They ran around in full view within about two hundred yards of me for several minutes before finally departing out of sight amongst gorse bushes further up the hill.

At this time of year it is quite usual to see bucks in close proximity to does and clearly following them, though definite rutting-style chases are less common. Indeed, we have watched bucks following close to does and staying in their vicinity on numerous occasions. One morning we watched a young buck follow a doe across a big open

space, only to see the doe returning rapidly whence it had come, still followed by the buck, a short time later. We then saw that the reason for this was a larger buck in pursuit. The latter stopped at the edge of the open space and started to feed, and as we watched the smaller buck reappeared and stood sideways to him, threateningly, and pawing the ground. The larger buck reciprocated, and I fully expected a fight to ensue, but the younger beast thought better of it and retreated out of sight, at which the older buck returned to his side of the clearing, where we saw that he too was accompanied by a doe.

As mentioned previously, a friend of ours living a few miles west of us feeds her roe deer daily throughout winter with vegetables of various sorts, mostly turnips, carrots and so on. The two regular does are very tame with her and the two dogs, which they see daily. The buck is more wary, but comes to the food in due course. These roe spend a lot of time close to her house, and she sees them on her daily walks with the dogs. As a result she gets to know their behaviour well, and has some remarkable experiences. Initially we were quite surprised when she commented one day, at the end of May, that the buck was back with the does, it being their mating time. We explained that the rut actually took place in late July or early August and that is mating time, but of course her observation was actually more accurate than many might appreciate, for quite clearly she was familiar with the spring false rut.

People tend to read and absorb ideas put forward by others, and if repeated sufficiently often these ideas may apparently become fact. As a result, observers may then interpret behaviour as being what they expect to see. I suggest that the autumn roe false rut falls into this category, and that suggestions that unusual deer barking, excessive scraping, and following the scent of other deer, and so on, is erotic are largely a product of imagination. At that time of year, when some of the older bucks may soon be casting their antlers, their testosterone levels will be low. Furthermore, whilst it is possible that an unfertilised doe might still be re-cycling, the likelihood of her still coming into oestrus in October is small, though perhaps possible. We have certainly seen a cow continuing to attract attention from a bull some weeks after she was satisfactorily served; the date of service subsequently being confirmed by the birth of the calf. On the other hand, it is known that roe bucks are full of sex hormones in spring after antler cleaning, and so, whilst again the probability of any doe being receptive to fertilisation then is rather remote, it is highly likely that bucks will display both sexual inclinations and aggressive tendencies. It is probable that much of the behaviour described as territorial establishment and marking actually results from the high testosterone levels experienced, in just the same way that similar hormones may lead to the manifestation of aggressive and sexual tendencies in young humans.

When the time comes to give birth, most animals have the instinct to be alone and seek some secluded sheltered spot. Cattle will wander quite a long way from the herd to calve, upon occasions, if they have the opportunity, which is not so common in these days of intensive farming. My own cattle calve on a fairly large area of hill and often I have to search for them when I find one missing. Sometimes they bring the calf to the herd when it is mobile, and at other times they leave it hidden for a couple of days, joining the other beasts to feed and returning to the calf subsequently. Red deer have this herd instinct, but roe deer do not. Consequently there is no motive for the doe to move far from the site that she has chosen, especially if she has no wish to come across a neighbour. With the kid spending more time lying down and not accompanying its mother, as a red deer calf does with the hind after it is about a week old, the doe is likely to stay close to the area. Therefore she chooses a territory in spring, possibly the same one as inhabited previously and perhaps one from which she never moved in winter in the first place, and keeps to this area throughout the summer.

One often reads, or hears people talking, about the territory of a buck. However, it seems to me that it is the doe's territory which is the basic part of roe society, if one can put it like that. It is usually the buck that seeks out the doe, and answers her call, as a stag seeks hinds, and not a question of a doe going to look for a buck, though a female in season will occasionally seek the company of a male if one is not already present. Moreover, in this part of the country, the bucks are probably polygamous because of the apparent disproportionate doe ratio, and so they are likely to move around more for this purpose. If a buck is shot in a particular place, or bucks frequenting a plantation are removed regularly, those does that inhabit the area do not go unserved that season but are likely to attract in other bucks.

These observations have formed my view that insofar that roe are in any way regular in habit, it is the does that are mostly so, and bucks, whilst they may frequent a certain area, are likely to wander more with occasional odd beasts passing through, even after the general movement of deer in spring when the winter family groups break up and youngsters are sent packing by their parents to go and look for new domiciles of their own, or perhaps move off spontaneously.

The behaviour of deer in different parts of the country is necessarily dictated by differing habitat. Roe in large areas of continuous woodland will not have the same behaviour as those in open country with small patches of cover or in hill ground, and beasts in twenty-year-old conifer plantations with a dense canopy and almost no ground cover or feed, other than in a few firebreaks or roadways, will have quite different habits from those living in large areas of deciduous woodland or more open trees with plentiful browsing everywhere. Roe bucks often seem to turn up and stay in a small area for a short time and then disappear. One season we had a buck appear in a small area of hill, just opposite our house and easily seen from the windows, which we had fenced off for our ponies. It consists of only perhaps one and a half acres with a few scattered birches and a couple of ash and rowan trees, but mostly open, adjoining thicker birch wood. A small stream runs through this rough paddock and there are a couple of nettle patches, and later in summer a few patches of bracken, though when the buck took up temporary residence this was not evident. One bottom corner is wet, with a small boggy area. I had kept a few sheep in this for a time during winter, and these, followed by the ponies, kept the natural hill grass pretty bare, for which reason we use it deliberately for summering the ponies at times when we wish to restrict their feed.

One morning I spotted a buck in this paddock. I watched him

moving about feeding for a while, noting with pleasure that he carried a particularly nice, well-shaped head, which I would describe as a classic good roe head. The next day I passed this paddock in the tractor, along the farm track that borders it, and I saw the buck standing motionless watching me about fifty yards away, presumably hoping that he had not been spotted. I carried on, and after parking the tractor in the farmyard I looked back and could see the buck feeding again. I was quite surprised that he was still there, since I would have considered the feed in the paddock to be poor compared to the adjoining hill, and the quite low netting fence around it presented no obstacle to a roe. I was even more surprised the following day, when I went to tend to the ponies in an almost adjoining enclosure, to see the buck running up and down the fence bordering the wood in an agitated manner. During the next few days this became a regular sight, and later I found a quite worn track alongside that fence. He was clearly not particularly alarmed, even when I walked within a hundred yards of him, not only because he could easily have jumped the fence, but also because a short while later I could look out of the house to see him feeding undisturbed. I do not remember now how long he stayed in that enclosure, but it must have been about two or three weeks at least, if not more. One day, having seen him earlier from the house, I could not see him when I passed by walking the dogs, so I decided to go and discover where he could possibly hide. I did not think that he had left the paddock, but so far as I could judge the only possible cover was a gully in which the stream ran for a short way, with hardly anywhere for a roe to hide, and two small nettle patches and perhaps a rock behind which he could lie. I crossed the fence with the dogs and I had not gone far when the buck appeared, agitatedly running along the end of the enclosure. I still do not know from whence he materialised. Although the dogs were at my side, he clearly did not like them, but ran down the fence towards me and then panicked and raced across my front and with a huge leap cleared the wire easily, at the highest part of the whole fence, and disappeared up the hill into the wood.

I expected that would be the last I should see of the beast, but to my surprise next day he was back in the enclosure running up and down the fence when I went to see the ponies. He stayed there for a day or two yet and then we saw him no more in his familiar place. What on earth attracted him to that spot I failed to ascertain. A couple of weeks later I spotted what I think was the same buck, with the distinctive, rather pale, nicely-shaped antlers, about half a mile away at the far end of another stretch of woodland. I did not see him again.

I suppose that most animals like clean territory and new feeding. Domestic stock certainly welcome this even if the new grazing is not especially attractive. So I presume that deer prefer a change too, and tire of one place. I have in mind several small shelter-belts that I have made on the edges of some fields. These have been created deliberately not as regimented forestry plots but as strips of wild rough with scattered hardwoods to form cover for wildlife as well as windbreaks for the fields. In some of these roe damage by fraying has been annoying and expensive, although mostly I planted sufficient young trees to afford to lose a number and still leave adequate for my intentions. Several of these shelter-belts we can see from the house or farmyard. In two of these it seemed to me that a buck took up residence for a short time and then moved off. Whether this had to do with activities in the adjoining fields, or was occasioned by wanderlust and a wish to seek a clean area, I do not know. However, both the ageing of the fraying damage and scraping, and the occasional sightings, suggested that the buck moved in for a few days and then departed.

This temporary residence is certainly a feature amongst crops. Once hay crops or cereals are tall enough to give them cover, roe spend a good deal of time in these. Does will often have kids in hayfields unfortunately. This siting of their territory is not so unfortunate when the crop is to be late cut hay in higher country, but on low ground farms where hay is cut early, and worse where the crop is cut for silage even earlier, kid mortality can be high. The young animals lie completely still and hidden and in a thick crop the only sign that the machine driver gets is a noise from the mowing machine as some object is lacerated. and perhaps he sees a small spotted skin protruding from that swathe as he comes round the field again. In late cut hay fields the kids may be old enough to be more mobile and the doe may lead them away when she hears disturbance. Presumably it is the thick cover that attracts the does, and in many cereal crops there is a good scattering of weed plants on which to feed at ground level, except of course in intensively sprayed crops. Bucks favour tall crops too, especially cereals, as a temporary residential area, and I often think that as well as the inevitable succulent feeding upon the ground level growing annual weeds, the shelter from flies in the summer must be a considerable attraction.

We see roe in our hay fields from time to time, and last season a young buck lived for two or three weeks in fields adjoining the back of the house. Several times we had splendid views of him from the kitchen window whilst doing the washing up, within fifty yards of us or less. We saw him further out in the hay quite frequently, and came to look for him whenever we passed the upstairs window that afforded views of these fields. This certainly emphasised to us what we have experienced so often with deer over the years, which is how one minute the deer is there in view and the next moment there is no animal to be seen. Watching roe in a hay or cereal crop also demonstrates just how small these animals are, averaging about 24 inches to the top of their backs, or level with the knee of a tall man. Most of the time that one looked out of the window there was no hint of any deer within miles, but every now and again there he would be feeding in the same part of the field, so presumably he spent much of the day lying down. This buck was the deer that even at the end of July merely had two bumps on his forehead that seemed to be little more than velvet-covered pedicles. We were not able to detect any outward sign of damage, except that at one stage he appeared to be possibly very slightly lame, and so far as we could see he was apparently in good condition, so the cause of his lack of antlers was a mystery. One might almost have regarded the animal as a roe hummel, since one could only detect the bumps on his forehead with difficulty when he was in profile, but his plumbing system identified his sex.

Deer become very used to their environment. It might seem astonishing that a roe would pass, and feed, within a few yards of a house, but animals adapt quickly both to danger and the lack of it. Deer that have been shot at from vehicles become very spooky at the presence of these, and deer fed from a vehicle on a regular basis get to know this and come close to it, just as do cattle. In Braemar, red deer, particularly stags, come into the centre of the town at night to feed on anything green, and all gardens in the vicinity have to be deer-fenced to avoid marauding. The roe that visited the clearings around our cottage in Surrey took no notice of the radio, which they must have heard from the house. Indeed on one occasion I experimented by playing an assortment of gramophone records to a doe, to see whether she reacted to different types of music. Typically Sassenach she finally moved off when I played a loud gramophone record of bagpipe music out of the window to her! The deer took little notice of the arrival of the postman in the morning or the dogs barking, or our talking to him on the doorstep. These sort of daily disturbances, especially those that occur at set times of the day, they recognise as familiar and harmless. Although they may stand and stare they never seemed to be unduly concerned. Some deer get so comparatively tame that their behaviour can become rather ridiculous, if not dangerous. Most people with knowledge of deer are aware that a hand-reared roe buck can be extremely dangerous, since without fear of humans they can give vent to their aggression, and sharp antlers can inflict bad injuries. Even a tame little roe doe can deliver damaging blows with her sharp hooves.

Our friend with the very attractive small nature reserve around her house, who feeds her roe in winter and talks to them, related two fascinating incidents to us appertaining to tameness in deer. The roe, particularly the doe that regularly lies close to the door of her house, though outside the deer-fenced garden, are quite used to seeing and hearing both her and her dogs. She takes her dog, a labrador, for a walk daily round the area, and he takes little notice of the deer and often goes within a few yards of them without either bothering much with each other. Quite recently she acquired a new dog, a six-year-old labrador bitch that needed a new home. This labrador is quiet and biddable and gets on well with her existing young dog. Shortly after the arrival of the new dog our friend was out walking them both when they passed close to a buck, who was in the process of cleaning his antlers and still had bloody strips of velvet hanging from the tops. The

66

bitch went up close to the buck, who stood his ground, and was clearly curious. Whereupon the buck lunged at the labrador and knocked her over onto her back with her legs in the air, as if to tell her to clear off and not pester him. The buck then stood looking at the dog seemingly rather astonished and then moved off a little way, while she got to her feet unharmed. It was fortunate for her that the buck had not finished cleaning his antlers and was not in full, hard horn.

The second incident also indicates the degree of roused curiosity indicated by barking. Our friend was in her house when she heard a roe barking a lot just outside, where the deer fence is only a few yards from her door. She looked out and saw that the doe was standing barking right up at the fence, staring fixedly at one of those child's large plastic footballs with which her dogs play, and which had been left lying in the grass close to the fence. There was a very strong wind blowing that was moving the light plastic ball about and had attracted the curiosity of the deer, who could not make out what this white round thing was that was rolling about on the opposite side of the wire.

# Chapter 4
# Acorns and Beechmast

In summer time the living is comparatively easy for most wild animals.
Their food supply is abundant, there is plenty of cover, and mostly the
weather is kind to them. This is especially so for roe deer in the south
of England, but applies elsewhere too. Spring is the time of recovery
from winter and the initiation of new life. Summer time is the period
for nurturing that new life and its growth into maturity. For roe bucks
the summer time is a period of rest when little demand is put upon
them, except at rutting time in late July and early August. They need
only to feed to maintain condition and assuage their appetite as the
mood takes them. With less demand upon their metabolism, once they
have sorted out their summer haunts from any rival claims, life for a
roe buck must be comparatively sedate in areas where thick cover is
available and food plentiful. Undoubtedly bucks spend much time
lying chewing the cud and resting in the warmth of summer, glad to
hide from the torment of flies in the heat of the day.

The doe, on the other hand, or rather the doe with a kid or kids at
foot, has a job to do in summer and as well as looking after her
offspring, guarding them as best she can, she has to feed them.
Providing an adequate supply of milk for her kids represents a
significant demand upon the doe, and her intake of feed has to be
sufficient both for the continuation of this flow and to maintain her
own body. Consequently the requirement of the doe for food is
higher than that of the buck in summer, and we see does
feeding more frequently, especially during the day time.
With the change of the season and the shortening of
the days the emphasis changes, and all animals
have the urge to store up food for winter when
the supply dwindles and the weather becomes
harsher. In autumn we watched from our windows
squirrels busily collecting acorns and nuts to store in

their caches as emergency winter supplies. Jays too are doing the same at this season, hiding nuts and acorns and other seeds as a store for harder times. Many of these caches will be forgotten, but the buried seeds are part of Nature's pattern for sustainable growth, since some of them will germinate to produce new young seedlings if left unconsumed in the ground. When we first moved to Scotland years ago jays were quite a rare sight, but now they are all too common, albeit not so abundant as in the south of Britain. Those creatures that cannot store winter supplies of food in this manner do so by storing reserves in the form of fat in their own bodies. Late in autumn rabbits begin to lay down internal fat. Throughout summer they are too busy with the strenuous activities of procreation to build up body reserves, but these cease in autumn, and survival through winter becomes the important objective. In autumn the building up of winter fat reserves becomes of paramount importance to the hedgehogs, for those without sufficient will not survive the winter. As the season turns, and the days shorten and colours change, we see young hedgehogs foraging avidly, even in the middle of the day, desperate to eat as much as they can before their food supply dwindles and the colder weather forces them to curl up in a nest of leaves in an old rabbit hole or a tussock of grass. Few of these half-grown hedgehogs will survive the winter simply because at that stage their bodies are still growing and excess food consumed is utilised for this rather than laying down the necessary fat reserves to enable them to endure long spells of inactivity, even at a substantially reduced metabolic rate.

So the building up of internal reserves is important for the deer as well, although they rarely lay down internal fat to the degree of rabbits or domestic livestock. One of their preparations for cold weather is the change into winter coats, comprised of longer and larger hollow hairs that provide them with both insulation and waterproofing. Whereas in spring the change to the lighter sleek summer coat takes place over several days, as the cast winter hairs fall out and gives both roe and red deer, but especially the former, a rather raggedy appearance whilst they still have patches of the old grey winter hairs on their bodies, the change to winter attire often seems to be much more rapid and suddenly one sees deer in winter pelage. Some roe deer take a few days to change completely and their coats darken as the grey winter hairs become apparent. With others the glossy grey coats, with their smart white gorgets on the throat and brilliant white rump patches, appear quickly. The change to winter coat in red deer seems slower and less obvious; but then the contrast in colour difference with summer coat is less striking.

I have pondered upon the question of coat change in deer. In spring it is obvious from the definite shedding of hairs, which one can find plentifully in places where deer have lain or gone through fences, that the winter coat falls out, or is pushed out by the new growth of summer coat. A knowledgeable Dutch friend of ours, who has written many books on deer, asked me some time ago whether the autumn coat change of deer is new hair growing or the summer hairs changing format and becoming the longer, hollow, insulating winter type. I was not able to answer the question with confidence. His view was that from the appearance of the deer, and the speed with which the change can occur in roe, the existing hairs actually changed format; possibly the catalyst is photoperiod, or the combination with weather conditions or temperature. I have asked other knowledgeable people and looked for comment in literature, but the question does not appear to have been examined or answered. Thus I took particular interest in observing our very tame red deer hind throughout two seasons of autumn coat change, being able to stroke her and brush her and part her hairs to examine the composition of her coat. Her grey autumn coat appeared first on the short hairs on her legs and gradually spread and the complete change took several weeks. During this time brushing and stroking her did not reveal any shed hairs beyond the very few that one might expect at any time. Parting her coat to examine the hair composition I was not able to discern two different types of hair, as one might expect if the winter hairs were new growth that either replaced or accompanied the summer ones. All the hairs looked the same at the base. Consequently I concluded that the summer hairs do indeed change format into the better protective winter version. This would be in accord with what I have read occurs in foxes, which actually shed hairs only in spring, and with the general observed experience of cattle, which appear to grow longer winter coats without shedding hair until spring. Sheep too, change their coat annually by a break in the wool in early summer, enabling the fleece to be shed. Although the change in red deer seems to take longer, there is little doubt that the mechanism is the same for all deer, and this would explain the rapidity with which some roe appear to change colour in October compared to their more drawn out spring change, that often imparts a somewhat moth-eaten appearance.

Though the feed value of much herbage available for deer has receded by autumn, as growth ceases, there is still a harvest for them to reap in the woods, and Nature provides opportunity for all these animals to gather this in the form of food to enable them to survive harder times ahead. Tree leaves now become available to the deer as they drop off. Perhaps those from the tops of trees, far out of reach hitherto, are more attractive for some reason, for instance having been at the growing points of the trees on the topmost or outermost branches, and maybe having a higher mineral content. Certainly

fallen leaves are an attraction, and especially ash leaves, if these are available. Roe seem to like ash leaves particularly. Perhaps all deer do, but most never get the opportunity to sample them. I recall a friend that reared a roe kid that was especially fond of ash leaves. We have several fields on the farm with ash trees at their edges, and when cattle are put into these they invariably go to see whether any leaves are within reach. In late autumn, when the ash leaves have turned to that lovely pale green which is enhanced by the yellows and reds of the birches, aspens and geans, hard frosts followed by sunny days cause the ash leaves to drop silently like gentle rain, and the cattle pounce on these and gobble them up with apparent relish. Similarly, at that time of year, sheep put into a new field immediately go to the edges where there are trees to forage for leaves. Ponies eat them too. Deer are no exception to this trait, and freshly fallen leaves are undoubtedly an attraction to them also.

I have often noticed that stock will eat other plants late in summer or early autumn that they will not touch earlier in the year, and undoubtedly this applies to deer also. Stinging nettles and docks will both be stripped by sheep late in the year, and cattle seem to relish cut and wilted nettles left lying in fields. Dried nettles actually have a good feed value, and some animals certainly seem to think so. Analysis has shown that they actually have a higher metabolisable energy and digestible protein content than red clover, and a significantly higher ME level than white clover, though a slightly lower level of digestible crude protein. A similar study has indicated that elm leaves have an equally impressive feed value content, though I have not seen the figures for ash leaves, which seem to be the favourite choice of most of the herbage eating animals. Ponies and deer will both delicately pick off thistle flowers to eat, as will young cattle. Since deer are rather more delicate feeders than farm livestock, the signs of eating that they leave, unless perhaps it is garden depredation, are less obvious and to establish what the former feed upon careful observation is often necessary to discern leaves or buds nipped off here and there as the deer wanders about.

Autumn is the time for a proliferation of fungi in the woods, and these too represent a welcome harvest for many creatures, including discerning humans that know the few which are delicious to eat. One often finds fungi that have been knocked over, trodden on or with apparent bites out of them, and I have long suspected that deer of all species eat certain of these, as well as other animals such as mice, voles, squirrels and rabbits. Though I have not actually observed deer eating fungi, their tracks to, and past, damaged fungi, or places from which these have clearly been removed, have led me to believe that these fruits of the forest are included in the diet of deer. This has been confirmed to me by a stalker friend who controls the deer on an estate in the neighbourhood. He always uses the tripe, or stomachs, of deer that he shoots as feed for his dogs and he tells me that the stomach contents of roe frequently include pieces of fungi. All deer are essentially browsers in that they like to vary their diet from grazing grass by eating leaves and forbs of many kinds, but roe are specifically so. When seen out in fields feeding, though they may consume a certain amount of newly brairded cereals, undoubtedly they will also eat a number of newly germinated forbs, or weeds, and later on as the crop grows broad-leaved weeds will be the main attraction for them. I recall the time when we had a small party of red deer feeding in a ripening oat crop directly behind our steading. Each evening they came into the field by much the same route, headed to a spot about a hundred yards out from our corn loft steps, fed there for a while, and then moved out further into the crop as darkness fell. I was able to identify very precisely the area of apparent main attraction for them, and during the daytime I examined this carefully. I could find no trace of any oats eaten, and the only damage was the small track that they made walking through the crop. What seemed to attract the deer was a low area of the field underneath which an old stone drain ran, so presumably this gave rise to moister ground, and here there was

evidence of the rather more lush broad-leaved weeds growing beneath the crop having been browsed.

As autumn proceeds and senescence overcomes many of the food plants, the diet of the deer has to alter. It is probable that the falling off in the feed value of many of the annual forbs on which the animals fed in summer is counteracted by the higher nutrition provided by the fruits of the forest harvest when good feeding is essential for the build-up of winter reserves in the body. Fungi, acorns and other nuts, seed heads and fruits will all be high in important food requirements and sought and relished by deer. Many plants retain most of their leaves throughout winter, of course, long after the trees have shed theirs and stand bare. Particularly in the south of England, where it is abundant, bramble will form a staple part of the diet of roe, and of other deer species, throughout the year, and the blackberry leaves provide a source of food throughout the winter, along with those other plants that hold on to leaves until new spring growth replaces them.

The leaves fall from trees and bushes and as the herbage withers the cover for the deer decreases, and this may serve to render them a little more nervous. Watching the deer from our windows it appeared to us that they spent less time on the clearings at each visit, despite feeding eagerly, and there seemed to be a little more movement in the population with individual animals occasionally being seen that we could not recall having seen before. Such observation was easier with bucks, of course, these having antlers by which they could be identified to some expectation of accuracy, even allowing for the possibility of other bucks with similar antlers and appearance being present in the area. With does only occasionally could we identify marks or peculiarities to assist us in differentiation between individuals. I reiterate this point since this uncertainty about identification is important, being relevant both to assessment of population and to the habits of individual deer.

As the daylight hours grow shorter and the weather cools the roe change into the plumper appearance produced by the thicker winter hairs. Usually within a few days of seeing the first winter coated roe they have all changed. The camouflage effect of the roe pelage is extraordinary, and the mixture of greyish brown hairs blends in well with dark tree stems in the woods and the darker herbage of the bare hedges. One would imagine that the contrast with the bright summer coats of earlier would be obvious, but this is not so. In the same way, the foxy red of the summer pelage might appear to be ludicrously incongruous against a background of green foliage, but it blends in surprisingly effectively. Somehow there is always a variety of colour in

74

any scene, and the deer watcher will constantly find himself or herself checking with binoculars what appears with the naked eye to be a distant roe only to find that it is a tree stump, a piece of dead gorse bush, senescent bracken or fern fronds, and even things like foxglove flowers, which at close range seem to have no resemblance in colour to a summer roe.

In the winter coat the white rump patch of the roe becomes very much more obvious. In many areas of England the pale rump patch of roe when in their summer coat is hardly visible until the beast flares the hairs on its backside when alarmed, and then it is buff coloured. In the north of Scotland there is a quite noticeable pale or off-white rump patch even when the animal is undisturbed, which is accentuated considerably when flared. In winter this patch is pure white in northern roe, but more of a dirty white in the south, and very visible on roe deer throughout the country, and especially so when flared in alarm. The white hairs on the backside of the winter roe provide a ready method of identification of the sex of the deer. Even from quite a distance, an experienced watcher of deer often gets an intuitive feeling about a beast, by the way it stands or moves, as to whether it is a buck or a doe. He or she may not need to see antlers or pubic tush to know whether the roe is a buck, though these may provide confirmation. There is always the chance that the roe could be a hummel, though these are rare. As I have said Diana has seen and sketched a young antler-less buck, whose sex was confirmed when he urinated, and we have read reports of another sighting of a roe hummel, so the absence of antlers may not be a totally reliable guide. In summer the pubic tush of a roe buck may not easily be seen beneath his belly, but in winter he has a substantially more obvious tassel. In winter coat the pubic tush of a doe is very obvious too, and this tuft of hairs sticks out from her white caudal patch like a tail, although it is at the bottom of the white area of the rump patch whereas of course the tail is at the top.

The white backsides of roe in winter coat are often what catches the eye in the poor light of early morning or late evening, especially when these move. Frequently at this time of year in gloomy or misty weather we looked out onto the clearings and would catch a tiny glimpse of white moving, and a check with binoculars would reveal a roe feeding away from us.

# Chapter 5
# Tracks in the Snow

Winter in the south of England is rarely a hard season, and if there are frosts they do not usually last long or penetrate deep into the ground as happens in the north. Thus the lives of deer in the south are easier in the winter months, with a plentiful supply of bramble leaves and other browse in the woods and along woodland edges and hedgerows. I always left patches of bramble in both clearings around our house, partly because we picked the blackberries from them, and partly as food for the deer. In some parts of the country, especially in more open ground, roe form family groups in winter, and often join these into winter parties. In some parts of Continental Europe winter parties of over twenty roe are not all that uncommon. However, in extensive woodland, the roe do not seem to group together so much in winter and mostly we saw only the doe with her offspring, and occasionally a buck with them in late winter. Quite probably harder weather causes the roe to join into larger groups, especially in more open country where the deer feed out in fields. In the north it is quite usual to see several roe feeding together in turnip fields in cold weather, but these are not necessarily part of the same group and mostly they arrive in the field separately or in smaller groups, and when disturbed they disperse in their individual ways rather than as one herd, quite unlike red deer.

Many people interested in deer, and in watching them, like to stalk about on foot through the woods and fields rather than sitting quietly to watch one area. On the basis of the idea that the grass is always greener over the fence they think that deer are likely to be found just round the corner in the next clearing or the field beyond. However, for watching and studying deer a high seat has considerable advantages. In some places where one can overlook an area from a vantage point a high seat is not necessary, but mostly it has the significant advantage of carrying one's scent at a higher level than that of the deer. Unlike

red deer, roe rarely seem to look upwards, and so it is quite often that one has the thrill of deer passing very close and even directly beneath one quite unaware of one's presence, unless of course they happen to scent the track made upon recent arrival at the seat. A permanent high seat is ideal since animals and birds get used to it and ignore it. Where that permanent high seat provides the watcher with considerable comfort it has the merit of enabling long watching periods without tedium, especially if one can be doing something else at the same time. Thus a conveniently placed house, with windows looking out onto areas frequented by deer, presents a splendid opportunity to study the animals over long periods without disturbing them and without great disruption to the watcher. Having been in such a position, by design, for almost thirty years, the great interest derived from watching a particular area over long periods of time becomes apparent.

One does not watch deer for very long before realising that they move about a lot when feeding, especially when feed is plentiful. In hard weather and in snow when food is in short supply deer may find a turnip crop, for instance, and stay feeding eagerly, but in areas where

they have plenty of choice they browse here and there and move on. Being small, and only the height of a medium-sized dog, roe deer can be difficult to see in long grass or crops, and can quickly vanish behind a bush or clump of foliage. For this reason, when looking for deer in the woods, it pays to move very slowly and to examine likely places carefully and patiently without hurry. Deer are quick to spot movement, and one has to learn to be vigilant for any movement on their part too. Sitting in a hide, or house, one has the great advantage in this respect, being able to spot the movement of deer within sight, be it that of a beast walking about feeding or merely the twitching of an ear of an animal lying down. Creatures moving about outside quickly attract our attention, whether it is a bird or animal. One then begins to appreciate just how easy it is to miss seeing creatures when one is moving about the woods and fields looking for them. A roe has only to lie down, or move behind a bush or tree and one would think that there was nothing there. So often one can glance out of the window and see nothing, and look a minute later and see a deer there. When this happens one begins to perceive the value of studying a particular area over long periods and throughout the seasons on a daily basis, and thus start to learn something of the variety of activity and the diversity of animals that visit the area. As with so many things, however, the problem arises as one realises that the more one learns the less one knows. Consequently sometimes one begins to question dogmatic descriptions of deer behaviour quoted by alleged experts on the basis of comparatively superficial studies, when one's own experiences do not coincide with what are regarded as being accepted characteristics.

Somebody wishing to learn about deer and reading what they can on the subject may gain the impression that deer are very regular in their habits. That is certainly not the experience one gains from constant observation of certain deer-frequented areas where the animals can feed and move about undisturbed. It may be the case that deer that maraud or invade gardens, or come to feed in certain places where they may be disturbed, develop regular habits when they learn that by visiting the area at night they can do so without fear, or that after people have gone home in the evenings they can emerge onto hitherto disturbed ground without hindrance. However, where deer are free to wander without interference and with a plentiful food supply their behaviour appears to be more haphazard and whimsical. We have frequently seen deer appear at what must be regarded as unusual times of the day, or in places where it is not usual to see them, and we see beasts that we do not recognise as having seen before. In winter the roe seem to be less territorial and to tolerate the presence of other deer with less disquiet. In summer when two does are feeding in the same clearing, albeit at different ends of this, the deer tend to keep a watchful eye on each other, constantly looking up as if to check that the other is not encroaching too near. In winter this slightly agitated behaviour is less apparent and the animals seem to be more tolerant of each other. This is especially so when some feeding area, such as a turnip or rape field, attracts in a number of roe from the surrounding cover, or when open clearings with re-grown foliage offer browsing when surrounding woods have only herbage and ground cover that has withered away under the dark canopy of conifers.

The contrast in the behaviour and habits of roe in various parts of the country with differing habitat and weather patterns can be quite marked. In Surrey there was a constant roe population in the woods around the house. By that I do not mean that the individuals comprising the population were necessarily consistent, since without marked deer it was impossible to be sure that does were regular or that bucks in velvet or with new antlers were the same as those seen in previous seasons, and we frequently saw roe that we felt sure were different individuals, and sometimes clearly strangers, using the same routes or feeding in the same places where we so often saw other deer which we thought were regulars. However, the numbers of deer in the woods remained high throughout the year and we saw them in the clearings around the house and in the woods habitually, although, of course, with the qualification that much shorter daylight hours gave less viewing time. We were just as likely to wake up in the mornings to see roe feeding outside the window in winter as in summer, or to see deer cross the open spaces browsing in the middle of the day. In northeast Scotland, with harder winters, poorer soil, and less abundant browse available in winter, the roe appear to have different seasonal behaviour. On our own farm, with an area of open hill and birch wood, and several thick bracken patches, surrounded mostly by conifer plantations of varying ages, the roe tend to retire into the shelter of the woods in winter, emerging to feed on more open ground in the evenings or at night, but also often during the day, especially in fine weather. In summer they move out into the more open areas of light shelter and spend the season there.

The roe bucks cast their antlers during the early winter, and commence the process of growing new ones almost straight away.

The antler growth, the drying up and shedding of velvet to leave the hard bone, and then the casting of the antlers at the end of the year, is all governed by hormonal activity associated with the male sex hormones. The pair of antlers are shed either together or within a short time of each other, and generally at least within a couple of days. The loss of antlers must inevitably cause the animal some disquiet, either by making its head feel a little unbalanced, or even perhaps tender for a while. Possibly because of this one seldom sees a roe buck in this condition and it may well be that they choose to rest in cover at such a time whilst they feel that all is not quite right. However, once the new antlers start to grow again the bucks move around as normal. Older bucks tend to cast their antlers earlier than the younger beasts, and finish growing them and clean them earlier in the season too. In the south of England older bucks start casting antlers in November, and sometimes earlier, whilst the younger animals may not do so until December. The new growth of antler takes from about three to four months to complete, and by late March or early April the older bucks in the south have clean antlers, and most young bucks are finished cleaning off the velvet and are in hard horn by mid-April. Any bucks seen still in velvet late in April may well be bad doers or be ill in some way. Further north in the country the timing is later, as one might expect.

The complete mechanism or the intricacies of the development of antler growth are not clearly understood by most people, nor precisely what it is that governs antler shape. Some people have had the opportunity of studying tame or captive roe bucks, but of course to study antler growth comprehensively it would be necessary to examine in detail antlers throughout development stages from a substantial number of individual animals, together with details of their food, living conditions, stress factors, and so on. It would appear that the condition and well-being of a deer has a significant impact upon the growth of its antlers, and that heredity may affect shape and characteristics in some ways. Roe in some areas tend to have antlers showing certain characteristics. For instance, in Surrey the bucks appeared to have rather narrower-shaped antlers, but with heavier pearling and thick heavily pearled coronets, than bucks in say Wilt-

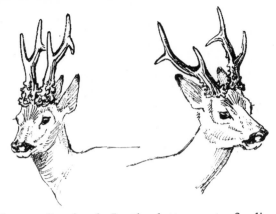

shire or in north-east Scotland. In the latter case, feeding may be significant as a factor in this, of course. However. this is only a very generalised observation, and by no means a reliable guide. What precisely determines that more growth is diverted to a rear or brow tine of an antler, especially if this is asymmetrical, is difficult to guess. Certainly a buck with fine-looking antlers at almost full growth but still with velvet, looks impressive since this furry skin covering exaggerates their size. It does not take a beast very long to shed this velvet once the blood supply is cut off and it starts to dry. This skin covering of the antlers is richly supplied with blood vessels whilst active growth is taking place, which somehow carry nutrients to the antlers to lay down the horn (it is not strictly horn, of course, since that is a different substance rather like fingernails, and is not shed annually, but colloquially deer antlers are often referred to as horns though they are actually composed of bone) beneath, and then at a certain stage hormones signal the sealing of the blood supply at the base of the coronet, and the velvet then dries and shrivels up and antler formation is complete. What predetermines their shape or the stage or size to which they will grow remains a mystery.

Certainly antlers of deer can easily become damaged whilst still in velvet and growing, and such damage is subsequently reflected by these when in hard horn. There is little doubt that a setback in the condition or health of the animal at a critical stage in antler growth can also affect these. Consequently there is no certainty, or possibly even likelihood, that roe antlers in consecutive seasons will either grow progressively larger or even show similarity to those of a previous season.

82

So until a buck has cleaned his antlers one can never be quite sure that one is seeing the same beast unless he is seen very frequently and progressive growth is recognised, or has some distinguishing mark.

One winter day, on 2 December, we woke to see a hard frost on the back clearing beyond our bedroom window. We were watching a roe doe and her female kid feeding there as we got up, at 7.45 a.m., when suddenly the kid bounded forward and fell on its back as if shot! We were astonished. The doe walked past her, ignoring her, fed briefly and then moved off. I dressed rapidly in order to rush out and investigate this strange behaviour. As I was putting on my boots to go outside, the kid raised its head, sat up, and finally got up, shook itself and walked slowly after its mother. I went out of the back door towards the clearing and as I walked up the path, making rather a noise on the frozen leaves under foot, the two deer crossed in front of me. The young doe fell twice but quickly got to her feet again, and they disappeared out of sight into the wood behind. We never saw any further evidence of this strange happening. The animal had certainly not been shot, and I examined where she fell to look for any sign but found nothing. The mystery remains unsolved. Perhaps she slipped on a frozen tree stump and knocked herself out, or perhaps she had some illness or mineral deficiency. I do not know whether we saw the same beasts again. There were two does on the clearing at first light a couple of days later, but we could not know if they were the ones in the earlier incident, and two mornings after that we saw a doe in the same place, but she had a pair of buck kids with her so was clearly a different deer. Indeed she appeared to be a stranger to us, for we had not seen a doe with two male kids there on the back clearing for a while. After those deer had moved slowly on into the trees, a fox came out onto the clearing. It pounced on something, but presumably failed to catch whatever it was, stood for a moment looking, and then sat down on a tree stump apparently admiring the view for a few moments before also moving off.

There seemed to be a high fox population in the woods around Meadow Plat, and in January there was often a lot of noise from both dog foxes barking and vixens screaming in a manner that must be rather hair-raising to someone unfamiliar with their noise and hearing this on a stormy mid-winter night. Though we saw foxes from time to time, their sign suggested more activity than our sightings indicated, and after the occasional winter snowfall we invariably saw tracks from their nocturnal forays. On the other hand deer tracks along the nearby forestry rides were always surprisingly absent in fresh snow, and it usually seemed to be a couple of days before tracks began to appear, and in that part of the world snow often did not lie that long. I always formed the impression that roe were rather disquieted or cautious after a fall of snow for some reason and tended to stay in cover initially, having plenty of scope for remaining in the shelter of the conifers without emerging onto the rides for a day or two. Whether this was coincidence, or whether the deer disliked the snow or felt conspicuous in it, I do not know.

# Chapter 6
# The Far North

Our holidays, as well as our daily lives, revolved around deer, and we spent these in the far north of Scotland where we had a long lease on a cottage at a tiny rent, almost as far away from Surrey as we could get on the mainland. This was situated at the foot of a mountain that towered 3,000 feet in front of us and next to a river with a couple of derelict green fields beside it. Although these fields were long abandoned and heavily infested with the rushes, to which they had largely reverted, they nevertheless represented a sort of green oasis in a huge area of peat and rock, which inevitably attracted the red deer from the hills behind. These deer came down every night to feed on the sweeter green grass of the old fields and along the river bank, both in early summer and in autumn, which were the times when we holidayed there.

The periods when we were able, or prepared, to holiday in our much loved remote haven of quiet and peacefulness were limited, since from late June, when the weather warmed up, until the end of September, when the days shortened and the weather cooled, with night frosts, the vicinity was uninhabitable in daylight hours, by human or deer, on account of the indescribable horde of fearsome midges. The female Highland Midge (*Culicoides impunctatus*) likes to feed on blood before laying her eggs in the damp peat. Many people are familiar with midges and their irritating biting habits; and a variety of different midge species is found throughout the country. However, until someone has experienced the midges that inhabit the north and west of Scotland, in peat bog country, I am confident that they cannot conceive either the ferocity, the persistence, or the quantity of these tiny pests, which descend in immense hordes on any warm-blooded animal rash enough to appear in their territory except in windy or cold weather when the midges are less in evidence. We once made the mistake of visiting that part in July and I vowed never to go there

again at that time of year. Being bitten was less of an ordeal than breathing in the insects in clouds. The first early frosts kill off most of the midges, and provide a welcome relief for the animals and people that live in the area.

Thus, in the summer months, the deer wisely shun the lower ground during the day and seek the relief of the high parts of the hill with cooler breezes where midges and flies bother them less. These high places do not offer much in the way of feed, so the deer trek down the hill in the evenings to seek the sweeter grass and to eat the green areas beside the river during the night. In June the nights in the far north are short, and for a period almost non-existent when skies are bright and the moon clear. I recall standing in the doorway of our little house at midnight some years ago, watching a stag down by the river in the moonlight, and I could see him better in his reflection in the still water of the pool on the edge of which he was standing than I could see the animal himself. In the summer, when the water was low, the stags used to wade across to a shingle island in the river to browse for a while on a cluster of willow bushes before moving on.

It was mostly stags that came down then. I imagine this was partly because the hinds were calving, or thinking about it, and not inclined to wander far from their calving areas, and partly because the stags are the wanderers anyway. Research has shown that hinds become hefted to areas near their place of calving, and seldom move more than a mile or two from there, depending upon the weather of course. A bad storm or heavy snow will shift all deer to shelter or to somewhere that they can feed. On the other hand, stags will wander long distances, and though they mostly join up into bands in summer, lone stags, or little groups of two or three, are quite usual. The beasts that come to feed where estates put out winter fodder for the deer are mostly stags. The marauders that cause trouble in crops or on crofting land, or in the gardens of houses, are nearly always stags. In the rutting season stags will travel very large distances in search of hinds, and it is nothing to a rutting stag to travel ten or twenty miles in a night. Many deer forests with lower ground have high populations of resident hinds, but few stags outside the rutting season. This may be because stags often prefer higher ground on which to summer, possibly because they are more troubled by flies and midges tormenting them on their velvet-covered newly-growing antlers, whilst the hinds need to summer in areas of better feeding to provide sufficient nutrients for maintaining a satisfactory milk supply for their calves, as well as more nutritious grazing and browsing for the young calves. Lactation is the biggest demand upon the metabolism of a hind, and the peak is about a month after calving. At that time she is having to provide most milk to the calf when it is growing fast and hungry but not yet supplementing its diet sufficiently with solid food. This is when the appetite of the hind, and her grazing activity, is at its greatest. When rutting time comes the stags then break out, as they say, and as they themselves come into breeding season so they leave the high ground in search of hinds also in season, often travelling long distances through neighbouring estates to hind territories.

The green grass in places along the river sides and the few trees and willow bushes growing along the edges of the banks, where the seedlings were able to germinate and grow out of reach of the mouths of sheep and deer, provided a welcome change of diet from hill grasses and heather, and the little fields around our house were a focal point as an oasis of green in a landscape that was predominately brown. These little fields had been used to graze a few cows and sheep, and even provide a meagre hay crop for the shepherd who had lived in the house in years past. Although they had deteriorated through lack of constant grazing and cutting, with a massive incursion of rushes and a reduction in the sward content of the sweeter grasses as a result of competition from the more vigorous coarser growth, they still provided preferable grazing for the beasts used to living on the hill tops. To reach these fields the deer had three regular routes, which were well worn tracks as a result of the passage of many deer feet over a long time. One of these tracks followed the river bank for a couple of miles downstream, passed by old peat workings, crossed the top of a badger sett in a high part of the bank, and over the burn that flowed by the house and provided our water supply, piped from higher up. A second track followed the long ridge that sloped down from the end of the higher ground behind the house until it reached the watering burn, and crossed over to follow along the burn side in the dead ground of a gully until this emerged into the open of the fields. The third track came from further out on the hill and followed the burn all the way down from where it was just a trickle high up on the hill; the path, cut into the hillside by many hooves, ran along the side of a steep slope while the burn coursed along the bottom of a gully some distance below, until both met again where they levelled out close to where our house water pipe joined up with the burn that fed it, a mile above the house. This deer path then joined the track from the settling tank beside the burn down to the house.

Where deer have a focal point that attracts them their habits have a regularity with a purpose. Here the green grazing attracted them, but the flying pests drove them away in daytime, so they returned in the evenings when the midges retired from the cooler air, and they retreated back up the hill again before the midges awoke with the dawn. We were able to watch the deer approaching from afar and wending their way down the hill in single file in the evenings, mostly down the last mentioned track, which was in full view from the sitting room window at the back of our house. In late May and early June, when the new grass is doubtless tastier and before the seasonal midge plague has got under way, the stags tended to come down earlier in the evenings, judged by the hours of light and darkness, though by the clock the hour was late. The deer seemed to favour the very closely clipped grass immediately round the house. It has always surprised me how ponies often favour certain patches of grass that appears to be so short that it would seem that they would have a job grasping the herbage at all in their teeth. So these deer favoured the little patches of grass just outside the house that were like close-cropped lawns. There were a few scattered sheep in the vicinity and these sheltered against the house in stormy weather when we were absent, and so this grass was clearly heavily fertilised and doubtless the close-cropping meant that any grass obtainable by hungry mouths was new and more nutritious growth.

In late May and early June the red deer stags in the far north are

casting their antlers and commencing the new growth. Those that came round the house were generally in all stages of growth. Some of the larger and older beasts had quite advanced velvet growth, which was already showing branching, whilst others had little more than large rather elongated gooseberry-like lumps on their heads, and some young beasts still had hard spikes. Sometimes the deer came so close, within a foot or two of the windows, that we kept still and well back from the glass and spoke in whispers inside the house to avoid disturbing them. During the day we used to look in the parks, and walk along the river banks and deer tracks searching for cast antlers. We generally found a few of them. Some had been chewed, for the deer will nibble them, presumably attracted by the calcium and perhaps other minerals, and if the cast antlers are left lying they may eventually be eaten completely by the deer. We picked up a few, since cut appropriately the antlers could be made into excellent coat hooks and walking stick handles. Unfortunately we were never there long enough to get to really recognise individual stags, but it appeared that the animals that visited the parks beside the house were the same regular animals.

We liked to go to the far north at the end of May, because we were then able to experience a second spring. At that time of year the bluebells and primroses, long since over in the south, were flowering in the far north-west of Scotland. The bluebells were small stunted stems, but a welcome patch of blue on the green sward where the river bends and soil brought down over the years had formed a bank of more congenial growing ground out from the peat that covered most of the area. The primroses always looked incongruous to me in the setting of the far north peat country. One would find odd plants or little colonies of them scattered about in isolation, such that one wondered how they had got there. Inevitably they grew on steep banks, or down the sides of gullies or on rocky ledges, where the ubiquitous browsing mouths could not reach them. I often wondered how much they would spread if protected from browsing by sheep and deer. The primroses, and other plants, would need to grow in the soil accumulated along the edges of the burns or on rocky outcrops, of course, and could not colonise the large stretches of wet peat.

Just what the countryside might look like there without the depredations of the sheep and the deer is interesting to speculate. In the early days when we first went north regularly there were no rabbits, but now these have spread and represent a menace to the growth of young plants and seedlings that might otherwise have colonised the area. Some clue as to what the countryside might have looked like a hundred years earlier could be gathered from the old game books of the estate, which I was allowed to borrow and read. From a study of these it seemed that the deer were always present in much the same numbers in that particular place, but that in the past blackgame were present in the vicinity of our house, and woodcock seemed to have appeared briefly in early December along the shores of the loch that lay between us and the sea. Both of these references to birds suggested to me that there was considerably more scrub cover and young birch in those days along the sides of the loch and the burns, where there was a degree of soil. In the early part of this century, especially around the time of the First World War, things seemed to change on this estate, and since then sheep numbers increased considerably, particularly after the Second World War. There can be little doubt that the increase in sheep numbers would have had a major impact upon the regeneration of trees and bushes, with seedlings in places acces-

sible to these animals having little chance of survival. At the same time, following the war, the successive governments encouraged afforestation, and many areas of better sheltered land in the High-lands that had previously served as wintering ground for the red deer became fenced off against them and planted with conifers. This certainly happened in proximity to the area with which we were familiar, and many of the deer that we saw coming down into the strath in the evenings, probably travelling several miles to do so, would undoubtedly have been able to move only a short distance downhill into sheltered corries and glens in the past that are now conifer plantations growing rather poor tree crops. Since we gave up our little house in the far north the trend of tree planting has accelerated, and much of the land in the strath where we saw deer feeding each evening, and which maintained a few hill cows, is now fenced in to protect acres of new trees, putting pressure on the deer to move even further afield to find food and shelter.

In days past, before the invasion of the sheep into the Highlands and the notorious Clearances, black cattle were grazed in the straths and glens and on the better slopes of the hills. These were Highland cattle, with long shaggy coats giving good protection against wind and wet, and small beasts able to forage successfully. Nowadays black Highland cattle are rare, almost all of the breed now being brown, and the breed itself is no longer in favour except as ornamental animals. Cattle and deer are complementary grazers and feeders, whereas sheep and deer are competitors. The effect upon grassland that is grazed by cattle as well as by sheep is noticeable, whereas that grazed only by sheep, especially on an extensive basis, has a different composition. In intensive situations, where fields are heavily grazed by sheep, they eat everything down, and the same is seen on the green patches in the hills where there are large sheep flocks, and even on the road verges. However, cattle eat both longer and coarser vegetation, whilst sheep eat the finer shorter grasses, clovers and other forbs. In winter cattle will eat rushes right down, especially where forage is limited, whereas sheep will not eat these. Thus rushes spread rapidly in the absence of cattle. Sheep and deer have very similar eating tastes given the same opportunities. One thinks of sheep primarily as grazers of grass, because they are kept under circumstances where this is necessarily the food available to them, but given the opportunity to roam wild, sheep will be seen to be browsers in the same way as deer. On the open hills the red deer have little opportunity to browse leaves of forbs and trees, but in their original woodland habitat this is their diet. This similarity between sheep and deer can readily be seen in the shape of their mouths, which are quite different from the squarer lips of cattle that are designed primarily for grazing grass.

The subject of natural regeneration is one that has come to the fore in the last couple of years as government policies have swung from encouraging intensive food production and food from our own resources to trying to restrict agricultural output and encourage a reversion to more extensive farming. The problems with trying to force people to adopt all these theoretical ideas are that of achieving sensible balance, and being able to foresee future consequences. Being a lover of trees and woods, the idea of a substantial increase in these throughout the country appeals to me, and unlike many other people it seems, I see merit even in large conifer plantations. For all their gloominess in their early years many of these plantations eventually grow into the lovely forests seen now in woods planted by earlier generations, and they offer habitat to a variety of different flora and fauna. Most crops look uninteresting or boring or even unsightly in their early stages. Ploughed fields, or newly brairded crops are hardly regarded as attractive to many people, and in their early years trees have the disadvantage of taking substantially longer to grow to acceptable stages of development. Governmental policies towards trees have had two stages of effect upon the deer population. Firstly, the best hill land has been fenced off and planted, which has forced the deer to adopt untraditional habitat and put pressure upon the animals to seek shelter and food elsewhere, particularly in winter, with continued fencing and planting steadily reducing the land area available to them. Secondly, the substantial increase in woodlands since the Second World War has provided significantly increased habitat for lowland deer of all species, resulting in a population explosion; though the massive increase in deer populations has taken place in many countries and not just Britain and is by no means a phenomenon particular to this country. Ten years ago an estimate was made that there were 1 million red deer and 6 million roe deer in Europe. I cannot imagine how this estimate was produced, but if there was any validity in it - and it is likely that it was an underestimate rather than the reverse, and the totals will have increased since - then it is worth noting that the Scottish red deer population represented over a quarter of that total of the dozen or so European countries aggregated.

There is a strange, but noticeable, difference in attitude of people, especially the newly-emerged ranks of those calling themselves conservationists, towards highland red deer and the other deer species, even including lowland red deer. Without doubt this difference emanates from the fact that the deer on the hills live on large estates,

mostly privately owned, and almost invariably by wealthy people. In days long past the deer were hunted exclusively by royalty and chiefs. Over the past century deer stalking acquired a cachet, as a sport for the wealthy, being available only to those estate owners and their friends, who holidayed in their impressive Lodges during the stalking season and then returned to their permanent homes in the south. Whilst this situation has now changed, in that deerstalking has become commercialised and is now available to those prepared to pay for the experience and is indulged in by those from all walks of life, nevertheless the cachet has somehow remained. Furthermore, since the shooting, and thus the control of numbers of the deer, is under private ownership in relatively few hands, highland red deer are very much regarded as the lairds' deer, and as such are often perceived in a light of jealous resentment. There is little doubt that in a few areas there are too many deer either for the good of the habitat or of themselves, and the poor specimens seen in many areas indicate this. In parts of the east of Scotland the red deer are little better in body size or antler growth (as an indication of condition) than in the much bleaker habitat of the north-west of the country. The deer that we watched feeding outside our windows in the far north were not impressive beasts on the whole, and most of them were small-bodied and had poor antlers compared to those seen in better environments. However, this is scarcely surprising when one examined the feeding and habitat available to the deer.

It seems to me that much of the rhetoric about the natural regeneration of native trees, and its prevention by the over-population of deer, is produced by people without much experience or knowledge of the subject, often encouraged by a few who are motivated by antagonistic feelings against the private ownership of large areas of land. In this context it is important to envisage what the land might look like under different circumstances. In some areas experiments are already taking place, under the jurisdiction of bodies like the Royal Society for the Protection of Birds and Scottish Natural Heritage. A good example of this is the Creag Meagaidh estate above Loch Laggan in Inverness-shire, which was purchased a number of years ago by the then Nature Conservancy Council. The sheep flock was removed, and an attempt has been made consistently over the years, at considerable expense, to reduce deer numbers and keep these low. Despite expensive rough terrain machinery, and even the employment of helicopters to facilitate carcass removal from the hill, together with the use of catching pens for trapping live deer for sale, and other costs that would be beyond the pocket of a private landowner trying to operate on any sort of commercial basis, there are still deer present, albeit in lower numbers. The main impact of the change in ownership and management, without doubt, has been the removal of the sheep flock. Examination of the effect of these changes on the flora and growth, especially with regard to the regeneration of trees, is of great interest. In places on the hill they have fenced small areas to protect these completely from the remaining deer in order to assess potential for natural unbrowsed growth. My own impression of the result of these experiments after several years was that they demonstrated the ability of birch scrub to appear and grow quite rapidly along the roadsides, and on the better low ground, where once the sheep had prevented this, but they also indicated that regeneration of rowan and birch seedlings could take place in the burnside gullies and sheltered areas, where there was better soil and some weather protection, albeit extremely slowly. Higher up the hill regeneration prospects were less favourable and would take many years before significant landscape change would be apparent. The growth inside the fenced blocks is certainly greater than outside, but by no means as impressively so as one might expect after the removal of the sheep grazing and a reduction in deer numbers.

It is difficult to picture the hills as they were a hundred, two hundred, or three hundred years ago, and even were one able to do so it would be a problem, and possibly even invidious, to decide what stage or period of countryside one might wish to re-create. Doubtless everyone would have different ideas. However, it does seem to me that the ideas promoted by some conservationists calling for the slaughter of deer in large numbers, but rarely calling for the removal of sheep or reduction in rabbit numbers, conveying a picture of attractive indigenous woodland clothing the lower slopes of the hills which is an unlikely one, are fallacious. My view is supported by two areas also managed by Scottish Natural Heritage near where we live in northeast Scotland. The first of these was declared a National Nature Reserve as a result of being a last remnant of natural oak woods in the area. Some years later research showed that indeed not only was

the wood not natural but man planted, but the seed was of foreign origin and not even indigenous! The second extensive site, also created a National Nature Reserve, once containing large areas of heather, with blackgame lekking grounds in clear open spaces in sparse birch scrub, now has large areas of thick birch scrub that has killed the heather, and is no longer good black grouse habitat, and which is unlikely to evolve into attractive birch woodland unless heavily thinned out by man and machine.

Much of the terrain surrounding our little house in the hills was wet peatland that would never sustain tree growth, even though timber remnants in the peat bogs gave evidence of heavy conifer afforestation in ancient times. Over the centuries the environment has changed too much to allow a return to woodland. On the slopes of the mountain in front of us, however, was a splendid indication of natural woodland possible under certain conditions. The whole of the bottom slopes of this hill were covered in birch wood, with a mixture of rowan and a few scattered holly trees. Most of the wood was growing on a steep slope and on hard ground eroded in the past from the hillside and not on wet peat. There were deer in the wood, both a few roe and red deer, but the latter probably did not live there permanently and only passed through because of the steepness, which explained the survival of the trees. Where the ground was flatter, on either side of the wood and held water, the damp peaty soil grew only deer grass, bog asphodel and other acid-tolerating plants. My judgement is that as the white-faced sheep, the North Country Cheviot, was responsible for clearing the glens of people in the north, when the lairds and chiefs saw profit in mutton and wool and cleared out the folk that eked a living there to make way for the sheep, so this animal too was largely responsible for stripping most of the straths and glens, and the burn sides, of growth and keeping them bare. In other parts of the Highlands the black-faced sheep played a similar role in gobbling seedlings and regeneration, and stripping the landscape of the many wild flowers that otherwise would grow there. Although they may share the trait with deer, sheep have a predilection for eating flowers, and continual destruction of blooms prevents seeding. As a farmer with sheep I have experienced at first hand the change in habitat that these animals can create.

There is little doubt that confronted with a few seedlings in an otherwise bare landscape deer will eat these, but I suspect that in many areas had the sheep not already devastated the herbage the deer alone would not have created a result that would attract the current criticism. Furthermore I believe that in many areas of the Highlands much land is not suitable for regeneration, and certainly not by the native Scots pine of which many conservationists purport to dream. Effectively these trees no longer exist naturally in most of the north and west now, with remnants existing only in central and eastern Scotland for the most part. If the area around our house in the north was cleared of sheep and the deer numbers were drastically reduced, as some would like to see, I believe that the few green patches of grass would be take over completely by rushes. Birches would grow along the banks of the loch and river, and on the steep parts of the burn sides, where there is soil and the water drained enough to avoid drowning the seedling roots, rowan would grow in similar places. Doubtless a few holly trees would take root too, but these exceptionally slow-growing trees would be enjoyed only by generations well in the future. In less acid places alders might also root on the river banks, but the overall result would be little more than fingers of scrub trees alongside the watercourses and roads and not the tracts of natural woodland apparently imagined by many.

In some parts of the Highlands, with more amenable environment and better soil, regeneration would undoubtedly be more successful (in the absence of rabbits, blue hares and sheep!), but then one is confronted with the problem of deciding whose picture of the ideal landscape should form the aim to be achieved. To some people the

open heather-clad hills, extensive blanket bog moorlands and stark bare hill tops are a feature of the landscape unique in the world and to be treasured. Many people would not care for the idea of the roadsides in the north thickly wooded with scrub birch that screened the views, and there are plenty of others that might prefer the opportunity of glimpsing a herd of deer, or a red deer stag, in preference to a distant dark green hillside forest. The dilemma, and the danger, is the decision as to whose perception of the ideal countryside in future years should become the goal if an attempt is to be made to manipulate changes by the action of man, and to be sure that the loudest shouts do not prevail only by reason of the volume and persistence of their noise. Certainly the pleasure that we derived from watching completely wild and free deer feeding contentedly a few feet from us, separated only by a glass window, was considerable, with an enduring memory of the many experiences of this nature that we were fortunate to enjoy.

Our autumn holidays in the north were generally at the end of September and early October. By then there had often been frosts, the nights were cooler, and the midges had departed for another year. Also by that time the red deer rut was under way, and it was a great joy to stand in the doorway of our little house on a still day in the early morning, or in the gloaming, listening to the stags roaring on the mountain opposite, their voices echoing from the hillside. With binoculars, or better a telescope, we could see different parties of red deer high up on the face and pinpoint the stags that were roaring. Some of the greens on which the deer fed and rested high up looked from below to be so steep that we wondered that the deer could frequent them. These green patches of grass, along the sides of tiny burns and where soil had eroded down the slopes in a cascade, were maintained as short green and presumably sweeter grass by the constant grazing of sheep and deer, whose droppings in turn served to fertilise the grass and maintain the cycle.

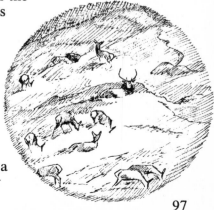

That far north the terrain and plant life on the tops of the hills was similar to that on the highest tops in Scotland even at much lower levels. Though the mountain in front rose to a peak of 3,050 feet, towering above our

97

house which stood at 50 feet above sea level, the hills behind us rose only to around 1,500 feet. However, at that level the habitat on the top was similar to that found at the 3,000 foot mark on hills further south. Proper cranberry grew here and on a small area, just at the top of the hills behind, small numbers of ptarmigan lived. If we walked on the very tops of the hills we generally disturbed two or three of these beautiful birds, and they either flew off uttering their amazing gruff croak to settle on the next hill top, or else they circled out from the hill and round to land a short distance away on the other side of the top of the hill. Their camouflage is amazing when they sit on the ground, with the mixture of greys and whites, browns and blacks blending remarkably with the colours of the rocks and lichens amongst which they live. In winter the birds turn white, with black tails, but in summer the male has a mottled greyish body and that of the female is grouse-coloured, though both retain the rather spectacular pure white wings. In this terrain there is nothing for the deer to eat, so the animals rarely rested right on the very top of the hill unless to catch the breeze on a warm day.

Sometimes in the early evenings in the autumn we would cross the river in the boat and take the car, which we often left parked on the other side to save the long drive round to the house, and motor a couple of miles up the road to watch the deer coming down to feed on the flats where the strath opened out into an area where ruins indicated there was once a settlement of a handful of dwellings, doubtless forcibly abandoned at the time of the Clearances. Some of the deer crossed the river and we watched them fording the shallows and got to know their crossing places. This information was valuable to me on one occasion later when a spate caused the river to rise to a level that made wading impossible, cutting me off from the vehicle on the other bank when the boat was not available. I walked two miles up the river bank to where we had often watched stags crossing, fording the current at an angle upstream. Here I found a

shingle bank running diagonally upstream where even at the high river level I was able to wade across, trousers tied round my neck, with the water only up to my thighs. It was interesting to watch the deer feeding in the evenings, in quite large numbers, and to hear the stags as well as the hinds making their little grunting squeaky calls to each other as they moved around, jostling for the choicest grazing.

We always made a point during our autumn holiday of driving to another strath an hour and a half or so away, because not only was it a beautiful place with forestry plantations and some mature trees on either side of the road, but also because we were always able to see sika deer there, and usually in an open patch of hill near the road we were able to watch several blackcocks in what presumably was a lekking area.

In early October the red deer came down the hill to the parks around the house just as it was getting dark. We could watch them filing down the track off the hill along the burn as the light faded, but by the time they neared the house the light was gone. Sometimes we could watch the first one or two jump the old sheep fence by the rough track and run down to the green grass and start grazing, but often it was too dark by then. One night a stag was roaring loudly and continuously in the dark in the early evening somewhere just behind the house. We had a friend staying with us who had never heard roaring before, nor even seen a deer close up, and had great difficulty in accepting that it was a deer making this loud bovine noise. So I took him outside with a powerful spotlight and I was able to show him the stag, which was lying down about fifty yards behind the house roaring. He was amazed. The stag was not particularly disturbed by the light. There were no hinds there, and he was just roaring because that was what he felt like, doubtless with his hormones at work.

I recall the first time I heard stags roaring. It was many years ago

# Deer: A Personal View

when I was still a student at university, and two of my friends there had vacation jobs as pony boys on a big deer forest. I think they had been grouse beaters earlier in the season as well. I was on my way north somewhere, but I do not now remember my destination. I do recall that I stopped off to see them and stayed a couple of nights in the beaters bothy in their company, joining them for the day as an additional pony boy, for which I was paid. I recall that we had stag's liver for breakfast, which was my first taste of this. The party shot one stag, which the friend accompanying me took home on his pony and that meant that I was able to ride back on my empty garron. I had a pleasant ride and got the pony home without incident, and subsequently was amazed not only to be paid but also to be complimented by the head keeper on my riding. I suspect that his ability to judge horsemanship was less good than his ability to flatter, and my wife would probably endorse my observation now! My friends drove me up the glen when it was dark to listen to the strange noises rather like cows roaring. More recently I was lying in the bath one October evening in our present house in north-east Scotland, enjoying the singing of a stag roaring on our hill outside when the telephone rang. The young man who lived across the valley behind us, who worked on the farm of the neighbouring estate, asked if we had not heard one of our cattle bellowing on our hill and sounding as if it was in trouble. He had been outside his house and heard it. Diana, who had answered the telephone, explained that we had heard it and it was actually a rutting red deer making the noise.

The roaring of a rutting red deer stag is one of those evocative and exhilarating sounds to me, like the calling of wild geese migrating high overhead. Our holidays in the north usually coincided with the time when the geese started to move south from their nesting

100

grounds in the remoteness of far northern countries, and often we saw and heard them flying quite low over the house. One year in particular we had skein after skein passing low overhead calling loudly. Friends staying with us left the following day to go south and told us later that they passed a loch near the road a few miles south of us on which they saw thousands of geese, obviously the travellers that had flown over us having a rest before moving on. We hear geese quite often and when we do we always look for them. In autumn they are heading south to winter in the more amenable climate of coastal Scotland and even England, and in spring we hear and see them returning north again to the barren tundra wastes to nest and breed. Perhaps it is something connected with their wild freedom that evokes the sense of excitement in some of us when we hear them, tinged with memories of watching cold dawn flights on lonely mud flats years ago. The roaring of stags is equally evocative to me, somehow encompassing the aura of unfettered wildness of the deer wandering free, and the picture of the majestic appearance of a fine ten-pointer or royal declaring his dominance and challenging rivals. There is an aphorism that simple pleasures are the last refuge of the sophisticated. There is certainly truth in the view that many of the simple pleasures provided by Nature are the most rewarding, and that the best things in life are free. Two of my simple pleasures are lying in the bath on an evening in October listening to stags roaring outside, and hearing the curlews calling on the hill on a lovely morning in early summer.

Listening to roaring is a good way of locating deer in woodland, and in places in continental Europe their woodland red deer are stalked in this way at rutting time. I remember visiting a friend a few miles away one evening, and while we were watching a glorious sunset with clouds of many shades of pink stretching across a darkening blue sky, we heard a stag roaring a little way off. I had always imagined there must be red deer in that area, but it was interesting to confirm this beyond doubt, and to be able to pinpoint the roars to where the deer had clearly emerged from the large block of woodland to feed at its edges, possibly crossing the road into fields. The motivation or instinct behind the act of roaring has interested me for a long time and I have been unable to decide what circumstances cause the stag to indulge in such vociferous activity during the brief period of the year while the rut is in progress. Without doubt roaring is influenced by hormonal activity, and though I have heard stags making other quieter bleats when feeding in groups, I believe they do not roar outwith rutting time. An occasional roar may be heard as

101

autumn passes into winter, but this is simply residual activity of the rut, perhaps from a beast that came into season late. I related how I showed a friend a stag roaring behind the house, lying down on his own. Sometimes one can see stags roaring when apparently alone. From time to time one sees travelling stags, clearly searching for hinds, stop to roar. Perhaps this is a challenge to provoke an answer from a stag that already has a harem in order to locate the opportunity of acquiring hinds. At other times one sees a stag that has clearly been rutting, and subsequently vanquished and banished from his hinds, lying roaring and looking tired and disconsolate. Whether he is hurling abuse at, or taunting his conqueror, or compelled by the flow of his hormones to continue roaring without much thought in mind, or feebly hoping to locate other hinds we cannot know.

If one watches a stag with a harem of hinds it is clear that the presence of another stag in the area, or even of young staggies that present him little competition, provokes him into roaring, and this assumes the gesture of defiant challenge. However occasionally one can see a stag with hinds, or even with only one hind, with no sign of any other male deer nearby, and yet he still roars. Perhaps somehow the roaring of stags is part of the trigger mechanism that causes a hind to come into oestrus. In many animals where both sexes come seasonally into mating condition the female appears to require some activity on the part of the male to encourage her to become receptive to him. Indeed one might say that this is the case with most mammals, and perhaps roaring is all part of the required display, such as involved in the association of most birds as a prelude to mating. I suspect this to be the case, and that roaring is not merely an aggressive challenge to other stags, but also part of the general rutting display, such as the growing of the mane and the increase in testicle size and so on, precipitated by hormonal activity, itself seasonally influenced.

The catalyst that precipitates the red deer rut is uncertain. It seems likely that the presence of a stag in mating condition, or in season, promotes the onset of oestrus in hinds in the same way that the presence of male sheep encourages ewes to come into heat. For this reason some shepherds introduce vasectomised tups, or rams, into the ewe flock a couple of weeks before putting in the breeding tups, which stimulates the ewes to come into oestrus ready for being served. It is said that a frosty night or cold weather gets the stags going and stimulates rutting activity, and in the north it certainly seemed that this was so. Mild warm autumns seemed to coincide with the red deer rut getting off to a slow start, but when the weather was colder, especially with frosts at night, the roaring of stags became significantly more apparent. I have little doubt that the factors that precipitate the rut and govern the timing of this are a combination of various things, which include daylight length as well as temperature. Undoubtedly the condition of the deer themselves also has a considerable bearing upon their sexual activities, which would explain why woodland or semi-woodland stags, having benefited from substantially higher quality and abundance of summer feeding, may often start rutting activity some time before the deer on the high hills, where temperatures are probably lower and frosts more likely. It is quite possible that the presence of other deer, and especially of any already starting to show signs of the mating activity, also has a sort of cumulative or communal effect of generally stimulating the deer to come into season.

The rutting activity that we could watch from the house in the north was often confined to distant deer viewed with the aid of a telescope. The hinds did not come down to the green parks by the river, and at that time of year the area around the house was visited at night only by the younger stags and beasts that were not otherwise occupied by their sexual proclivities. The bigger stags either had hinds to guard from rivals, or were themselves rivals hoping for a chance to move into a herd in an unguarded moment on the part of the master stag and drive out a few hinds for their own procreational ambitions.

Autumn in the Highlands is a wonderful experience for those privileged to appreciate and enjoy the beauties of wild Nature and the peace and solitude of the environment. Our little house had few facilities that might be regarded as modern conveniences. However, we had running water, piped from the burn, and proper washing facilities including a bathroom, and even two loos. The hot water system was excellent and efficient, this being heated by the coal or peat burning cooker and circulating into and from a copper hot water tank situated in the loft above. One might describe the water system as a modern convenience perhaps, but there was little modern about it, the stove being ancient and the water tank of similar vintage. We had introduced the bath and a second loo when we added on to the house after I got married. However, there was no electricity in the area for many miles, other than a privately generated supply at a house five miles across the hills, and no telephone within similar distance, and we preferred to keep it that way. It would have been a simple matter to install a generator, especially if used only for our short holidays, but I resented the idea of the noise of an engine sullying the peaceful quietness of the setting, where the only sounds outside were the wind and the noise of the river and the roaring of stags. Tilley lamps and Calor gas stoves made a certain noise, but not an unpleasant one, and much of our lighting was provided by candles which gave a soft relaxing light. We used a Tilley lamp where we wished to read, but candles were adequate otherwise, and gave a pleasant light that enhanced the warmth and cosiness of the house on a stormy night.

# Chapter 7
# Curlews on the Hill

We knew that there were plenty of roe deer on the farm when we moved to north-east Scotland in 1974. I walked round the boundaries early one morning after we had bought the place but before we had taken possession of it, and saw as many roe as I might have expected to see on a similar walk in Surrey, even if I do not presume the population in the vicinity to be so high. Though wooded in places, the more open ground gave better visibility at a distance than in the south. One of the first things we noticed about the roe in our new area was their white rump patches that are visible on undisturbed animals even in summer, unlike the southern deer we were used to seeing where the pale patch is noticeable in summer coat only when the backside hairs are flared in alarm. With our northern roe deer, when they are in red summer coat, the rump patch is not so obvious as when this is flared and displayed as an alarm signal, but nevertheless is visible as a smaller white or pale off-white patch below the tail on most roe. Not as white as in winter of course, but often still very obvious.

We did not see any red deer on our farm for a while, but we knew they passed through because the local keeper told us they did so, and they had been in the area in small numbers for a good many years. Our predecessor, the tenant farmer, and a neighbour, both told us that they had shot big deer in the past on their respective farms. Red deer are present in quite large numbers on the hills within ten miles of the farm, and even within five miles some of the year, and it is clear that many deer choose to winter in the adjoining woodland, which stretches unbroken to the farm, especially when their numbers are swelled by deer migrating from the high ground further up the valley when the weather is severe. Some of these beasts undoubtedly remain in the woods rather than returning to the hills when conditions improve, reverting to what is after all their more natural habitat.

I can recall very clearly the first red deer that we saw here, and indeed Diana painted the scene subsequently, so that we have this recorded. We were sitting having a cup of tea late one afternoon in spring when I looked out of the window to see Diana's Highland pony staring intently at something. As she continued to watch the object of her interest I decided to relieve our curiosity by going outside to see what it was that had captured her attention. Going cautiously into the farmyard I went over to the side of the sheep pens and peered across to the farm road in the direction that the pony was still looking. To my amazement and delight I saw three stags grazing in the small paddock beside the road. I crept away without disturbing them to fetch Diana to watch them too. On subsequent evenings, for several days, we kept an eye out for these deer and saw them come down the hill and pause cautiously on the edge of the tarred farm road before crossing this to jump the low fence and graze on the green grass of the paddock.

From then onwards we saw more sign of red deer about the place. We found tracks here and there, not only on the hill but on the farm road and in the fields too. Occasionally we glimpsed red deer on the hill and began to see them more often from the house. A little later that summer we were having breakfast, our chairs facing the large window to enable us to watch the continual entertainment provided by the bird feeding table outside during winter and early spring, when I spotted a movement under the trees on the hill two hundred yards in front of the house. As I looked I realised that there were three red deer hinds there, quietly browsing on the leaves.

Having taken on the responsibility of running the farm on my own, with Diana's help, the opportunity for us to get away to our little house in the north, let alone to do so together, became increasingly remote as stock numbers of various kinds built up. Much as we loved the wild but peaceful solitude of the north, with the red deer as our neighbours, the environment in which we now live is so lovely that in comparison some of the magic of the north dimmed, and moreover we also had red deer near at hand, as well as the plentiful roe. The escalating price of petrol made the long trip north, which took five hours even from our new home, increasingly costly, and finally we decided to part with the lease of our little house there. Thus, although in subsequent years we often had many opportunities to see and watch red deer in various other places, most of our observations have been on our own farm, and a great many of these were from the comfort of the windows of our house.

Spring in the north is a very different affair to that in the south. When we first came to north-east Scotland an acquaintance told us that there is no spring here, or at most a very short one. However, that is an unperceptive observation. We have a spring, and even a long tantalising one for a farmer waiting for the grass in the fields to grow sufficiently, anxious to cease feeding his cattle and sheep their winter rations. Nevertheless spring in the north is quite different from the season in the south. There spring appears gently, with the first signs hardly noticeable except to the observant countryman watching for new growth and evidence of the fresh start to the year. In the south winter is very short, and there is a comparative abundance of feed for deer throughout the winter. If there is hard weather, this does not last long, and never has the severity of that experienced in the north. Here, the grass does not start perceptible growth until May, wood anemones, or windflowers as Diana likes to call them, do not appear until early April, and violets only show towards the end of that month. The roe deer do not shed their winter coats until June, and we have to continue feeding cattle until well into May, by which time farmers in the extreme south of the country are already thinking of cutting grass crops!

Winters here vary in intensity of cold and duration of snow, but mostly we get long periods of frosts at night, often lasting throughout the day, and usually periods of snow cover lasting several days. Even in the milder winters these have the effect of reducing herbage and food supply very considerably. The milder damper winters in fact seem to be more detrimental to domestic stock than hard bright weather, and one supposes that the effect upon deer of all types would be similar. On our hill there is a certain amount of grazing

107

and browsing available through until late January or February, but then there is a lean time, and March well deserves the reputation of being the hungry month. This period of March and early April, when food must be scarce for deer, has two adverse effects upon the health of deer. The first is the lowering of their condition. The second, which is speculation upon my part, is because of this the eager feeding upon newly emerged green growth in late April and early May deer suffer from, and succumb to, the same mineral deficiencies as domestic stock, of which staggers or hypomagnesaemia may be the most critical. This would certainly account for the corpses of roe that I find at this time of year. Generally we come across the remains of at least a couple around the farm each year. Though natural and unfertilised herbage is less prone to a shortage of mineral uptake than forced heavily fertilised grass, and forbs or broad-leaved plants may contain a higher mineral content than grasses, the problem arises because rapidly growing spring foliage has a much lower mineral uptake, and thus content, in the spring, and to a lesser extent in the autumn. With magnesium, for instance, which is a mineral necessary for the body in tiny quantities, cattle cannot store reserves in their systems and need a daily intake. With the lower content of magnesium in spring grass they cannot absorb enough material to satisfy the requirement, and the result of this is an occasional beast which literally staggers uncertainly, then goes down and finally deteriorates rapidly into convulsions and dies unless treated promptly. I often wonder whether the deer suffered a similar fate when I find a carcass in spring.

When I was actively collecting deer books twenty-five years ago, one of the very few that eluded my searches was a copy of *Some*

*Account of Jura Red Deer* written and published privately by Henry Evans just over one hundred years ago. Consequently when I learned that a limited reprint had been made, though I am not too interested in reprints, I rapidly obtained one of these new copies. It is a slim little volume that can be read in an evening, but in my view it is one of the most remarkable books ever published on Scottish red deer, and one that most people interested in this subject would find fascinating, not least because so much of what Henry Evans wrote a century ago is all too familiar in the more recent publications of researchers. This remarkably astute and painstaking observer of a century ago, in the role of many notable natural historians of his time and earlier, knew well then what some of our modern experts have just discovered.

Most of the work on deer, especially pertaining to health, has been carried out on deer farms or the equivalent, or in special environmental circumstances such as upon Rhum. I am not aware of any post-mortems taking place on a wide basis into winter deaths of wild red deer, especially where these occur on a significant scale. Without such work the cause of death cannot be established, and can be attributed easily to starvation in a generalised way. A hundred years ago Henry Evans wrote "The death rate of sheep in the western portion of Argyllshire is lamentably heavy and is largely due to parasites. It is probable that careful study, accompanied with special knowledge, might lead to very interesting and valuable discoveries, and perhaps to changes of management which would greatly reduce the death rate, both of sheep and deer."

A major problem, recognised by Henry Evans is that "We seldom find dead deer quite fresh enough to open and examine them." This was written by a man who went to great lengths to find, examine and count dead deer. He believed that very many deer in the wild die of lung worms, or husk, but acknowledged that some may die of liver fluke. One wonders whether such comments are equally applicable today, and indeed perhaps more so with increased deer numbers. Liver flukes might well be undetected in deer livers if no lesions were visible and the small bile ducts were not cut open for examination. In those deer found dead it is probable that such a detailed post-mortem would be unlikely unless the carcass was reasonably fresh. Certainly young sheep can die of heavy fluke infestation with the liver outwardly appearing normal and without lesions, and I see no reason to suppose that the same would not occur with young deer.

I suspect that very little is known about the true health of wild deer on a wide scale. Most deaths are put down to starvation and bad weather. I have seen references to the view that deer are not as

waterproof and well insulated as cattle and sheep and thus much more susceptible to bad weather, especially heavy, cold rain. This may be true, but it is dangerous to generalise as a result of comparison of captive deer in a field with those with freedom to roam and to find shelter or keep warm by moving or whatever. One definite difference between deer and domestic stock is that it has been shown that even with those offered ad lib food, there is a loss of appetite in winter that occurs naturally, and this is coupled with an animal that does not lay down great reserves of fat like cattle and sheep, or even rabbits. It has also been shown that like most of these other animals, and possibly more so, stress is a very significant catalyst for precipitating acute disease. In many animals the bugs exist naturally in their bodies in small quantities, but stress somehow can cause these to multiply fatally. Anybody that keeps sheep knows this only too well!

Staggers, or hypomagnesaemia, is one affliction that can be precipitated by stress though basically it results from a deficiency in the daily intake of magnesium necessary from ingestion of large quantities of lush vegetation in spring. Bad weather or frost may precipitate a case that otherwise might have survived. Although I have not seen staggers in deer myself, two people have told me recently that they have observed deer suffering from it, despite a vet suggesting that deer do not get it! Since death is rapid, only careful post-mortem analysis could reveal it as a cause of death in wild deer, but it is so common amongst cattle where adequate extra magnesium is not fed that it seems likely that deer suffer too. Likewise the suggestion that mastitis is associated only with high productivity is extremely rash. It may seem more prevalent in high-yielding dairy cows, but the problem is widespread amongst low yielders too. Cattle and sheep of all kinds get mastitis, and so do humans, and even ferrets. We had a 28-year-old mare who had not had a foal for fifteen years contract mastitis in one quarter, with ultimately fatal results. All mammary glands are susceptible, and heifers as yet uncalved can get it. I suggest that it is highly likely that wild deer suffer too on occasion, and this might well explain some calf deaths. It is extremely unlikely that if culled hinds were examined for mastitis the situation would be readily apparent, even if those researching knew how to establish if infection had taken place earlier in the year.

Whilst overpopulation and excessive deer numbers would clearly accentuate other problems, I am much concerned at the generalised way so many people seem to blame high red deer mortality on bad weather and starvation without research having been carried out into precise cause of deaths. Perhaps heed should be taken of the wise writing of Henry Evans a century ago suggesting that careful study might lead to very interesting and valuable discoveries and result in changes in management and reduction in the death rate of deer. Evidence that deer deaths are not caused merely by excessive numbers and population *per se* may counter the strident ululations of those who claim that some of the sporting estates are so overrun with red deer that the remnants of the ancient Caledonian pine forest cannot regenerate, as I have read.

Certainly in spring time deer are very evident at the edges of fields in the mornings and evenings, and often during the daytime too. In early May if we drive anywhere during the evening before it gets dark we invariably see winter-coated roe feeding hungrily at field edges, mostly in grass fields, though of course the deer are more readily seen against the green background and are probably eagerly feeding along the sides of other fields too. I imagine that their attraction is the young growth of many forbs, or broad-leaved plants, rather than the new grass, for the roe are primarily browsers rather than grazers, but they may be glad of a bite of young grass too when hungry. For many years the roe emerging into the fields has been one of the signs for which I look with anticipation in spring, for this, together with other indications such as the greening of young larch trees, has always suggested to me the beginnings of steady growth of grass, heralding the nearing opportu-

111

nity for taking the cattle off their hill wintering ground back into the summer grazing fields.

In spring I eagerly await the emergence of the wood anemones. In parts of our birch woods these flowers literally carpet the ground in great patches of delicate white and pinky purple, but the flowers are to be found all over the hill to a lesser degree. Deer, and sheep, seem to favour eating flowers. It may be that the flower has a higher feed value than the rest of the plant, though I am not familiar with the chemical composition differences. However, it is accepted that the time to cut many weed plants to weaken them, and hopefully to eradicate them eventually, is when they are emerging into full flower, and this suggests it is at that point of growth the plant has concentrated most nutrition in its flower head. Roe, in particular, are fond of wood anemone flowers and one can often watch these dainty animals feeding on them with delicate fairy-like movement through the woodland. I always find the emergence of abundant wood anemone flowers heralds the appearance of the roe from their winter shelter in the warmer conifer plantations out into more open ground, eager for the fresh growth that appears earlier and in greater profusion in the more open birch woodland than beneath the dark canopy of the conifers.

We see roe regularly from our window in spring, both in fields, where sometimes they will feed for long periods and at any hour of the day, and on the hill opposite, especially on the open areas that I cleared in the past to give us a wider view and where I feed cattle in winter, so the grass is shorter there and thus with higher content of the wild white clover much loved by deer and sheep. Through May the roe are much in evidence. Although we see signs of them, the red deer are not so apparent in spring and we see them less regularly than later in the summer. Careful observation reveals signs of nocturnal visits to fields unoccupied by stock, though.

The differences in habit, as well in size of body and antlers, and coloration, between the roe of north-east Scotland and Surrey are quite marked. Although we have seen roe in many different parts of Britain, without long study it is difficult to surmise regional differences, but I should imagine that all deer, as with other animals, adapt themselves to their environment to some degree, and so the behaviour of deer in the wetter west or bleaker far north, let alone the much milder and lusher south-west of the country, no doubt have idiosyncratic characteristics that are discernible to those that watch them. Thus whilst in extensive Surrey woodlands the winter and spring movements of roe are undoubtedly governed to some extent by the expanding population and .he young of both sexes wandering off to find their own patches of ground where they can live in solitary peace, after being chased off by the mother, in the north the weather is a factor of at least equal importance. Cold winds, heavy rain, snow and hard frosts all affect deer adversely, not surprisingly, and shelter is of great importance to them. Consequently, where these are available, deer of all species will seek out thick woodlands that offer cover and shelter from the elements, and perhaps a dry bed. In this area there are plentiful conifer plantations of varying ages and stages of growth, and thick plantings of perhaps five to fifteen years old provide ideal shelter. So the deer tend to retire to these in poor weather and when the days grow short and cold, emerging to feed often at night. Ruminants divide their 24-hour day more or less equally, but not necessarily consecutively, between feeding, ruminating and resting or sleeping. In summer when food is plentiful, one can see, if one watches deer for long periods, that they alternate between these activities if one can so describe resting, quite frequently, eating for a short while, and then lying down to ruminate, occasionally dozing off. In winter and spring the pattern changes through necessity, for when food is in short supply the deer need to intake as much as they can whilst the opportunity presents itself, until, when their stomachs are full, rumination becomes the priority.

The curlew is the herald of spring to me. I am not sure quite when winter ends and spring starts, nor where it merges into summer, for the calendar dates for the official commencement of the seasons do not apply in the north-east. Perhaps March, April and May might be regarded as spring here, though the early part of the period is still the hungry time for farm stock and wild creatures alike. The grass and other herbage does not start to grow properly until May is well settled in, and this period is a dangerous time for deer, and many of the deaths of red deer in the hills occur at this time of year, just when the new season shows promise of arriving. Often by this time the long hard winter has taken its toll, and severe weather now can be too much for deer in low condition. March is often a stormy month with cold spells, periods of driving wet rain, and devastating snow squalls that take a heavy toll of new-born lambs in the fields as well as upon deer on the hill. The first lapwings or green plovers often appear in the field

in front of the house at the end of February, but these usually vanish again when the seemingly inevitable coarse weather re-appears. They return again at the end of the month, albeit unfortunately in decreasing numbers in recent years, and often bring with them the teuchat storms (teuchat is the local name for peewit). I have always said that we get snow when the daffodils first appear, and this generally is the case, if only for a couple of days. Then, after this final fling of winter, the better weather comes, and the wood anemones appear eventually to carpet large patches of the birch woods, and the birches themselves start to show green.

The curlew is the bearer of hope for better weather to come and fresh life starting, however, and once we hear the first one we hear him or her again daily, for they come and stay. Gradually more curlews appear, until quite a large flock of them comes down each evening into the field behind the house to feed. We love to hear their wild call on the hill and around the house, and to lie in bed on a spring morning and listen to the curlews on the hill is one of my great pleasures. The first oystercatchers appear within a few days of the curlews, as do the blackheaded gulls that nest on some of the ponds that I have made on the farm. We love to see them, but somehow they do not have that magic wild appeal of the curlew calling far out on the hill. The far-off bubbling song of a curlew is a lonely, haunting cry, evocative to me of the similar call of the smaller whimbrels in the uninhabited areas of northern Lapland, where we searched for nesting lesser white-fronted geese many years ago.

The appearance of the windflowers is a sure sign of the time when the roe appear out from the shelter of the thick conifer woods to take up summer residence in the more open parts of the hill where the feeding is better, and where the does will have their kids and raise them. By the middle of May the grass has started to grow continuously in the fields and I take the cattle off the hill and back to graze the grass there. This leaves the hill undisturbed, and the deer take advantage of this. By the end of May, when spring is merging into summer, the roe are re-established in their summer haunts, and an occasional red deer hind will soon be taking up residence. The first swallow usually arrives outside the house at the end of April, generally a single male, identified by his longer tail. Most years we wonder if he regrets his early arrival, as there is so often inclement weather at this time; but this does not last long, and by the start of May the incessant call of the cuckoo on the hill indicates that summer has come. The deer are feeding hungrily, with the pregnant does and hinds heavy with young, both due to give birth in the following month and their growing foetuses placing greater demands upon food intake.

# Chapter 8
# Orchids and Knapweed

One of the delights of our hill, to us, is the plethora of wildflowers that grow there in summer. I am no botanist, but I have listed 238 species growing on the farm, and I have little doubt that a knowledgeable botanist who made the effort to maximise the record of plant species on this ground could increase this number significantly. Orchids, of at least eight species, grow in large numbers all over the hill, and if one was competent to assess the niceties of identification and distinguish those that have hybridised one might well find others. In summer, large areas of the open parts of the hill in front of the house are covered in swathes of striking Trollius, or Globe flowers, like enormous pale yellow buttercups, but readily distinguishable from these, even at a distance, not only by their greater size but also by their softer colour. From the house, parts of our hill in front appear as a carpet of yellow, and it is a joy to watch a red deer hind feeding in the patches of yellow Trollius, up to her belly in flowers, with a new calf just visible beside her. The deer favour the Trollius flowers, and I have frequently watched roe picking off the yellow blooms.

As summer progresses, the wetter parts of the hill become tinged with the golden yellow of bog asphodel, and subsequently the dark orange of the attractive seed heads of these flowers. Later in summer other patches of the hill are blue with Devils Bit Scabious, and in places these are mixed with the purple of Black Knapweed. The former acquired its curious name because of its strange root with a broken off appearance. The legend is that once the plant had a long root that provided useful cures for all sorts of ailments, but the devil did not like it being useful and bit off the root! The background of the hill is one of constantly changing colour throughout the seasons and in differing weather conditions. The grasses and rushes change from bright green in early summer, to pale fawn and grey, and then a darker brown sometimes almost purple after a rain shower, and the bracken in September gradually changes to brown and yellow, and then orange-brown that is almost roe coloured, as autumn replaces summer, with sporadic senescence of the fronds often confusing the enquiring eye on the outlook for deer.

Against this background the variation in the apparent coloration of both red deer and roe is often remarkable. Much of the time one wonders how it was that red deer got their name, when they do not look to be red at all, whilst the little roe in summer coat is bright foxy red-brown. But from time to time one sees the red deer in mid summer, when an animal is standing appropriately and sunlight catches it right, and then one sees a deer worthy of its name. The light reflection from the hair of deer is undoubtedly a wonderful aid to their camouflage, and a group of red deer standing feeding at differing angles presents a variety of colour depending upon how they are positioned in relation to the viewer. Sometimes, especially when wet, the reflection from a deer's coat can make the animal appear to shine, and one can catch the movement from a long way off. At other times it is difficult to distinguish the deer from adjacent rocks. Years of watching deer have taught me that however well I consider that I know the view from the house, and despite the thousands of times that I must have examined through binoculars particular bushes or stones or lumps of rushes and so on, if something catches my attention for some reason, then it is better to investigate with a glass to ascertain for sure whether there is a deer present. On countless occasions it is a false alarm, and I wonder how I can continually peer at the same gorse bush or rush clump, but light and weather conditions seem to be infinitely variable, and the persistent watchfulness is rewarded from time to time by spotting an ear twitching in the grass, or the top of a back just visible over the bush, or a dim shape on the skyline, which must have somehow caught my attention.

In June both red and roe deer change their coats into summer pelage in this part of the country. At this time of year the deer often look very scruffy because of the change, and one can find tufts of winter hair lying where deer have rested, or where they have crossed or crawled underneath fences. It is remarkable how deer, especially roe, prefer to crawl underneath a fence or through a hole in it if they can possibly do so, rather than jump one that is easily within their capability. On many occasions we have watched a deer, both red and roe, walk up and down a fence line, like a caged animal, seeking a place to go through it or below it, before finally jumping over. Red deer do not bother much about conventional stock fences, which they can jump with the greatest of ease, when they know just where they are heading, although calves are frequently reluctant to jump and will often spend a long time running up and down insisting that the wire presents an insuperable obstacle. However, when unhurried, deer will invariably halt at a fence, sometimes walking up and down a few yards as if looking for a better place to cross, or trying to buck up courage or energy to make the jump. When one observes how effortlessly they can clear the fence their hesitation seems absurd, but often the hindmost deer in a herd, particularly young beasts, still seem to be reluctant to jump even when the leaders are well across, and perhaps feeding eagerly on whatever has tempted them over. When alarmed, all the deer, except an occasional calf, will jump instantly and without hesitation. One evening I watched a group of red deer hinds and calves feeding near and in a paddock at the bottom of our hill where we often keep the ponies. Half a dozen hinds and yearlings were in the paddock, with the remainder out on the hill with the calves. Those in the paddock moved along inside it until they were opposite where the settling tank for our house water supply is surrounded by rushes and lush vegetation due to the ground being wet from the overflow pipe. One older hind obviously thought that this herbage looked tasty and jumped over the fence, which is normal stock height, so low for a red deer. The other hinds wandered up and down inside the fence for some minutes, occasionally appearing to buck up courage and being about to jump over to join her, which they could have done with ease. Finally they decided against it and moved back along the paddock and jumped out onto the hill again in the place where they came in, where the fence was very little lower than by the settling tank.

Roe deer always seem to prefer to go under fences or through holes rather than jump, and we have frequently watched them squeezing under the bottom wire, where a dip in the ground presents an opportunity, or through the lower strands, like a dog. I recall sitting up a high seat watching a doe feeding towards me one evening, and then observing as, to my surprise, instead of climbing through the rather loose wires of the fence in front she clambered between the lower bars of a wooden gate, one foot after the other just as a dog

would do. Instances such as this serve to remind one just how small an animal a roe deer is, being no bigger than a good-sized dog, and standing no higher at the top of its back than the knee height of a tall adult human; something that many observers forget, or perhaps never realise.

I should imagine that temperature may have some effect upon the timing and rapidity of the coat change of deer as well as daylight length, but undoubtedly the condition of the animal also has a considerable bearing upon this, with a beast in good condition changing more rapidly than a poor specimen, just as occurs with cattle for instance. The change over to summer coat often seems to be more rapid with red deer than with roe, but it may be that we see more roe in spring and the early part of the summer, or because the contrast in coat colour between winter and summer is much more marked in the latter. Grey hairs persisting in the coats of roe, usually in the back part of the body, are more obvious against the bright reddish brown summer pelage. Unlike cattle and sheep, which frequently rub on trees and rocks if provided with the opportunity when shedding their winter coats, evidence of which can be seen in tufts of hair or wool caught on the object used or lying on the ground, I cannot recall having seen a deer scratching its body thus, nor finding evidence of one having done so. They do nibble at their coats a lot though, and clearly find the change over itchy. However, I have watched a hind rolling upon its back, with her legs in the air, just like a horse would

do, clearly relieving an itchy back. This was actually quite a bit later in summer and long after coat change, so I presume that it was just an itch, or maybe even *joie de vivre*! Certainly I have only once seen a deer rolling upon its back in this manner, just as our ponies sometimes do when they have been turned out into a paddock after being out on a ride, pushing herself onto her back with legs kicking straight in the air, and repeating the manoeuvre several times. We have watched a stag rolling, but not quite so pronounced and not flat on his back with legs vertical. This was not wallowing, for he did this on hard dry ground, and since he did it twice he may well have been relieving an itch. He was a big black beast that had just come in to join hinds, and the first big stag that we had seen that year, on 16 September. Through the telescope I saw him roar a couple of times at a smaller beast, but did not hear this because he was far up the hill and the window was shut. He then lay down, and I watched him chewing the cud for a few minutes. I called to Diana to have a look, which she did, and then went out to her studio to look at him through her telescope and sketch. Whilst she was going out I saw the stag lie on his side and kick his legs a couple of times. He then got up and moved downhill a few yards and started to feed. I then had to go and feed the dogs, so desisted from observing him. Meanwhile Diana saw him lie down and roll again, but this time he also thrashed briefly with his antlers on the ground as he did so.

Stags like to anoint themselves with smelly material at the time of the rut of course, and wallow in wet mud where they find suitable places at the edge of ponds, or peaty puddles and so on. They add to the smell of the mud by urinating first in the patch before rolling in it. One evening I was watching a stag through the telescope from my study window. He was lying chewing the cud in full view on short turf. He suddenly twitched his head back and dug his antlers into the ground and then rose to his feet. He stood gazing into some trees for a moment and then attacked the turf where he had been lying, spiking and thrashing it with his antlers with apparently considerable force. He paused and stared again at the trees, and though I saw nothing I imagined that there must be another stag in the cover unseen, but perhaps winded by the animal that I was watching. I presume that he may have then urinated on the patch, for he suddenly lay down, had a quick roll, and then got to his feet again and proceeded to gouge and rake the grass with his antlers, dancing around as though fighting an adversary. All of a sudden he stopped and ran twenty yards down the hill, and as this was rutting time I supposed that either he had some hinds out of sight below him, or he

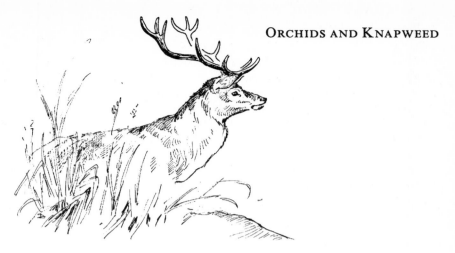

had spotted a rival and was off in pursuit. However, he stopped and to my surprise started to graze. He fed for a few moments, and then stood facing downhill chewing the cud. I then saw him raise his head and roar a couple of times, before resuming cud chewing. I suppose that this behaviour was merely manifestation of the growing rutting urge.

We keep binoculars or telescopes in most rooms in the house, having acquired a number of these cheaply at farm and house sales over the years, but the telescope in Diana's studio is a special astronomer's instrument. It is not particularly powerful at a magnification of 50, but has the merit of an eyepiece at right angles to the telescope, which means that she can look down into the instrument mounted on a tripod, instead of having to stoop to look through it, which makes it much easier and more convenient for sketching as she observes. I generally keep a powerful zoom telescope mounted on a tripod on my study window-sill, and a pair of binoculars handy on my table to grab whenever I glance up and see something of interest. I also keep a pair of binoculars by my bed to enable me to lie and study deer on summer mornings, and a smaller tripod mounted telescope on the dressing table in front of the window. The advantage of having these aids ready for instant use is the opportunity of watching many things that otherwise one might miss. One day I glanced up to see a buzzard flapping into a tree on the other side of the field, and was able to grab the glasses in time to identify the white rump patch and feathered legs of a rough-legged buzzard. These birds are migrants that sometimes visit north-east Scotland, but whether they breed here or not is debatable. Certainly we had had a good view of a rough-legged buzzard sitting on a dead tree in front of the house the previous year, and with the telescope we saw clearly its feathered legs. On a

number of occasions we also saw one, perhaps the same
bird, a short distance away, perched on a telephone
pole beside our farm road, watching for rabbits.
The rough-legged buzzard apparently prefers
larger prey, such as rabbits, to the smaller insects
and voles most often taken by common buzzards.

We have a great many buzzards in the area, and the population of
these birds seems to have increased in line with the significant increase
in rabbit numbers, which now appear to be up to, if not exceeding, the
numbers prior to the introduction of myxomatosis in 1952. I have
watched eight buzzards circling above the house, and one day Diana,
out riding on the hill, watched ten of these birds circling and wheeling
high above her. One day I noticed a large white bird sitting on a
favoured dead rowan tree across the field in front of the house. I might
have thought at first glance that such a large white bird sitting in a
field would be a blackbacked gull, but clearly being on the top of a
dead tree it was not. The telescope revealed a large raptor and I called
to Diana to come quickly to look. Our first reaction was that it was an
osprey, being almost completely white underneath with a pale head
and black eye stripe. However, it had yellow feet and, although I could
not see its legs, this made us wonder whether it might possibly be a
juvenile rough-legged buzzard, since ospreys have grey-blue feet.
Unfortunately, after sitting for a long time, peering around, the bird
vanished completely when I turned to check with a book, so I never
saw it fly off. We did not see that bird again, and with its dramatically
white under parts we would certainly have recognised it. Checking this
later with an ornithological expert we came to the conclusion that it
was a young osprey.

The simple pleasures afforded by wildlife often provide the most
wondrous and memorable experiences, and for the country dweller
there is so much activity and so much to see for anybody that looks
and observes. The hillwalker or rambler that marches steadfastly on,
clad in bright clothes and heavy boots, often talking noisily to

companions, will see little of Nature's wonders, for the wild birds and animals will flee from him or her, as will the true country loving watcher of wildlife. I remember standing one evening in very shallow water at the edge of a little river in the gloaming fishing for seatrout when two otters came splashing upstream along my side of the water and passed me almost paddling over my boots. They glanced up at me as they passed but otherwise seemed to take little notice of me. I could have touched them with my landing net had I wished to do so.

One day in summer I happened to notice a stoat beside the garden wall, and I called to Diana to look. Curious as to its activity I investigated with binoculars and found that it had stolen a bantam's egg from a nest at the base of the dyke. It was rolling this egg in front of it with its nose, guided by its front paws. We watched with amusement, quite content at its acquisition of the egg, since we generally have trouble locating the nests of the bantams anyway. To our amazement, as we watched with increasing fascination, the stoat rolled the egg to the corner of the small garden in front of the house, and then turned and rolled it across the gateway and continued to push it alongside the bottom of the stone wall for the whole length of the garden, a distance of perhaps twenty-five yards, until it came to the next corner, whereupon it changed direction yet again. The stoat rolled the egg halfway down the side wall, and then finally reached its chosen place and pushed it into the dyke and disappeared from view.

Stoats are fascinating creatures, and we love to see them. Indeed we are glad to see them about the farmyard, since though they may steal an odd egg small enough for them to tackle, they prey on rats that do far more damage, and so overall benefit the farmyard. Unlike mink, which are a feral menace in some areas and can do great damage to poultry as well as to wild birds and their young, I doubt that stoats do much harm. If they do indulge in the occasional misdemeanour, this is inevitably outweighed by the good they do in preying upon damaging rabbits, voles and rats. I doubt that a stoat would tackle a very large rat, and indeed a much larger ferret can sometimes suffer from a fight with a large rat, but young ones are undoubtedly a welcome addition to their menu.

On another occasion we watched a stoat in the garden for quite a long time. It was an ermine, having changed into white winter coat as a result of a previous fall of snow. In this part of the country, where we see stoats frequently and have the opportunity to observe them under many conditions throughout the year, we have concluded that their change of winter coat to white, which usually takes place overnight, is dictated by a combination of day length, temperature and whiteness by which I mean snow cover or a heavy hoar frost. Sometimes stoats do not change their entire coat to white, but mostly they do. I have no idea of the reason for incomplete changes, but it may be that the animal was holed up in a warm den and did not emerge such as to respond to the coat change mechanism completely. However, regardless of the situation, after a snow fall or heavy white frost in late winter we invariably see ermines running about hunting where we saw brown animals the previous day. A fall of snow in early winter, say November, and perhaps early December, does not seem to precipitate coat change, which indicates that light or day length is also a governing factor, as it is in much animal behaviour, including that of deer. Anyway, on this occasion the snow had gone and the white stoat, or ermine, that we were watching was very conspicuous. He or she had the remains of a rabbit carcass, and was dragging this along inside the garden wall. She arrived at a gap in the stones and proceeded to drag the remains of the corpse into the dyke. After several minutes of repeated attempts at pulling the rabbit into the small space the stoat decided to change tactics and came round and pushed the carcass from behind. This was a more successful manoeuvre, and after several more attempts it succeeded in getting the remains into the dyke and all disappeared from view.

The most remarkable experience that we have had of a stoat pushing rather than pulling, we also watched from our window. This was one Boxing Day, but there had been no snow and the stoat was its normal brown and white colour. Perhaps I should say brown, white and black, for the back part of the tail is noticeably black both in the stoat and its white ermine winter attire, and this black tail end is the easy distinguishing factor from its much smaller cousin, the weasel, which has no black on its tail. I happened to glance out of the back window as I came downstairs at midday when I saw a stoat and a crow in the middle of the field, both trying to claim the carcass of a rabbit. It was a field of short grazed grass and though a hundred yards from the house, all was easily visible. I opened the window and made a noise and the crow and stoat both cleared off. However, as I watched, the stoat reappeared from the dyke at the edge of the field some forty yards to the right and came back to the carcass and started to drag it. The corpse was evidently a large rabbit, and was clearly stiff. I do not know how much heavier it must have been than the stoat itself. Clearly the little animal had difficulty dragging the stiff corpse, and to my astonishment it came round behind this and seemed to push with its shoulders and the rabbit rolled over. I called to Diana to come and look, and we watched this performance for fully half an hour. From time to time the stoat ran off back to the dyke, but came out again and continued pushing and rolling the stiff rabbit over and over, until finally it reached the long grass at the edge of the field a couple of feet from the dyke. At this point it resumed dragging the rabbit, and with a great effort pulled the carcass into a hole in the dyke and out of sight.

Strangely, one of the enemies of a stoat is a cat. I cannot imagine why this is so, but cats will kill stoats, though just leave them lying and do not eat them. I have not seen this happen, but quite often in winter I have found dead stoats lying near the Dutch barn, where we store the hay. This hay attracts both rabbits and rats, which live amongst the bales, and these in turn doubtless encourage visits from both stoats and cats. The dead stoats often have traces of blood on their fur. One day in summer I found a young stoat lying in full view on the grass at the edge of the farm yard. The corpse was still warm and blood at signs of a bite was still wet. It had not been there a few minutes earlier when Diana had passed with the dogs, and she would certainly have seen had they been responsible. I presume that the cat had killed it. I have watched our cat chase a stoat, but unsuccessfully. We had been watching this stoat in the field in front of Diana's studio attacking a rabbit and drinking blood, and, as we discovered subsequently, eating one eye, from an unfortunate, but undoubtedly stupefied, rabbit. The cat had clearly smelled the stoat from the farmyard down wind about a hundred yards away, and appeared stalking the stoat and ultimately giving chase. After the cat had seen the stoat off down the burn bank, and probably into a hole, she came back and sniffed the rabbit, which was still breathing (which I was able to detect with the aid of a powerful telescope), albeit in a coma, and took no further interest in it. On another occasion I was watching a stoat from the back window as it dragged the remains of a rabbit carcass to the fence. As I had seen two crows at this earlier I imagine that there was little left, and in due course the stoat abandoned it, and started down the fence towards the steading. The cat was lying by the field gate just inside the field staring intently at the stoat. However, the latter thought better of it and turned and ran off across the field whilst still some distance away.

Life in the north is not only harder in winter for deer, due to more extreme weather and a less plentiful food supply, but also in summer when their conditions have disadvantages in the form of extra parasites and irritations. Though ticks are found in a number of areas populated by deer in the south, they are very prevalent in the north, and in this part of the country all deer carry heavy tick burdens. Any animals in poor condition, perhaps as a result of liver fluke infestation, can be lowered even further by heavy tick parasitism. Noticeable to the watcher of deer is the significantly greater irritation to deer by flies and midges in the north of the country as compared to southern parts of Britain. Though nowhere near approaching the torment that these tiny horrors represent in the north and west of Scotland, where the Highland Midge (*Culicoides impunctatus*) bothers all warm-blooded creatures in the warm weather of summer. As I have men-

tioned, the female midge seeks a blood meal before laying her eggs in the damp ground, and deer are as much of a target as humans, though possibly more resistant to the discomfort. In bracken areas and in birch woods small flies are attracted by animals and are intensely irritating. So in warm weather during summer deer often seek breezy places to alleviate the attention of these pests, and as a result of them their ears are constantly flicking. This movement is often a give away sign to a watcher of deer. Often we scan the hill in front of the house and spot a suspicious patch in a group of tall rushes and watching this we see an ear flick and know that a deer is there.

Although we can, and do, see deer at all times of day on occasions throughout the year, during the summer we do so consistently. This is probably because they are under pressure to feed heavily to regain condition lost during winter and to promote growth, especially the nursing females that have to produce a milk supply as well as sustain their own bodies. No doubt the longer grass and rushes and other vegetation also give the deer reassurance in the form of cover in which to lie and feed. Although red deer in parks or deer farms may give the impression of being grazers, these animals are really browsers, being basically woodland species. In spring and early summer buds and shoots are undoubtedly richer food value and perhaps with higher mineral content, and we can watch the red deer delicately picking off the lengthening male birch catkins. I recall watching a group of hinds and yearlings feeding around the old branches of a birch that I had felled for firewood in winter. Through the telescope I could see that they were eating these twigs, and later in the day, when the deer were long gone, I went to look where they had been, curious to see the signs that they had left. Not only was it very difficult to identify that any deer had been in the area despite the damp ground, with few signs of tracks or droppings, but only by close examination of the branches did I realise that the animals had very delicately been nipping off the immature male catkins on the ends of the twigs. Had I not watched them doing this I should never have discovered that these were missing and eaten.

In the early summer the red deer hinds tend to keep in groups of varying numbers. One of the great frustrations with watching these deer is the inability to know which animals one is looking at. We may think that we can recognise a few particular hinds by some characteristic, such as an unusually white rump patch for instance, but one can never be certain that the deer is the same one and not an identical animal. Similarly we can never be sure whether groups of hinds of differing numbers are the same animals in different groupings or others altogether. Woodland or semi-woodland dwelling red deer move around a great deal, it seems, and I suspect differ in habit quite a lot from those on the open hill. Some stalkers reckon to know hinds that live in certain corries or on particular greens on the open hills, and sometimes they can be sure of this when the deer have some identifying characteristic. However, whether they can be sure that others in groups are always the same beasts living constantly in restricted areas, or if there is movement amongst the animals, seems less certain. One sure difference that undoubtedly affects the behaviour of the deer in the differing habitats is the available food supply. In the hills the deer are naturally attracted to the sweeter green grass near burns and springs and in sheltered places, and so tend to congregate in such spots and stay in the vicinity of such places in daytime, though they may travel to feed elsewhere at night. It is possible that the deer return to rest in the same places in daytime. However, in the woods feed is more abundant and varied and it would appear that the routine of the animals is much less consistent and certainly more eclectic. This results in the woodland red deer seeming to move a good deal rather than staying in the same spot, and they appear to vary between resting and feeding with greater frequency, often lying down for a short time to ruminate before being up and feeding again. Consequently it is unusual to be able to watch any particular group of animals for long periods, for they move away into cover. They give the impression of being more restless than beasts settled out on an open hillside, but when one compares their feeding behaviour with cattle and sheep grazing lush fields one can observe similarity of pattern, for domestic stock tend to graze somewhat eclectically moving steadily from one end of a field to the other, and spending much time feeding whilst the grass is abundant. Deer, of course, are not limited by the fenced field boundaries, and so probably graze and browse around the vicinity, varying their movements according to wind and weather conditions.

The variety of food plants eaten by red deer in a woodland setting must be considerable, and infinitely more than their less fortunate counterparts on the hills. It is known that deer browse conifers and strip bark from the trees in commercial woodlands, thus incurring the ire of foresters. In such woods the food variety is more limited than in natural areas of hardwoods. Certainly there is evidence of a browse line on the lower branches of birch trees, and I have watched red deer feeding on birch leaves, and even rising on their hind legs to reach foliage higher up. However, they rarely dwell for long eating the same type of leaf. As seems to be the case with all grazing and browsing animals, ash leaves are evidently a particular favourite, though probably deer rarely get a chance to eat these. We have also seen hinds eating rowan leaves, and one evening we stood outside the house

128

watching a hind on the other side of the small field standing browsing the lower leaves of a rowan tree growing in the dyke at the edge of the farm track. She then proceeded to stand with her front legs on the stone dyke, in order to grab large mouthfuls of rowan. Finally, to reach other leaves on the side of the tree nearest to us, she actually climbed completely onto the dyke and stood on top of this munching away for a few minutes. By this time her companions had moved off down the farm road and so she hastened to rejoin them. Willow is another tree of which the leaves are readily browsed, as well as any aspen twigs within reach. Seed heads of various kinds are readily eaten, being almost certainly more nutritious than other parts of plants. I have watched hinds picking the seed pods off broom bushes, and I have no doubt that they eat the flowers too in season, since all deer, like sheep, favour many flower varieties in their diet. I have certainly watched roe picking the yellow flowers of broom bushes early in the season. In late summer thistle buds are sometimes picked off and eaten, especially those of creeping thistles and marsh thistles. Horses and cattle seem to like these too, and pluck them carefully from the stem. Throughout the summer, but especially in dry periods, when presumably they are more succulent than alternative food, and also late in autumn when much herbage has started to deteriorate, bulrushes or Greater Reed Mace leaves are favoured and the deer will wade out into water to reach these. Many annual plants feature in their diet, and one summer I was intrigued to learn what plant appeared to be the attraction to a group of red deer hinds that came regularly to feed on a part of the lower hill where I feed cattle in winter, and which gets churned up in wet weather so that many weed plants infiltrate. I carefully observed specifically where the beasts fed and went the next day to examine the spot. Without doubt the attraction to them was a crop of knotgrass.

Probably, like most browsers, deer of all species are ready to try browsing most herbage and flowers. One only has to have a pony or cattle able to reach over a garden fence to discover the variety of plants that they are happy to nibble, and a pet lamb turned loose in a garden can be a disaster. So there is no reason why a deer should differ. Roe will certainly eat fungi of various kinds and I should imagine that red deer will happily do the same. Red deer will also strip bark from trees in plantations, and seem to have a preference for some varieties, such as Lodgepole pine. To what extent they will strip bark from hardwood trees in natural woodland I am unsure. Certainly ponies will strip the bark from quite large rowan and aspens trees in winter, as well as willows, and kill these. Rabbits will eat the bark from rowans in hard weather, and occasionally do the same on a few young birch trees, though mostly they do not attack wild trees and seedlings during normal weather, unlike planted saplings that they will attack wantonly if given the opportunity. Presumably deer too would strip bark from such trees if the necessity arose in severe weather.

On the open hill, deer have much less choice of diet, and so tend to concentrate their feeding in certain areas paying particular attention to wind and shelter. Red deer often favour certain areas in differing weather conditions, and so can be found quite regularly in these spots according to wind conditions and so on. The green areas of better feeding or sweeter grass are at a premium, and a change of location may involve a trek of some distance over the hill. Thus the deer watcher can get to know places on the hill where deer can be expected to be found in certain wind conditions. In the woods, with food more abundant and shelter less of a problem, the deer tend to move about a lot, in a rather restless manner, and their habits are much more irregular. This is all too obvious to us as we watch from our windows. In the same way that cattle graze steadily from one end of a field to the other and then back again, rather than simply standing eating all round them, given the situation of plentiful and extensive food the deer will follow the same behaviour. However, there is a slope in front of our house where I feed cattle in winter, being harder ground. These two factors favour shorter grass, with a wild white clover content, and both red and roe deer clearly prefer this particular spot and often tarry there for a while, obviously finding the grazing there to their liking. On the open hill the deer will stay near one small area of favoured feeding simply because there is little alternative. The roe may appear on the hill or in the fields at any time, and they may be seen in the same sort of spot several days in succession, or they may not. This is apparently neither dictated by disturbance nor by weather conditions, but rather by mood or eclecticism, or maybe just haphazard. Similarly red deer may appear at certain times for a day or two, but one can never rely upon their doing so, nor be certain that when they do show themselves the beasts are the same animals as seen previously.

All animals seem to follow tracks instinctively. Sheep grazing permanent pasture will make very noticeable tracks from one area to another, as a result of one following another, even if they move at differing times, despite the field being open and featureless such that there seems no reason for a specific path to be followed. Deer will do

the same. Red deer tracks are far more obvious of course, not only being larger creatures but because usually there are several in a party, but roe will follow the same routes as other roe or as they have done previously, and all these will follow existing paths and tracks by preference. However, when walking in the woods, or on the hill, or even across fields, one often finds that one is instinctively following a track made by deer or sheep. Sometimes this is because the route taken seems to be the best, or sometimes because the worn path is easier walking, but often for no obvious reason. Where there is a food supply of particular attraction the paths to it are more obvious and the route taken more easily defined. Parts of woodland with little feeding attraction tend to have paths through them more than areas of good feeding, where the deer scatter a bit to browse or graze. It is probable that the greater variety of diet and the reduced attraction to limited or restricted areas of browsing renders woodland deer more healthy than those on the hill in open ground. This is possibly because when drawn to feed regularly on greens and burn sides the parasite burden must increase as a result of the accumulation of deer in certain places, and the lack of what the stock farmer would describe as clean grazing (that is grazing that has not had animals feeding on it for perhaps a year, during which period hard weather and lack of suitable hosts may have reduced the levels of parasites contaminating that place).

Deer tend to be crepuscular to a degree even in quite undisturbed areas. This seems to be a natural, and possibly atavistic trait. Domestic stock too seem to be inspired to activity in the gloaming and especially in spring and summer as the light first shows signs of failing, or about the time that deer very often emerge to feed in some places, younger cattle and sheep often take to playing about. In spring this is a time of day when lambs can be seen to race around in groups beside field edges or along the top of banks, in a last expenditure of energy before settling down for the night. Young cattle, especially bulls, will also playfully spar with each other then. Deer tend to feed a lot at night of course, although whether they do so more than domestic stock given similar circumstances I do not know. In the case of most deer the circumstances are different from that of domestic beasts, either as a result of caution because of disturbance and danger, or because they change habitat at night. This they often do both because during the daytime they have sought the shelter of high ground or thick woods from both parasitic pests and from human disturbance, and because they are tempted by feeding in places such as grass fields, turnip crops, and so on, from which they are physically deterred in daylight hours.

The time of orchids on the hill is the time when the new deer generation begins. Very occasionally we find a new roe kid lying tucked up in a clump of rushes or long grass, sometimes discovered by the dogs, which stand pointing the young creature, but mostly we just see a doe feeding on the hill with a new kid at foot, or less often in this part of the country with twins. The red deer hinds, being more mobile than the roe doe, who stays in her area with her offspring for much of the summer, have their calves follow them almost immediately, or certainly within a day or two. Red deer, as cattle, prefer privacy for calving, and the groups of hinds seem to break up at this time, re-forming again after they have their calves at foot. Whether the hinds regroup with their previous chums or relations, or do so by chance I do not know, since it is impossible to tell with any degree of certainty without specifically marked and recorded beasts, and again this may differ between deer on the open hill and those in woodland. I recall particularly seeing a single hind on the hill from my bedroom window one evening. She was quite close and easily visible, and I watched her through the telescope. From her behaviour I felt certain that she was about to calve. It is difficult to describe what formulates this intuitive feeling, but years of tending cattle and sheep and watching for signs has perhaps instilled a sort of instinct for these things. She was restless, and scarcely feeding but standing looking this way and that. I thought it unlikely that she would calve in just that rather open spot. I went and had my bath, and by the time that I re-emerged, some time later, she had gone. The following morning, as I dressed, I spotted a hind emerge from some trees just below where I had seen the beast the previous evening, and then, as I watched her, a little spotted calf trotted out from the cover too and joined her. I have little doubt that it was the same hind and that my prediction had been correct.

Gradually one begins to see more hinds together and more calves. It is a little difficult to make out the composition of these groups sometimes, because in an area of good feeding such as this the yearling hinds can be large and young hinds tend to calve at a much earlier age than on the hill. Just as, from a result of bad management and failure to have a watchful eye, I have had cattle heifer calves served by my bull on a couple of occasions, so yearling hinds in good conditions can produce calves. Some people say, with cattle, that this stunts the growth of the heifer and that she will never grow as a cow. Undoubtedly carrying and raising a calf sets back her own growth rate, since the food intake is divided in use between herself and her growing offspring, but my experience is that her growth is slowed only temporarily and in a couple of years time she will be of the size that she would have been anyway if calved later. I would expect the same to apply to deer. It is possible that the first calf, cow or deer, is itself small either being from a small dam, or as a result of the mother giving less milk in her first lactation, but thereafter there is no reason for differentiation.

Many of these points that seem unclear will doubtless have answers established as a result of behaviour and circumstances recorded on the proliferation of deer farms, from which much evidence has already emanated to disprove long held and quite illogical theories about deer promulgated by stalkers and deer forest owners. In the last ten years or so a considerable amount of research has been done into many aspects of health and growth and the reproductive cycles of farmed deer, and a good deal of this new information is undoubtedly applicable to wild deer also.

# Chapter 9

# The Lazy Days of Summer

The summer is a time of growth for red deer. The hinds are busy raising their calves and feed a lot in daytime, perhaps to encourage their offspring to follow suit or perhaps to ensure a good flow of milk as well as replenishing their own reserves. The stags are busy growing their antlers. Roe bucks already have their antlers, of course, having grown these during the winter in a completely different cycle to the red deer. This difference may be connected with the varying breeding pattern, whereby the roe does cycle is governed by delayed implantation. Thus the hormone cycles in roe, and the way that these are influenced by light factors, are different from those of other deer. Female stoats have delayed implantation too, which basically means that embryonic growth does not start soon after mating but waits until early spring. It is curious that this applies to stoats and not to their cousins the weasel. The result is that stoats only have one litter a year, whereas, given a plentiful food supply, weasels can have several litters in a year. This was particularly evident when, in the 1950s, myxomatosis was introduced into this country and within a year or so wiped out 99 per cent of the rabbit population. The absence of rabbits enabled herbage to grow in places and at rates not seen for many years, and long grass and cover provided an ideal habitat in which voles and mice proliferated. These are the main food prey of weasels, which in turn responded to the rapidly expanding food supply by successful breeding, thus increasing their own population. Stoats, on the other hand, were unable to increase their breeding rate, and, moreover, suffered from the drop in numbers of their main prey, the rabbit. Being significantly larger than the tiny weasel they are unsuccessful in pursuing the small rodents down their tunnels and stoat numbers fell. As rabbit numbers have increased again, so have those of stoats, whereas weasel numbers have declined in comparison, and in this area though weasels are relatively uncommon and we remark when we have seen one, we see stoats frequently.

Another strange behavioural trait of stoats is worth mentioning, since it helps to explain the reason why nature may have ordained delayed implantation. During the first winter the young female stoat grows more quickly than the male. This is because she is in preparation for giving birth to a litter. If the embryos were growing inside her, some of her food supply would be diverted to the growing young and delay her own growth. So Nature has designed things so that she can grow well before her young start to develop. Strangely, and indeed incredibly, young female stoats are apparently mated whilst still blind in the nest. Research suggests that this occurs, and that the adult male, finding a nest of young, discriminates between the sexes and serves the young females. It is said that the noises made by the young stoats at this time indicate that actually the baby females are receptive, and tests done subsequently on young stoats have shown that they are mostly fertilised then. Though such behaviour, distasteful to humans, does not occur with roe, the purpose of the mechanism of delayed implantation may well be the same, which is to enable the doe to build up her body ahead of, and in preparation for, parturition. Thus, on account of the different timing of mating cycles, and therefore the variation in the increase and decrease of hormone circulation affecting this and antler growth, the roe bucks grow their antlers at a different season from red deer stags; the roe antler growth starting almost six months earlier in the year than for red deer. Whereas the red deer stag is antlerless when his offspring are born, the roe buck is in full hard antler when he becomes a father. Not that the description father is particularly appropriate for male deer in this context, since they take no part whatever in rearing the young, not even being in the company of the dam.

Our impression is that in this part of north-east Scotland most roe kids are born around early June. Red deer calves are also born during this month, with most probably born in the middle or second half of June. But unless one is constantly scouring the hill, and thus disturbing the deer, in order to obtain a sample large enough to be meaningful, it is difficult to be sure of this. Calves from young hinds may be born later. Both the kids and calves are spotted in colour initially, the white spots on the

135

browny-red coat giving a sort of dappled appearance that assists camouflage considerably when the young creature is lying curled up in undergrowth. Although initially the markings may be as strong as those on a summer sika or an axis deer, the spots soon fade, though not completely for a good while. By August spots are still detectable, but not very obvious. I recall sitting in a high seat one evening late in the roe rutting time hoping to call a buck, since I derive a certain pleasure and excitement from enticing both bucks and does to within a few yards by calling them. The rut here in Aberdeenshire goes on quite late, sometimes being obvious well after the middle of August, depending upon the weather. On this occasion most of the evening was spent watching two roe kids ambling about and feeding in the clearing in front of me. There was no sign of a doe, but when I descended from the seat I was barked at by a roe in the trees below, in which direction the kids had finally departed, and I assumed that this was their mother. I noted that both kids still showed spotting on their haunches, which seems to be the last area of deer to shed moulted coat. Similarly I have noted red deer calves still spotted at the end of August too. The spots are lost completely when the young deer grow their first winter coat towards the end of September, although a few very faint spots can sometimes just be detected on the backs of even quite old hinds.

Summer is a time of plenty for most deer, except perhaps in some areas where populations are too high or disturbance or habitat destruction too stressful, and it is a busy time for the does and hinds, for they have young to rear. The raising of offspring places quite a burden on the females, which may not be immediately obvious to those that are not familiar with rearing animals. Despite the fact that young deer will nibble herbage within a few days, the overwhelmingly important food supply is the mother's milk. Initially, during the first couple of days, the mother supplies her young with colostrum, which is the thick first milk, and is not only very rich but also supplies various antibodies from the dam to safeguard her young baby. What many people seem to forget, or perhaps never realise in the first place, is that this vital food supply can be affected by all sorts of factors, and can have a dramatic effect upon the performance of the young deer, perhaps throughout its life, and even influence whether it lives or not. Cows, ewes, and even human females, can get mastitis for instance, and this has a major effect upon the young. Mastitis is basically an infection of the udder, perhaps as a result of dirt or flies on the teat, or some other source. Heifers can get mastitis before even parturition occurs, and, as mentioned, we had a 28-year-old mare that had not had a foal for years, which suddenly developed mastitis. Sheep are particularly prone to developing mastitis at lambing time. If they give birth to twins this will inevitably result in the death of one lamb if it is not fostered elsewhere, for the young become conditioned to feeding from their own teat, and not sharing these, and the one producing no milk means that the lamb on that side starves. Sometimes a ewe or cow becomes badly infected and is in great pain, and thus does not allow the young to suck, even on a neighbouring unaffected teat. In the case of ewes the udder can burst completely on occasions. There is no reason at all why these mastitis problems cannot occur with deer of all species, and undoubtedly they do so. Once a cow has had a calf she maintains a visible udder thereafter, of whatever size, but a ewe's udder contracts annually once the milk flow ceases and it can be difficult to tell in winter, without handling the animal, whether her udder is fully functional. Clearly it may be impossible to tell this in wild deer. With four teats the loss of one may not be disastrous with a single offspring, provided that other quarters of the udder produce sufficient milk. However, they may not do so; and if others develop infection there will be no milk at all. A cow has four teats, and so can still raise a calf with one or more non-functional, but a ewe is limited. With small teats and a compact udder a deer may be more sensitive. It is easy to forget that a roe doe or a red deer hind without a calf may be yeld for a variety of reasons. She may have failed to hold to service as a result of ill health or poor condition, or perhaps even the sire is infertile, just as she might be. Experience with other animals suggests that equally likely is that her milk supply might be at fault.

For those involved with the management of deer, insofar as one can ascribe this word to the duties of those involved with wild deer populations, the task of choosing hinds for culling or any female deer for that matter is fraught with difficulty. It is impossible to know why hinds are yeld without examination, and a beast that has lost a calf for some reason and is now in good condition as a result of not having this burden may be potentially a strong breeding dam for the following year. She may have failed to conceive, or have

137

aborted, due to poor condition the previous winter, but now in good condition could be ready to produce and rear a fine calf. On the other hand a female with a poor calf at foot would be a strong suspect for having a poor milk supply, whether from previous illness or simply just being a low yielder. In which case such a poor raiser of calves might well be the least desirable breeding hind to leave in the herd, and there could be a strong case for giving yeld hinds a second chance, as is the policy on perhaps the best known deer farm in this country. The difference between deer on a farm, where the animals are all marked and recorded, and those in the wild, where they may not be recognised, or even seen again, of course, is apparent, and one probably has no idea which hinds have been yeld in a previous year.

The importance of this milk supply, the only nourishment of the calf or kid for the first few days of its life and the main food supply for many weeks, cannot be overstated, and has a major effect upon the new generation of deer. This importance is obvious to any shepherd or stockman. A friend was telling me of his experiences as a young man on a big cattle station in the far north of Australia. He commented upon the amazing difference between calves born to cows that gave birth in drought conditions before the rains came and those born a couple of weeks after the herbage had been greened up by rain. Once green food was available the cows obviously milked substantially better. Similar effects are well known in Texas, where the proportion of poor spike bucks (yearlings without forked antlers) amongst white-tailed deer rises dramatically in drought years. The influence of feeding at this very early stage affects not only bodily growth of the young deer but also on occasions the antler development of male deer in future life. It appears that both sexes of deer have detectable pedicle growth in embryo stage. Of course, with the exception of reindeer or caribou, female deer of all species do not grow antlers. However, as the skull bone tissue develops, this obscures the pedicle growth and is not apparent at parturition. In the early stages of growth, sex hormones are produced in the young animals, principally testosterone in young males, and this results in the development of pedicle tissue. Later in the first year a renewed circulation of hormones results in the growth of a small antler on the pedicle. It appears that the production of testosterone can be affected by nutrition, and it is thought that this is the cause of hummels, or antlerless stags. This would explain why hummels are rare in continental Europe or in woodland or low ground populations, but common in the poor feeding areas of north and west Scotland. I use the word common loosely of course, for the hummel percentage is very small relatively,

but these are far from unusual.

People often refer to large hummels, but work has been done to show that there is no difference in average size between hummels and antlered deer. There are big hummels, medium-sized hummels and small hummels. The explanation for those hummels in areas of plentiful food, or indeed otherwise, may lie in the lack of availability of an adequate milk supply and nutrition of the calf due to inability of the dam to supply sufficient for some reason, and in poor feeding areas this may result simply from the hind being in low, under-nourished condition. The explanation for large, heavy hummel stags could well be that whilst a period of under-nourishment occurred at the critical stage of initial pedicle development, this was subsequently redressed by adequate food supply, and the young deer thrived well. The suggestion that a hummel grows large because he does not suffer the strain of antler growth is perhaps spurious, since it is doubtful that this places much strain on the stag in most circumstances, and certainly not in comparison to the developing foetus inside a preg-nant hind, or the burden of producing milk to feed young. Certainly a stag without antlers growing, in velvet, may be less pestered by flies in summer and so less tormented and driven to the relief of high breezy ground or dark woods, and thus able to spend more time feeding in summer. Moreover, without tender growing antlers he may have advantage at this time in establishing his rank in the pecking order, which undoubtedly has a substantial bearing on the outcome of his success at the time of rutting.

So the emergence of plentiful summer food supply is vital to the hinds and does, and in the weeks during May and early June they take maximum advantage of the new herbage growth to prepare themselves for the birth of their young. In this area roe twins, though not uncommon, are far less usual than in some parts of southern Brit-ain. In Surrey, where we used to live, twins were the norm, with a few single kids and occasional triplets. Red deer twins are uncommon, but they do appear from time to time, and just as occasionally a cow will have twins. In the past twenty years we have had a cow with twin calves on three occasions. I have only observed a red deer hind with twins one season, and I saw her twice on different parts of the hill within a few days. Though there were other deer in the vicinity, I watched closely to satisfy myself that one of the calves did not belong to another hind and was convinced that they were twins.

As the red deer calves grow, so the hinds come together in groups again. Their behaviour is similar to cattle in this respect, in that when the hind feels that parturition is imminent she moves off to privacy and finds a sheltered place to give birth. Cows do exactly the same given the opportunity to calve where there is cover. Sometimes one of my cows, which calve on the hill, will appear at feeding time with a new calf at her heel, but at other times she will appear clearly having calved, and anxious, for a brief period in order to feed, and then return rapidly to locate and tend her calf. Very often she will do this furtively, and if she is aware that I am following her, in order to find and check the calf, she will not go straight to it, or she may even lead me away from it. Red deer tend to leave their calves hidden for quite some time whilst they go and feed, both in terms of the spell away from the calf during the day, and in terms of the period of growth. That is to say that the young calf may be quite a few days old before it accompanies the hind permanently, though undoubtedly this is to some extent idiosyncratic, depending upon individual hinds or calves, and the calf will accompany her when she moves to a different feeding area. Roe seem to be much the same, and perhaps more so, since they are relatively static and so do not move far from a hidden resting kid, whereas the hinds seem to be on the move a lot through woodland areas, which necessitates the calf accompanying the mother before too long, or for parts of the day at least.

In the first few days or weeks of life, before they follow their dam continually, calves tend to lie down after they have suckled. They often wander off, sometimes quite a few yards, and curl up in long grass or under a bush. The mother remains watchful, and I should imagine that a fox would stand little chance against a hind, particularly having seen one advance purposefully on my Irish Water Spaniel, and knowing how very aggressive hinds can be on deer farms and in parks. People tend to regard hinds as gentle creatures, but a beast rearing up and striking with its forefeet can be very dangerous. However, a fox sneaking up on a very young calf, undetected by the hind, is another matter. Red deer calves and roe kids suckle for a very short time each feeding session. Bigger stronger calves may suckle slightly less long than smaller ones, but mostly the period is only a couple of minutes for young calves and less as they grow older. Whether this is because the milk supply tails off or because the calf is more adept at milking the udder I do not know. As with cattle and sheep, male calves tend to be larger than hind calves, and either because of this, or to enable this, stag calves usually have a gestation period a day or two longer. Similarly the offspring from first calvers are generally smaller than those from dams that have had young previously.

With such a short suckling period each time, the hinds milk is rich, rather like that of rabbits where the supply is even more restricted since the doe rabbit only suckles her young once in 24 hours, and then for only three minutes. This has been borne out by analysis of the milk of hinds at the Rowett Institute, which has shown that the milk of red deer hinds has about twice the solid content and protein of cows milk and almost three times the fat. They found that after a couple of months the volume of milk dropped off from around 1500–2000 grams per day, but that, unlike in cattle and sheep, the content of fat and solids increased. The composition of hinds milk is much more akin to that of a ewe than of a cow, and hand-fed red deer calves were better reared on ewe milk substitute. Young deer tend to run straight to their mother for a feed, and if she stands they go straight in and suckle. Lambs and cattle calves often go round in front of their dam to stop her, before they start suckling. When feeding cattle or sheep this trait can be tiresome, since the beasts tend to follow similar action, even when adult, and cross round in front when one is trying to put out food for them. As with most similar animals, female deer tend to lick the backsides of their young offspring when they are suckling to encourage them to defecate. In their first few weeks the faeces consists largely of processed milk, of course, and whether the dam is attracted by this cheesy substance, or whether as a precaution against adver-

141

tisement of the presence of young to predators, she eats it. Most farmers are aware that their dogs are partial to the creamy faeces of calves of their cows in the first few days of their life, before increased intake of solids changes the composition.

Milk

| | fat % | crude protein % | lactose % |
|---|---|---|---|
| red deer | 8–10% | 7–9% | 4–5% |
| cow | 3.75% | 3.4% | 4.75% |
| mare | 1.2% | 2.0% | 5.8% |
| ewe | 6.5% | 5.8% | 4.8% |
| human | 3.8% | 2.1% | 6.3% |

The speed with which lambs grow is impressive, but red deer calves and roe deer kids seem to grow even faster. This is not really surprising when one thinks that a red deer calf has a much shorter period in which to grow. A lamb is born in April or so, disregarding those born earlier as a result of planned management, and has until perhaps October before the feeding becomes more difficult with the cessation of the grass growth and the weather deteriorating. A lamb strong by then will stand a good chance of surviving the winter in the hills. A red deer calf is born in mid-June and has to be strong enough by the same time of year, and so may have up to two months less time to grow. The above table shows the richness of red deer milk in comparison to that of sheep, and even more so to that of a cow or human. The importance of this early food supply to a red deer calf can thus be judged. Bearing in mind that the early growth of the stag calf is influential in its initial production of testosterone, and it is the first flush of this hormone that causes the pedicles to grow, ready for the subsequent growth of antlers, it could well be that mastitis is one of the causes of the development (or should one say the lack of development) of a hummel.

Watching red deer calves suckling, especially those a couple of months old, I have been interested to note how rough these can be, bashing the hind's udder and almost lifting her back leg off the ground. I have often watched lambs doing this, and when there are a pair of well grown ones sucking they really can lift the back end of the ewe when bashing the udder. Anyone who has fed orphan lambs with a bottle knows just how strong they can be, and these are generally weaned comparatively early and so not so strong as an older lamb. I am sure that Nature has things well organised, but I often wonder what effect this violent bashing has on the udder and whether it has any influence on the possible development of mastitis in the dam, particularly if she already has a slight sore on the teat for instance.

Unlike a cow, where the udder when dry may shrink a little but remains obvious, that of a ewe retracts completely when out of use, and it then becomes difficult to establish, late in the autumn, what the udder was like and if it functioned properly during the summer. In other words, picking out ewes to sell as sound in udder for sale as cast is largely a matter of faith or imagination. I recall a ewe where one quarter developed mastitis and burst. How sheep can survive such a ghastly looking wound, let alone escape the flies, astounds me, but they can do so, although no further use for breeding of course. When we came to pull out ewes for sale in the autumn I was astonished to find that had I not marked this animal's ear at the time I should never have been able to find her as the udder had healed. Deer are similar to sheep in this respect, in that by the time of the hind season it must be very difficult to assess a beast's udder function. I have never examined the udders of dead hinds, but I rather wonder whether anyone has actually done so and recorded any detail.

I do not know what the prevalence of mastitis in deer might be, but I should imagine that red deer are as susceptible to the problem as any other mammal. All mammals can get mastitis, even well protected humans, so deer must do so at times, and especially hinds exposed to the torment of flies. I imagine that deer farmers have such a situation under control to some extent because they may be able to detect a hind with mastitis, either because she becomes temporarily lame, or she refuses to allow her calf to suckle on one side, or maybe she just has no milk and the calf dies. Undoubtedly that hind would be culled. With wild deer the situation goes quite uninvestigated in the vast majority of cases. Nobody seems to have any idea how prevalent mastitis might be in wild deer, nor how many calves die as a result of lack of milk caused thus, nor indeed how many of the yeld hinds are yeld for this reason. I do not suppose that this information would have a dramatic effect upon management policy, but it would assist the build-up of our knowledge if we knew the level of incidence and if it was a significant factor in causing hinds to be yeld.

It is difficult to see clearly the udders on deer, and so not easy to assemble information on a significant sample. However, in May one often sees roe does and red deer hinds with noticeable udders, indicating that parturition is not far off. The development of the udder is rather idiosyncratic, with some animals, especially first calvers, not bagging up until only a day or two before giving birth, and others showing signs of increasing udder size perhaps up to three weeks beforehand.

The fecundity of deer varies considerably. In good feeding areas the incidence of twins in roe is high, but in poorer places single kids are more usual. I do not know the probable incidence of yeld roe does. In the south of England it was rare, and I suspect that in this part of north-east Scotland most does, perhaps excepting yearlings, will have kids. With red deer the incidence of yeld (barren, temporarily or permanent, i.e. not giving milk) hinds is higher. This varies considerably with habitat. The situation is exactly the same with sheep. In rich agricultural ground, where ewes are flushed or put onto good grazing to ensure that they are in rising condition at tupping time, thus producing plenty of ova, the lambing percentage might average 200 to 250 per cent, with triplets common and occasional quadruplets. In bleak hill country, of say Caithness or Sutherland or on the west coast, the lambing percentage might average only 70 per cent or even as low as 50 per cent. The fecundity of the sheep is dependent entirely upon the habitat, the food supply, the weather, shelter, and so on. So it is with red deer. Research carried out by the Red Deer Commission suggests an average percentage of live calves in summer for red deer at around 30 per cent, with few hinds calving before three years old. Many of the yeld hinds may have given birth to calves, but mortality rates are high for a variety of reasons, and it has been shown that hinds in poor condition, and thus presumably not in a fit state to produce enough milk to rear calves, will reject their offspring. Perhaps this should be interpreted in another way by saying that without the pressure of milk in the udder an animal lacks the desire to be suckled and to encourage its offspring to do so. Amongst semi-woodland red deer in this area I would imagine that the calving rate is probably at least twice that of hill beasts, or more, and I would expect most of these hinds, including a high proportion of yearlings, to raise calves. In 1890 Henry Evans noted on Jura that more calves were raised on the better ground, and that mortality rates, especially of calves, were higher on poorer areas, though a high proportion of dead calves were never found. Presumably those little corpses that were not rapidly cleaned up by scavenging ravens and gulls could easily disappear into holes or peat hags or burns. His estimate then, for the overall Forest calving rate, was 30 per cent, the same as thought to be the rate covering much of Scotland. This was based upon counts in February. He noted further that this estimated calving percentage was based upon the total of all hinds, but if one excluded estimated yearling and 2-year-old hinds from the total calculation the percentage went up to

144

37 per cent, and if one excluded the poorest area with the lowest rate, which brought down the average, then the greater number of calves raised on the good ground might raise the average for the better areas to 66 per cent.

By the middle of summer we can see hinds and calves feeding at any time of day, sometimes lying in view of our windows for long periods ruminating, alternating this with some beasts getting up to feed. It is when I have the opportunity of watching hinds lying chewing the cud that I am reminded strongly of the extraordinarily long faces of old hinds, and the considerable differences in face length of red deer of different ages. I paid particular attention to this aspect one afternoon, since I was comparing the faces of actual hinds with those in a painting that Diana had just completed. This picture was of a specific scene that we had both watched together from her studio. A small group of hinds was on the hill in front, in clear view, with three beasts feeding amongst the yellow Trollius plants and a single old hind lying in the foreground. Just to the right of these, from the background of yellow of the globe flowers, the head and neck of a roe doe emerged from time to time. As we watched, a roe buck came out from the trees on the right and moved towards the doe, and then stopped, staring uncertainly at the old hind a short distance from him. She merely turned and looked disdainfully in his direction, still chewing the cud. It was this scene that Diana painted. When I saw this I confess that I thought she had rather exaggerated the face of the old hind and made it a bit too long. With the picture now on the wall of my study, and my telescope mounted on a tripod in front of the window, I spotted a group of hinds and calves feeding on the hill quite close to the house. These then lay down in full view to ruminate, giving me the ideal opportunity for prolonged study of their faces. In the group was one old matriarch, and after careful observation I was pleased to satisfy myself that the proportion which Diana had painted was quite correct. Her face seemed to be almost twice as long as that of a young hind, and of course contrasting in the painting with that of a roebuck it appeared to be even longer. I have little doubt that, despite not having Diana's artistic eye for close detail, were I to have such a group of deer

permanently available for observation, such as being fenced in, I would in time be able to distinguish individual animals by idiosyncratic characteristics in precisely the same way that I can distinguish ewes in my flock, just as any shepherd can, despite these sheep all appearing to be similar animals to an inexperienced outsider. However, I would not care to see these deer fenced in, for incarceration, even on quite an extensive basis, somehow changes the animals and alters their appearance in an undefinable way. I suppose that somehow they lose their instinctive alertness, ever wary for danger, and their demeanour seems to me to lose that somewhat haughty wildness that is so attractive in these lovely creatures.

One afternoon I walked up the hill from the farm track to admire the orchids and other wild flowers growing in abundance. Halfway towards a small, ancient but now abandoned field near the top of the ground, I saw three hinds feeding. I did not attempt concealment but walked on a few yards, whereupon one hind saw me. All three stood and stared at me and I halted and remained motionless. I think the group consisted of an older hind, a younger one and a yearling. Suddenly the old hind let out a bark, like someone banging a stick on an empty forty-gallon oil drum, which evoked startling resonance from the adjacent birch wood, and all three ran and jumped the fence onto the adjacent part of the farm. I could still see them in the trees, seeming reluctant to go, and I guessed that there was a calf nearby. I walked on, and sure enough a red deer calf sprang from behind a gorse bush and ran off up the hill. Coming to the fence of the old field it turned back and ran towards me again, following the fence that bisects the hill ground, close to which I had been walking. The calf ran down the fence line past me with that lovely ground-gobbling trot so characteristic of these deer, and reminiscent of American trotting horses. It passed me about twenty yards away, and as I watched another calf appeared from the same sort of area and it too came back down the fence line. I could see the hinds fleetingly in the background of the trees keeping watch on the calves, so I knew they would join up again as soon as I departed and left them in peace, which I did.

When walking on the hill, or indeed anywhere in the area, we are always on the alert for deer and their signs. Mostly the deer follow set paths, but they always seem to be aware of open gates and make use of these when there is an opportunity, rather than jumping fences. Knowing just how often and where we see deer I am always fascinated to see signs in these places and look for evidence of deer having been there. By several of the ponds I have made, patches of bog myrtle grow. One of these is in a small damp hollow in the woods, and I have noticed that not only do the ponies browse off the tops of bog myrtle when given the opportunity, but also deer seem to like it. So far as I can tell this applies to both roe and red deer. Constant browsing has a deleterious effect upon bog myrtle, and whilst I do not grudge the deer their snack, I do find it irritating that this injurious pruning renders it very difficult for me to find in the spring a twig or two of the tiny deep red male flowers, which I generally like to pick for the dining table at that season. One spring I was intrigued to discover which of the two deer species was the culprit, or whether perhaps both red and roe were responsible. Although the ground was wet and peaty and one would have thought ideal for footprints to show, I was astonished to discover that I was quite unable to find clear slots in the patch, and only on a small deer path away from the place could I locate clear hoof marks, which had been left by roe deer. However, I also found a small tuft of red deer hair in the pond, evidence of the start of winter coat shedding, and nearby some red deer droppings or fewmets. Thus I was actually little wiser as to where the responsibility lay for the browsing of every single bog myrtle plant in that patch.

I am always amused when I read of quasi-scientists doing research into deer habits and populations that try to locate and count deer droppings as part of their factual evidence. So many of these people, as I see it, show little evidence of knowledge and understanding not only of deer and their habits but also of other species of animals and their traits too. I confess that I have never held in high regard many so-called qualifications, including what I have seen so appropriately described as that contemptible German degree, which is how the PhD was described by some British academics when it first came to Britain from Germany soon after the First World War. This particular qualification, which encourages all manner of people to title them-selves with the prefix Dr which to me means a doctor of medicine and nought else, is awarded for a thesis based on two or three years of original research. Since the subjects chosen are often abstruse, and the examiners little qualified to judge the validity or usefulness of the content, and the newly qualified PhD often no longer pursues that particular subject, I find myself totally unimpressed by the qualifica-tion. Consequently I am concerned when I discover such people researching deer matters, not as a result of a passionate interest in the animals but as a mode of employment and acquisition of income. I came across one such fellow doing research on the utilisation of an area by deer, who based the level of use upon the counting of deer droppings. The criterion was that deer defecate 18 times a day. I questioned whether frequency of defecation was related to volume and quality of food intake and was told that this was the case, but that he had to work upon some standard and somebody somewhere had counted the number of times a day that a deer defecated so this was taken as the yardstick. Having frequently watched deer feeding, lying, and moving about, including our own tame red deer hind, and having gone deliberately to the specific places to look for subsequent signs, I am of the opinion that taking any such findings as a yardstick on which to base fact is highly suspect, even if carried out daily for a long period. There is no substitute for long hours of painstaking observation.

Deer tend to defecate when they rise, after lying chewing the cud. If one watches a group of deer lying until they all get up and gradually move on this can be seen as they get up, stretch, and walk off a few yards to start feeding again, often defecating either soon after they stand up or as they walk off. Sheep and cattle do exactly the same, and as a result of this it is easy to see in a field of cows where they usually rest. A sheltered spot behind a stone dyke or a dry corner of the field where the beasts have lain will have a concentration of cowpats. All these animals will also defecate or urinate if mildly excited or disturbed. One only has to move a flock of sheep or a herd of cows for this to be quite obvious. Deer, too, will often walk stiffly with a few steps, tail out, and defecate, if very slightly worried or uncertain. There is nothing unusual about this in the animal world, of course, for even humans can feel the urge to take similar action in certain situations of extreme excitement or concern. When watching red deer their tails are quite obvious, and it is very easy to see when they raise these. With roe, with a tail perhaps only an inch or so long, this is less easy to see. However, it is quite obvious when one looks for it.

One aspect of markings that can assist somewhat in attempts at differentiation between red deer hinds is the coloration of their caudal patch. As a generalisation the pale tail patch of red deer is a fawny, dirty light brown colour, varying to off-white on occasions, but some deer seem to have extremely white rump patches. We have often commented upon the considerable variation in the coloration of these caudal patches when watching a group of deer, and one summer we saw regularly one hind with such a white patch that she seemed almost that she might have sika blood. We assumed it was the same deer that we saw, over a period of a week or two, and then we saw a hind with a bright white patch no more. There is also variation in the black markings that border each side of the caudal patch. In most red deer the pale patch on their backsides extends up over the base of the tail and well onto their back; but this is not the case with all red deer, especially those that may have continental blood.

This comparison of deer behaviour with that of other animals seems to me to be important in trying to understand their lives a little better. As a stock farmer, many similar actions in sheep and cattle are so commonplace as to be taken for granted, so that one comes to expect the behaviour from deer under certain circumstances. Those unfamiliar with the everyday lives of other animals are at a disadvantage. This is often recognisable in comments by researchers with a narrow-minded or blinkered approach, such as those who believe that counting deer droppings in a certain section of a wood at infrequent intervals, or without taking into account seasons, weather, food availability, disturbance (even by the researchers' presence) and so on, is a satisfactory way of establishing deer numbers and regularity of use of that area. A similar sort of interpretation by a scientist, whose knowledge of deer, both captive and wild, impressed me considerably in the past, rather disappointed me. In this case there was an experiment being conducted in an attempt to discover whether young red deer stags could recognise that superior antlers meant a dominant stag. A prime stag was put into an enclosure with five young stags, in which a pecking order had already been established. The leader of the

five, unimpressed by the new arrival's fine antlers, attacked him but was defeated. He attacked again several times with the same result, and finally the other young stags all joined in and defeated the new arrival. The same experiment was repeated a year later with the same result. The interpretation was that the young stags failed to recognise, or remember, the superior antlers of the prime stag and be warned that he was dominant. However, my interpretation would be that when introducing a new animal into the territory of others, this sort of behaviour is inevitable whatever the size of the newcomer. One sees this frequently when introducing a new cow, or tup, into a group of others, and particularly if the new animal is put into the territory already established by the others rather than introducing them into his territory. The same behaviour occurs even when one removes a tup, or ram, for only a day or two and then returns him to an enclosure with erstwhile companions. I would expect just the same performance as occurred with these red deer stags to happen if one introduced a three-shear tup into a group of tup lambs or shearlings, and recognition of superior horns has nothing to do with it. There can be a great danger in trying to read into behaviour or signs less obvious or less familiar interpretations, or to consider that these apply to deer alone. The dominant animal in the pecking order is not invariably the biggest or best looking.

One of the problems with the opportunity to watch deer from the comfort of one's house for long periods is that one can so easily devote a great deal of time to this when other work needs to be done. I suppose that it is a question of getting priorities right. My view of this generally is that the deer might not be there another day so it is best to take the chance to watch them and leave other chores until a time when the deer are not readily visible, if that can be acceptable! Sometimes in summer this can mean a whole afternoon spent peering through the window with telescope or binoculars. I never consider this to be time wasted though, for there are always moments of interest or amusement. The passer-by seeing a farmer leaning on a gate watching his cows or sheep may think, unwittingly, that the man is being idle. This is not the case. Much can be learned from watching the animals in one's care, in order to be familiar with idiosyncratic behaviour and recognise anything at all unusual to enable problems or illness or difficulties with parturition to be recognised in the early stages. So watching deer helps build up knowledge of these animals in order to understand them better. A herd of hinds has many similarities to a flock of sheep or herd of cows, especially in a mixed herd of hinds, yearlings and calves. However, my impression is that amongst the deer

150

there tends to be a more rigid pecking order, and a good deal more bickering, than with domestic stock. This seems to be completely logical amongst wild animals where a degree of alertness and some discipline is likely to be of considerable importance to their well-being. Much of the chivvying about stems from the young deer, particularly the yearlings. Some of this is caused by older hinds chasing these out of the way, and in particular hinds that are ridding themselves of the proximity of their previous season's calf in favour of the new one, but in other cases it is probably the establishment of the pecking order, where the more dominant young hind is telling the socially lower animal to get out of its way. In a larger group of deer moving around feeding there is often a constant movement of this sort.

One morning I watched a small group of hinds feed across the slope in front of the house, and as they were disappearing into the trees off to the left, two hinds and a calf raced onto the slope from trees on the right. Quite clearly one hind was chasing the other, and with firm intent. I was not able to establish whether the chaser was older than the chased, and neither could I make out to which hind the calf that ran along with them belonged, despite their crossing the slope twice, before disappearing off to the right again and not returning to rejoin the original group, which had now disappeared.

I was watching a party of hinds and calves feeding further up the hill one afternoon when suddenly the whole bunch ran off for a hundred yards or so, and then stopped. I wonder what had spooked them, but they did not give the appearance of being alarmed by looking fixedly in any direction, and to my surprise they all settled to feed again and continued to do so. Whether one beast had been spooked by a warble fly, or perhaps by a rabbit startled under its feet, or some such, I do not know: perhaps it was just a sort of communal frolic. This behaviour reminded me of the movement of a flock of sheep temporarily disturbed by some triviality at the side of a field.

Roe deer kids occasionally appear to have a little frolic, especially if there are twins, but their behaviour is rather more sedate compared to red deer calves. The latter have more need for speed and stamina than roe of course, and this is undoubtedly the motive for their occasional exercising in the form of a mad sprint across a clearing and back for no other apparent reason. From time to time we see several calves racing across the hill, backwards and forwards a couple of times and marvel at their grace and speed, and at the hinds apparently totally oblivious to the activity. I remember one lovely early summer morning some years ago going out to the back of the house and spotting a small group of red deer in a field next to the one behind our steading and house. This was newly sown with grass and well rolled, giving a flat surface of soil. I watched with fascination as a red deer calf raced back and forth across the field kicking up little spurts of dry dust, whilst the mother and other deer ambled very slowly across before disappearing over the dyke into the wood.

One especially enchanting scene that I watched one morning was from the comfort of my bed. I had seen a number of deer feeding on the short grass of the slope in front of the house when I awoke, and having taken the pair of binoculars that I always keep handy by my bed I was watching these. Some were in the longer grass at the top of the slope, and I saw two young spotted red deer calves there feeding. Suddenly I was aware of a roe doe in the long grass. She had obviously been lying there and was disturbed by the proximity of the red deer.

Quite slowly she started to amble downhill away from the red deer towards the trees. The two red deer calves stared in fascination at this other animal, clearly not one of them, as she passed within a few yards

152

of them. It was interesting to note how small the doe looked in comparison to these young red deer calves, and how angular they looked in comparison to her daintiness. As she walked off the two calves stalked slowly after her. One stopped and stared after a few yards, and the other played grandmother's footsteps behind the doe, at a distance of twenty yards or so, following behind her until she disappeared; at which point the calf lost interest and returned to graze near its chum.

Watching young creatures is usually full of fun, and deer are no exception. The young are always curious. Sometimes rooks alight on the hill amongst the deer to peck at this and that, and it always amuses me to see a young calf spot this black thing walking about and stalk it, walking towards it, pausing while the bird jumps off a few yards, and then resuming its approach, until finally the rook gets fed up with the attention and flies off. One often sees young lambs following after rooks and jackdaws, of course, for these birds are much attracted to lambing fields, no doubt in a search for wool for nests as well as insects and choice feasts like bits of afterbirth that the shepherd may have missed removing.

Corvids favour deer hair for nesting material, and occasionally we see a jackdaw on a deer removing parasites, presumably ticks and keds. We very often notice a magpie or a jackdaw hopping about on a resting ewe, sometimes pecking about its ears. I can imagine that the light feet of these birds might not be noticeable to the sheep on thick fleeces, but they must be conscious of their presence when the magpie is standing on its head or neck, and one can only presume that the ewe is aware that the bird is doing it a service by the removal of these parasites, like an oxpecker on a buffalo or giraffe. Rooks and crows do not carry out this cleaning service to sheep and deer so far as I am aware. Perhaps they are too heavy. Jackdaws and magpies are lighter birds. The crows in this part of Scotland are carrion crows, and only very occasionally do we see some of these birds with faint brown markings, suggesting a cross with the hoodie crows of the north and west of Scotland. Crows have few loveable characteristics, but rooks

can be much admired on close observation, despite the fact that they can be a menace in the lambing field, since they are as ready as a crow to peck out the eyes of a feeble lamb, and tiresome stealers of eggs from the farmyard. I once watched a rook walking after a very tiny baby rabbit pecking at it with murderous intent. Despite my constant vendetta against rabbits, which do so much damage on the farm, I intervened to rescue the young bunny and allow it to return to the safety of its burrow. Rooks seem to have a higher requirement for protein in their diet, particularly at nesting time, and can be somewhat of a pest in spring.

Often I spend a few minutes watching rooks strutting about in the field just outside the kitchen window, looking glossy and sleek. Unlike crows, rooks consume large numbers of wireworms, leatherjackets and other farm pests, and thus do a great deal to compensate for occasional attacks upon lambs or pilfering of cereal grains from flattened crops in autumn. They appear to be such clumsy and ungainly birds on the wing at times, as they come to and fro past or into the fields, but at other times their aerobatics are spectacular and we often watch their amazing antics on the wing in wonder at their aerial skill. Even when they move steadfastly to a definite destination across the fields in a strong gale, flying low over the ground, hopping over dykes and hedges, their flight is impressive, but when they play in a high wind, or whiffle down from a great height in the manner sometimes displayed by wild geese, one can stand and stare in amazement at their skill. There is a large rookery in some clumps of tall Scots pines over our march, beyond the end of the farm. This rookery used to be all in one wood until a few years ago, but the trees were mostly felled for timber, leaving a few standing scattered about to encourage self-seeding. In the following winter gales many of these now exposed trees blew over and few remain. The rooks changed most of their nest sites to several nearby small clumps of tall pines, and the population still inhabits the vicinity, albeit rather scattered. These

154

rooks forage in both the valley in which our farm lies and also the neighbouring, larger valley to the south. Often in the spring and autumn, when dawn is at the time I waken in the mornings, I can lie in bed and watch the rooks in a compact group, which looks rather like a flock of pigeons in the distance, purposefully flying high towards the south over the hill for their daily foraging on the farm land in the next valley. Later in the day, sometimes when I am out feeding cattle, I see odd rooks returning from across the hill to the rookery. I am constantly astonished at the speed with which they do this. Having gained the height to cross the hill they seem to set their wings, with never a flap, and angle down from the height to their pine trees near the river in a long, fast, breathtaking dive, extraordinarily different from the rather clumsy flopping about from field to field that one so often associates with the rook. On a number of occasions I have watched a bird circling and hovering, puzzled as to its identification and unable to judge its size accurately against the background of the sky. I have thought that it was a buzzard from its mode of flight, but somehow it does not appear to be quite right in shape and perhaps too small. Then suddenly it sets its wings and swoops down to land in a tree and I realise that it is a rook after all.

A good many years ago I stopped applying artificial fertiliser to my grazing fields, preferring to rely upon the natural nitrogen fixation of the indigenous wild white clover, enhancing this by grazing the fields with sheep. More recently I abandoned the use of chemicals alto-gether, even on my hay fields, since I found that the increased yields so obtained were of doubtful economic advantage in my circumstances. It is possible that the more natural unfertilised herbage on the farm is more to the liking of deer. Certainly it is noticeable that where cattle are introduced to a new field, if there is rough natural grass around the edges, they will very often concentrate upon this with a seeming preference for it. Reluctance to use chemical sprays does create some problems with weeds such as dandelions and stinging nettles. The latter are relished by stock when cut and dead, or when withering late in the autumn, and have been shown by analysis to have a good feed value. The dandelions appear in the hay fields behind the house in early summer in profusion. The growing grasses soon swamp these, but the dandelion seed heads remain for some time below the grass canopy and provide a considerable attraction to seed-eating birds. For some weeks we derive great pleasure from the constant presence of a large flock of linnets feeding on these dandelion seeds, flying up at intervals to perch on the electricity cable running overhead across the field, and then swooping down again to disappear in the grass. The flocks usually comprise a mixture of birds, with a few greenfinches, and occasional redpolls feeding amongst them, and often joined by a number of goldfinches. Towards the end of the summer the latter delight in the thistle seed heads just in front of the kitchen window, and the groundsel seeds growing in the weedy gravel below the washing line in front of the dog runs (rarely used, since our dogs spend most of their time in and around the house!).

The opportunity to be able to watch both red deer and roe deer feeding in proximity is fascinating from various aspects. In practice the roe usually seem a little uncomfortable in the presence of the bigger deer, but I suspect that this is probably simply because roe do not really like the presence of other deer, being rather solitary beasts much of the time. The red deer, on the other hand, are gregarious by nature, with a herd instinct, though the groups are quite probably family based to some extent. When one sees the two species of deer together not only is the size differential apparent, with a mature roe being much the same size as a young red deer calf or a little smaller, but also one really appreciates just how small and dainty are the roe.

One summer I was turning the hay crop in the field by the steading when I spotted a lovely roe buck on the slope in front of the farmyard, only about 150 yards away, taking no notice of the noise of the tractor. I paused and watched him for a minute or two through the monocular that I always carry. He was what I would describe as a perfect roe buck, probably just reached his prime, with a large, perfectly shaped six-point set of antlers, looking so graceful as he browsed around the edge of a clump of bracken. Some days, perhaps a week, later I was closing the gates across the yard preparatory to getting the sheep into

the pens when I looked up and saw this buck in the same place, a hundred yards in front of me. He ignored me as I walked back to the house, and I was able to find Diana and tell her that he was there. Obligingly he lay down, and Diana took a stool, sketchpad and binoculars into the yard and sat drawing him. I deferred my sheep operation whilst she had this opportunity of sitting in the sun and sketching. As it happened, she sat drawing him for over half an hour, for after a bit he rose again and then fed, moving gradually towards a clump of bracken into which he finally disappeared. Although I think he might have been the buck that we saw being chased across the slope in front of the house a couple of times in spring, we did not see him again on any other occasion.

The deer that we see in the fields certainly vary, with different deer being seen in the same spots in the field. Sometimes it is a doe with a kid, sometimes a doe with two kids, and sometimes we have seen a good buck there, not far from the doe. We have also seen a small spike buck in the same part of the field, and all of these sightings are within days of each other. One day there was even a red deer hind feeding there, with the roe doe and kid not far away, and the big buck further down the field.

Roe like hayfields, particularly those that are composed of more natural grasses and herbs and not heavily fertilised. As I have said, I have not used artificial fertiliser on my hayfields for some years now, and all of these fields have been used for a hay crop for some years consecutively. The longest sequence is one field from which a hay crop has been taken annually for twenty-four years in succession. All of these fields have a good clover content and a significant number of forbs that some modern farmers might describe as weeds. These plants undoubtedly attract deer. The long grass offers cover to roe too, and these small animals are difficult to spot in tall hay. When we have roe resident in the hay behind the house, for much of the time there is no evidence of deer there at all. Then, as we glance out of a window, we might see an ear flick, or a head appear. One of the more interesting sightings of a rutting roe buck we watched, from the landing window, in the hayfield behind the house. The hay had been cut, but lay in swathes, untouched since mowing because of incessant rain. We were doing the washing up after lunch in the kitchen when I spotted a doe trotting across the field a hundred yards away, followed a little distance behind by a small buck. He had only a small pair of spikes as antlers, and one might have guessed him to be her kid of the

157

previous year. However, as they came to the fence that divides what was once one field into two, I saw him sniff at the backside of the doe and, since it was the end of July, I reckoned that he was rutting. We moved upstairs to the landing window to obtain a better view. They trotted down the fence, and at the far end, where this slopes down a steep bank to the march burn, the fence is lower and she jumped over. The little buck hesitated briefly before jumping too. The doe then set off diagonally across the field towards the open gateway into the hayfield beyond. However, the buck did not seem to like this idea and trotted round in front of her and headed her back towards the fence for a few yards. This happened a couple of times, until finally the doe set off determinedly towards the gateway at the far side of the field. The little buck was nosing about in the grass, and then looked up and saw her halfway across the field and took off after her. He raced flat out towards her and swung round in front of her to head her off, just like a sheepdog. Unfortunately, in executing the sharp turn under her nose he skidded on a wet swathe of hay and fell! Quickly he rose again and herded the doe, who was bigger than him, right back across the field to the burn bank, where they disappeared.

The roe deer rut is always of interest, and we see bucks and does together at any time of day, sometimes with the buck chasing the doe. I generally like to try my hand at calling a roe buck at some stage in the rut, as I have done for many years now. It always gives me a thrill to call roe right up to me. I notice that calling deer in this part of the country is more difficult than in southern England, but I do not know why this is so. It could be the different terrain, but I suspect that it is more likely to be the apparent high proportion of does to bucks. The rut tends to be later than in the south, perhaps by as much as two weeks or so, but clearly the weather plays a considerable part in dictating activity. Warm muggy weather seems to be typical roe rutting conditions, and I tend to associate this with just the sort of humid day that precipitates the emergence of the flying ants on their once a year appearance. I well recall returning from an evening watching roe rutting, and walking along the farm track in the gloaming where there seemed to be toads every few yards presumably gorging on the annual eruption of flying ants. As a guide, we usually start seeing signs of roe rutting activity in the last week or so of July, and this goes on until well after the middle of August. Like other forms of calling or decoying, calling roe has to be carried out in the right circumstances to succeed. Most of the commercially available calls can be successful on occasion, and some people that can make noises by blowing on a strip of grass held between their thumbs, which I cannot do, have even called roe bucks by this method. Indeed the German name for the roe rutting time is Blattzeit, not Brunftzeit as it is for the rut of red and fallow deer. Blatt is German for leaf, and blattzeit means leaf time, referring to the older practice of calling roe by using a young beech leaf held against the lips. I have not seen this done, but knowing the strange shriek produce by a hard squeeze on my rubber Buttolo call to imitate the geschrei, which is apparently regarded by some people as the very insistent sex call of a roe doe, and the dramatic effect that this can have upon a buck in certain circumstances, I can well believe that it succeeds. In fact geschrei is short for angstgeschrei, which is German for cry of fear. This shriek is sometimes made by an as yet unreceptive doe being harried by a buck. I have called roe with a number of different calls into which one blows. One of the cheapest, a little black plastic call, with a small metal rod that one can move with a fingernail to adjust the reed and thus the tone, is effective. By making a higher pitched squeak it imitates a kid's call and so is effective in calling does, whilst the rather deeper note that imitates a doe will lure a buck under the correct circumstances.

I have only ever heard the doe making what is described as a fieping noise. The other deeper, and seemingly rather un-deer-like shrieks, I have not knowingly heard and associated with roe, except rarely with injured or terrified deer. However, one does hear such noises in the woods on occasion and I have not been sure if it was a bird of some kind, perhaps a raptor, or something else. Nevertheless the loud geschrei shriek can have spectacular results sometimes and so I presume that the buck must recognise it. Often when one watches a roe buck running a doe (or is it a doe leading on a buck?) they are silent. I have quite often had them run rather close to me in the woods and heard only the sound of their feet, and perhaps heavy breathing if they are very close, but from time to time I have seen and heard them running through the trees and heard the doe squeaking or fieping. Years ago I was told that the doe peeps every second step. I have not been able to confirm that for sure, but this would seem to be about right. As they weave in and out of the trees and change direction, so the peeping fades and disappears and then one hears it again as the deer come close in one's direction again. Thus the idea of peeping a few times on a call at intervals seems realistic. Sometimes a roe buck will come at full gallop when called, and I have quite often been aware of their approach by hearing literally a thunder of hooves and a sort of snorting or heavy breathing. This has more often been the reaction to using the loud geschrei shriek in desperation either because a visible buck has taken not the slightest notice of frequent peeping, or because after much calling without success I have got fed up and decided to try desperate tactics. However, mostly the buck attracted by peeping approaches stealthily, downwind, often circling the source of the noise. I do not know whether he does this to check what sort of buck is running the doe that is making the noise, or whether he is just cautious to see if there is another buck around, or whether he is suspicious because the squeaking is coming from some immovable spot. Whatever the reason, it is advisable to have good visibility around one when calling roe, and especially downwind. For this reason a high seat, or a perch in a tree has a great advantage, since one's scent is carried away above deer level, and visibility is usually better too, whilst roe rarely look upwards, unlike other species of deer.

A buck that already has the company of a doe is unlikely to respond to a call, since his interest is already engaged. However, I have called a buck with a doe, even though she also had her kid with her too, by peeping with a high-pitched kid's call. This attracted the doe right across a newly-planted area in the wood towards me, and the buck followed after the doe and kid. Calling deer close in this manner of

160

course gives ideal opportunities for photography, as well as the thrill of having deer really close.

The first buck that I ever called was at a roe ring. I discovered this in a young plantation of beech trees on the Surrey North Downs. The trees were perhaps only six or eight feet high, and the ring was in a small area where they had not taken so well and which was fairly open, just inside the planting. Fortunately the foresters had left a reasonably substantial birch tree on the edge of the ride and I was able to put a seat in this. The effect of squeaking that evening was dramatic, with a buck appearing with snorting and a thundering of hooves. Roe rutting rings, or tracks worn by the feet of the constantly circling deer, usually formed around some central object such as a bush or tree stump, are comparatively rare in relation to the number of rutting deer. Sometimes they are in the form of a double ring or figure of eight. No roe rings that I have found ever re-appeared in following seasons despite carefully searching for them. I suppose that in some stable and restricted habitat, where herbage and trees are not constantly changing and growing, perhaps where there is an open space containing a rock or tree stump, and where roe are naturally attracted to the place, the site might be re-used, but I am not familiar with this.

My own observations suggest to me that when a buck is chasing a doe (or should one say driving a doe, or even that the doe is leading on the buck?) mostly they do not circle, but sometimes when attracted by some pivotal point they may do so, or perhaps in thick cover they circle around to avoid losing each other. I learned recently of a buck and doe chasing round and round a telephone pole. One ring in my wood was formed round a large bush in which a child had made a small hut or shelter in the past. It does not take a great number of

161

passages of a deer's feet to create quite a beaten path. I have never found a roe ring other than at rut time, or soon afterwards, and mostly the evidence disappears as the herbage and undergrowth grows. Most of the chases that I have observed have been in the open, across clearings in woodland, or in mature woods, either hardwood or conifer. The rings that I have found have all been in woodland, and one in particular in a very thick area of undergrowth. I have watched roe chasing around isolated gorse bushes on turf in the open, but the action was not especially continuous circling, and the turf would not show traces of their footmarks since it was fairly resistant to the frequent passage of sheep feet. I have watched a buck mount a doe in such a situation, and on another occasion I watched a buck chasing a doe in the typical rather slow fashion, somewhat haphazardly around a turnip field in the middle of the day, and finally mounting her. The slow chase then resumed. A keeper friend told me of finding a roe ring in a turnip field close to his house, but I did not see it, and do not know what, if any, central focus point there might have been.

I imagine that whether a roe buck chases a doe or is led on by her is dependent upon the state of the sex hormones of both animals. Just as stags in season round up their hinds, some of which are clearly unhappy with his attentions when they are not cycling in season, so the same will apply to roe, with the male coming into a longer, and more continuous, season than the female. So far as I know little research has been done into roe, and certainly not into the doe hormonal activity. Why some roe form a rutting ring and others do not, and whether the doe or the buck is influential in its formation is presently unknown

Sometimes when we are outside in summer we hear a roe deer bark. They rarely bark in winter, and in spring we are usually conscious of hearing the first bark of the season up on the hill. Red deer rarely bark except when actually disturbed by a human, and they seem to bark as a specific warning. The bark of an old red deer hind in a wood can be quite startling, being loud and resonant in the trees, sometimes sounding like someone striking hard an empty metal dustbin with a heavy stick. On the other hand the bark of roe is often more quizzical than an alarm, and they seem to make the noise when uncertain or slightly disturbed, whereas when alarmed they silently melt away, or race off with the sound of clicking hooves. We often wonder what has caused the roe up on the hill or in the woods to bark. Was it a fox, or another deer, perhaps a red deer? Sometimes we hear a jay giving its squawking raucous alarm call and wonder what caused this commotion. We have seen jays dive-bombing and mobbing roe, perhaps mistaking them for a dog or fox. At other times, in spring or early summer, a curlew on the hill starts off a series of loud alarm calls and we wonder if this has been upset by a fox or wildcat, or just by a passing deer. I remember one time I was in the woods watching a pair of roe kids from a high seat when I heard a roe bark from behind me. At least I thought it was a roe, but was unsure. It barked two or three times, but was rather high-pitched, and I came to the conclusion that it was Diana up another high seat on the other side of the wood, having gone to watch for deer and sketch, and trying to imitate the bark of a roe. When I returned to the house after the light had gone I saw Diana and asked if it had been her trying to mimic a roe bark, but she told me that she had not left the house that evening! So I never did discover what had made the noise.

I see roe very often as I go about the farm, and it always amuses me when I see a deer first, before the animal sees me, and watch its reactions. They are clearly well used to the noise and passing of a tractor, and often will step behind a bush and watch me go past, following me with their gaze. Sometimes I disturb a deer feeding out in the open, and whilst they will mostly run off, feeling exposed, occasionally one will stand stock still, hoping that lack of movement will enable it to escape detection, rather as a rabbit will crouch low and frozen like a model until the last moment. When I see a deer doing this, standing like a statue, following the passing vehicle with its eyes and a barely perceptible turning of the head, I realise how often one must pass deer in cover behaving similarly but totally undetected. I have passed a roe buck lying in long herbage beside the farm track but only fifteen yards from it, clearly presuming that he had not been seen. Had I paused he would have been up and off, but as it was he never moved. One day I was checking cattle on my rather noisy little three-wheeled All Terrain Vehicle motorbike, and parked this by a gate into a field, next to a low stone dyke that fenced off an area of rough ground. It was not until I started to open the gate with a clanking of the chain,

two or three yards in front of the motorbike and just beside the dyke, that a roe doe leaped up, almost within reach, and sped off. Despite the noise she thought that she was well hidden, until I must have almost loomed above her.

At the top of our ground is an area of damp birch woodland, with patches of rushes, coarse grasses and sphagnum mosses. In summer this seems to be a favourite place for deer of both species to rest up in the daytime. I suppose that it is cool and sheltered. In autumn, and even late summer, it is a place of fungi, and I go there to pick chanterelles that grow in profusion under the birches, though in this place they often appear later than other sites lower down the hill. I was walking close to the edge of this wood one summer afternoon with our Irish Water Spaniel, Paddy, and he ran off into the wood hunting rabbits - with my approval, I should add! He had not gone more than fifty yards into the wood when I noticed a red deer hind standing beyond him looking intently at him, and a couple more hinds and calves behind her. I stood quite still and she had not seen me; neither had Paddy seen her. He was snuffling around in the rushes, and she advanced purposefully right up to within a few yards of him, where-upon he looked up and saw her, to his disquiet. He ran back in my direction, not especially scared, and the hind trotted after him. Paddy came back to the fence, outside which I was standing, and the hind came up to within twenty yards of me but then spotted me, gave one of those deep resonant barks, wheeled round and ran back to her companions, and they all vanished into the wood. Paddy was rather astonished, and I called him to heel and we left the scene.

It was in this damp patch of woodland that I saw a woodcock carrying its young. I had taken Diana and a friend up to see the Coral-root orchids, which grow in profusion there around the end of June. They are tiny flowers and really rather insignificant, but rare. They have no leaves and are symbiotic with birch roots. We were looking at some of these and the friend was photographing them, so I wandered a few yards away to find better ones, when suddenly a well-grown woodcock youngster fluttered up from my feet and flew off into thicker wood. Then an adult woodcock rose five yards from me, clearly carrying another of her young between her legs. It looked ridiculous and burdensome, for the chick was almost her size. I was reminded of two vast mating flies as they flew off! I called to Diana and her friend to look and they both had a clear view.

164

The birds landed about a hundred yards away at the edge of the open area, but I had no inclination to follow up and disturb her again. As I turned, another large young woodcock rose close to me and flew off, and I was astonished that the mother would be bothered to carry her chick when it was clearly well able to fly on its own. Diana had seen this twice before, so was not so astonished as I was. It is one of those often discussed matters that one never seems to be able to believe completely until witnessing it oneself. She had not previously seen such a large chick carried, but twice out riding, both times when accompanied by friends, she had witnessed a woodcock fly off carrying young and was in no doubt about it.

Diana has always found that her ponies are excellent watchers for deer. Often when we have been in the house we have seen the ponies standing on the hill looking at something with ears pricked, and we have followed their gaze and seen deer. Out riding, Diana can almost rely upon the ponies to tell her when deer are about, even before she spots them herself. Their eyesight is very sharp, and they have the added advantage of a superior sense of smell. In summer the ponies are kept in small enclosed areas of an acre or two, mostly at the bottom of the hill, but in winter they have the run of perhaps a hundred acres through the woods to an open area of heather at the top. They must come into contact with deer quite often, and both must get used to each other. Certainly the deer feed quite happily close to the ponies. Diana has the theory that the ponies detect a difference between regular deer and strangers somehow, since she believes that the ponies react differently to some deer. Sometimes they seem slightly nervous or alert, and perhaps they pick up reciprocal feelings from deer that are unused to the ponies and are themselves cautious and uncertain. Very often she is able to sit on the pony within perhaps a hundred yards of hinds or roe, sketching these while the pony stands

or feeds. Perhaps the deer do not recognise that there is a human on top of the white pony if she is down wind of them. The ponies are a good mobile high seat for other animals too, and Diana has ridden right up to within a few yards of a wildcat and had an excellent view of this on two occasions, as well as good views of capercaillie and other creatures.

I have often found it remarkable how observant both ponies and cattle are, as a result of their large eyes, placed on the sides of their faces to give better all-round vision, and when one notes this it is easy to understand how much more observant are deer, where the acuteness of their eyesight is so much more important. Cattle grazing in a field, apparently engrossed in feeding and seemingly not even facing in one's direction, will suddenly look up as one approaches, even at quite a distance. However, it is not just movement that catches their eye, and certainly the ponies are able to spot deer standing still or lying down at quite a distance, or even the face of a roe peering out from behind a gorse bush.

It is remarkable how deer get used to noises that one might expect to disturb them. I have been up the hill in Sutherland, lying watching a stag rutting with a group of hinds at the top of a steep slope down into the strath, when an aeroplane has zoomed past along the strath below us, making a noise that gave me a fright, almost causing an involuntary evacuation of the bowel, and yet the deer, instead of taking off at speed as I expected, seemed to ignore the terrible intrusion into the quiet of the wilderness. Clearly they were not unfamiliar with these low-flying aircraft. Deer that live near traffic often seem to disregard the noise of vehicles and continue to feed without even looking up, unless a vehicle stops. The deer on our farm are clearly used to the noises in our farmyard and to the sound of voices there, and of dogs barking. When I have been watching deer from a high seat on the hill I have heard the noises of Diana calling to the dogs and the ponies whilst I have been observing deer, and I have seen that they take no notice. Occasionally if they hear a distant shot, or a metallic bang from the neighbouring farm, or some such, they may pause briefly to listen, but no more than that. One morning I was watching some hinds and calves on a bank quite close to the house, some lying and others feeding. Diana was out in the yard with the dogs, and I heard these start to bark at the turkey stags, as they often do when these birds start to make aggressive noises at the dogs. Diana shouted loudly at the dogs to stop. Although these deer were not only within earshot of the noise, but they were actually in full view of the yard too, I saw no reaction from them at all to the barking and shouting except for one hind looking unperturbedly in the direction of the yard.

It has always amazed me how my cows can recognise my vehicle on the road. We have a few fields at the far end of the farm on the other side of a road, and when I go over to check the cattle or feed them I generally take a vehicle. This may be a tractor, an old Land-Rover, or a car. I can understand that if I approach along the farm track the cows would realise that it was my vehicle coming, or if I approach by road and slow down or stop I would expect them to take notice. However, what surprises me is that when I drive past at normal cruising speed without any sign of stopping, just as all the other traffic that uses the road, invariably I see several of the cows look up, and perhaps moo, quite clearly knowing that the vehicle is familiar. Undoubtedly their senses are honed more finely than we can appreciate, and they can recognise the noise of the engine of my vehicle or maybe it is some form of telepathy that animals so often appear to display.

The hinds that calve on our hill must be familiar with the ground, for it has been found, as a result of tagging calves, that hinds become hefted to the area within the vicinity of their birth, in much the same way as sheep do. I gather that the little Herdwick sheep of northern England, perhaps one of the hardiest of the sheep breeds, become very hefted to their place of birth and will travel miles to return to almost the precise spot on the hill where they were lambed. Probably the deer also become aware of the feed available at the different times of year in their choice both of place to calve and the area in which to raise their calves. Many animals and birds return to the same place to have their young, of course. Swallows are a good example of this instinct, and many raptors use the same nesting sites in successive seasons.

The subject of choice of place to raise young reminds me that a favourite place for birds seems to be one of my tractors! One year a wagtail chose to nest behind the seat of my largest tractor, gaining entrance through a partly open back window. Fortunately I did not need to use that tractor whilst the birds were in residence. The following year a wren decided to use the cab of another tractor. I

167

spotted her slipping in through a crack in the partially open rear window with a beak full of food, and when she left again I investigated and found a nest in the corner of the cab roof jammed against the foam rubber lining. She hatched before I needed the machine for hay making. The following year a wren nested in the front corner of the same cab! I wondered whether she was the same bird. That summer, after the young had fledged, I discovered another wren's nest in a shed where we keep hay for winter feed for the ponies. There were half a dozen small square hay bales left in the shed in a stack from the previous year, and when I went to move these to the front, in order to fill the back with fresh bales, I found the wren's nest amazingly attached to the side of a bale and hanging there reminiscent of a swallow's nest on a wall. Since I believe that wrens are the most numerous nesting birds in this country I suppose that one might expect to find their nests quite frequently.

Deer do not tarry close to their exact spot of calving though, with the atavistic instinct to move quickly away, having licked the calf clean, eaten the afterbirth and removed other obvious traces of parturition that might be spotted by predators. Having moved a short distance away from this spot, the hind tends to feed or rest a little way from the calf, with the young animal usually wandering off some yards to thick cover when it decides to rest. Again this separation is an aid to hiding the calf, though the adult remains fully watchful and alert, albeit at a distance. I was watching a small party of hinds with young calves one afternoon when I noticed one hind suddenly run off about a hundred yards to where her calf lay. I do not know what caused the temporary panic, but she quickly settled and the calf rose and suckled briefly.

As the hinds reappear with their new calves, the parties of hinds join up again, and are accompanied by their yearling offspring. These often accompany the hinds right up to rutting time, when the male yearlings tend to be chased off by the stags, and so form their own parties. Often we see a small family group of a single hind accompanied by a yearling and her calf.

Watching the deer through the summer I have long been fascinated by the growth of antlers. At this time of year we rarely see stags, which disappear after the rut and reappear in the following September. Undoubtedly these older stags seek relief from flies irritating them, particularly on growing antlers, and other parasitic horrors such as Deer warble flies (*Hypoderma diana*) and nasal bot flies (*Cephanomyia auribarbis*), by seeking the cover of thick woods and especially shady conifer plantations, of which there are plenty in our area. They may

leave the immediate district altogether to seek the relief of breezes on the tops of the hills. Warble flies lay their eggs on the legs of deer, and these hatch into maggots, which then burrow through the skin into the flesh of the deer. Over the next few months these maggots migrate through the body of the deer and finally emerge as large grubs, the size of big caterpillars, in cysts with air holes through the skin on the backs of the animals. Nasal bot flies are even more unpleasant, since the huge maggots fill the nasal cavity of the unfortunate deer and render breathing difficult. The fly is viviparous, which means that it lays maggots already hatched rather than eggs. It hovers in front of the nostrils of the deer and deposits the little maggot into these, which then crawl inside, fasten on and grow. It is small wonder that the deer seek refuge from these parasites, and probably the stags, under less pressure to feed, having to accommodate only their appetite to achieve bodily growth or recovery of condition from winter, do not have the additional burden of providing for a growing embryo and then a milk supply for a hungry calf, and so may be able to shelter more and spend less time eating.

Even though we do not see the mature stags in summer, we see the antlers of the yearlings growing, and occasionally those of stags that may be a year older. With good feeding and shelter available, these young stags grow antlers noticeably bigger than their peers on the open hill with less ideal conditions of habitat. As we see these various young stags through the summer, and watch their antlers forming, initially from knobs resembling rather misshapen velvet-covered gooseberries, and gradually growing into more defined shapes, I find myself wondering at the marvel at this strange growth, unique amongst mammals, in that not only are the antlers bone, but they are shed and regrown annually. Detailed experiments have shown that the antler growth of deer, as with other rhythms of their lives, is controlled by what are known as photoperiods. Once the basic mechanisms of antler growth are set in motion, then food supply is the factor that dictates the extent of growth. In this semi-woodland area with some access to farm land at night, a two-year-old stag can carry a pair of ten-point antlers and weigh 16 stone, but a stag on the open hill in the west or north might not display these attributes until five or six years old, if ever. We have seen stags taken nearby, where all the adjoining estates operate commercial stalking, which prove these ages by tooth examination. A fine royal head, with twelve points, was shown by its molar teeth to be no more than four years old.

Unfortunately unless red deer are artificially marked and thus of known age, there is no method of assessing age accurately, particularly once the rutting features of enlarged neck and rough mane have appeared, except by examination of the teeth, which can only be done once the animal is dead. Thus live age assessment is largely guesswork and a matter of comparison. A person used to seeing red deer on the north-west coast would undoubtedly be confused and misjudge deer in this area, in the same way that when I went to visit a friend on a large west coast deer forest I made a slightly embarrassing error. As I arrived at his house I saw some hinds and calves feeding in a small rushy paddock in front of it. My goodness! I exclaimed, those must be very late-born calves, or are they sick? My host was rather surprised at my somewhat uncomplimentary, but genuine, enquiry, for those calves were normal for that area. The effect of availability of good quality feed and shelter is dramatic.

In the case of sheep, cattle and horses, the age of young animals can be judged by the incisor teeth, the ones at the front of the mouth and used for cutting the herbage. For instance, in sheep the central of the four pairs of incisor teeth are replaced by larger permanent teeth at

170

about fifteen months old. The next pair of milk teeth are replaced by the larger permanent ones at 21 months old, and the next two at intervals of six months or more until it has a full mouth at four to five years old. Thereafter the teeth of the sheep tend to wear or become lost, depending to some extent upon the type of food available. However, deer replace their milk incisors much more quickly, and as yearlings red deer may have one or two of the pairs permanent, with a complete set as a two-year-old. Research has shown that incisor eruption varies with the rate of growth and weight of the animal, and may take place fully at any period between 19 and 26 months, by which time all young red deer should have a full set of front teeth. Thereafter age has to be judged by the molar teeth, which can only be seen properly by an operation to enable the mouth of a dead beast to be opened sufficiently to see the very back molar, or wisdom tooth, which is the last permanent tooth to appear. This occurs at two years old, at which age the roots of the premolars are also still open and fragile; though examination obviously necessitates removal. The third cusp or point of the back molar is just emerging from the jaw at two years old, and at three years old is starting to become stained. Thereafter judgement of age is made by assessing tooth wear, or else by sectioning teeth, which apparently have growth rings similar to that found in tree growth, though I am not personally familiar with such sectional examination. The judgement of tooth wear is rather arbitrary, and variation will depend not only upon type of food eaten regularly, and even type of soil (sandy soil, for instance, may accelerate tooth wear), but also on individual idiosyncratic tooth performance, just as occurs in humans. Moreover, I have read that stress increases the magnitude of dental asymmetry, so pedantry can be dangerous in this respect. Unfortunately this exact ageing of deer can only be performed in an autopsy, and so judging the age of live animals has to be arrived at on the basis of experience.

# Chapter 10
# The Fascination of Antlers

The importance of food supply to young deer of all species is no different from that to all young of all creatures at what is a critical time of their lives. A good deal of research has been carried out into the phenomenon of antler growth. It is a unique process where each year, in a normal male deer, this bone tissue grows out of its skull and subsequently ossifies or mineralises into hard effectively dead bone, which remains connected to the skull by the pedicle until at the appropriate season it is cast and new growth starts again. Antler growth occurs only in male deer, except in reindeer or caribou where females also carry antlers, albeit smaller. Reindeer are also unusual in having either only one brow tine, or one that is asymmetrical and much larger than the other, either palmated or just a spike. This brow tine tends to stick out well forward, and it has been suggested that it might be useful for digging out lichens in the snow for them to eat. The hormone system of reindeer might work slightly differently from those of other deer, since castration does not have such a dramatic effect upon the males.

Man has been fascinated by the antlers of deer from the very earliest of times. Some of the earliest primitive tools were made of antlers, and all through history antler bone has been used in tools and implements for handles, and still is used today. The earliest cave paintings depicted

 stags with huge antlers, and magnificent antlers have always inspired admiration. Sometimes antlers are referred to as horns, which is technically incorrect, since horns are composed of tissue rather like fingernail material, and these are not shed. Cattle, sheep and antelopes have horns, but deer have antlers.

Though the use of antlers for tools goes back infinitely further in history, their attraction to man for medicinal reasons goes back a long way, perhaps for a couple of thousand years. For centuries the antlers in velvet, or whilst still growing and covered with furry skin, have been used in the far east. Possibly the original attraction was because of the connotations associated with the mysterious annual growth of these adornments to the head of male deer. Whatever the reason, the use of antler in velvet has featured importantly in the medicines of various far eastern countries throughout modern history. The principle users of the material are China, Tibet, far eastern Russian countries, and Korea. China and the Soviet Union produced their own antler products, and there have been domesticated deer in parts of Siberia for a long time. However, the production of antler in velvet was always on a small domestic scale until the 1960s. In more recent times it was discovered that there was a lucrative market for the highly valued product, and supplying this strong demand created a boom in deer farming in New Zealand, at a time when the expansion of the imported deer population in that country had reached proportions where the animals were regarded as pests causing habitat destruction and erosion. Thus wild deer were caught and farmed rather than simply shot.

Contrary to apparent popular ideas, the use of ground up and dried deer antler in velvet is not as an aphrodisiac but as a tonic, though such an effect might promote greater activity in elderly men, and in a great variety of medicines, including those for young children. Seemingly in Korea powdered velvet antler is an almost weekly purchase for most families in some form. The growing antlers are living tissue, so their removal has to be done surgically and under anaesthetic. For this reason the operation was rightly regarded with disfavour in this country, and elsewhere in Europe, and legislation prohibited it. I understand that the dark velvet grown by sika deer is most favoured in some countries, allegedly having superior qualities. This was the species of deer perhaps better known in the far east, but the farming of sika deer has not caught on, possibly because they are allegedly a much worse tempered species than red deer and so less easy to handle. Red deer are the most commonly farmed, in various parts of the world now, sometimes with wapiti blood introduced to improve body and antler size; though wapiti cross deer have the reputation of being substantially worse tempered, and more difficult to handle, than red deer. The antlers of the latter are much like those of wapiti, albeit smaller, and I gather that the Koreans prefer wapiti material. Other species of deer have been used for this trade, including Rusa, that are supposedly more easily trained, and chital (axis) that are said to be more flighty, as well as reindeer, which of course already have a long history of domestication.

I am glad that the trade in antlers in velvet was prohibited in this country, since the idea of removing growing bone tissue from the animals in order to supply mystical medicines to the people in eastern countries, however lucrative, is as abhorrent as the similar supply of rhino horn and tiger bones. Nevertheless the interest generated in deer farming has undoubtedly assisted knowledge of the mechanisms of antler growth by research.

Thus, in one way or another Man has long been fascinated by antlers and made use of them. Undoubtedly deer antlers are impressive, whether on a dainty little roe buck or on a majestic-looking stag. Nevertheless it would be unfortunate if, despite this fascination for antlers and tangible trophies for hunters, the beauty of deer was overshadowed, let alone overlooked, as a result of this. So far as I am concerned, one of my most memorable experiences of red deer was not gazing at a superbly-antlered stag, though I still carry in my mind the picture of a superb royal with dark antlers and even white tips which rutted on the farm some years ago, and which I hope was not shot by trophy-hunting neighbours or a farmer angry at depredation of his turnip crop, but of a young hind. I was sitting up a rather low high seat that I had made in a birch tree from a few planks. Two hinds

appeared further up the hill from me, and at much the same level as myself but upwind of me. They were feeding upon broom pods, which I suppose are highly nutritious. In due course they jumped a fence and grazed towards me, the older hind moving off a little way to my right, whilst the younger hind plucked grass audibly to straight underneath the tree. As she stood below me, perhaps only six feet away, she looked up and stared at me. I dared not breathe visibly or flinch at all. She gazed at me for an uncomfortably long time and I noted her huge eyes. Finally she decided that I was part of the tree, or at least not dangerous, and resumed grazing,

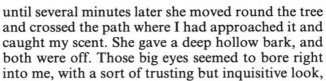

until several minutes later she moved round the tree and crossed the path where I had approached it and caught my scent. She gave a deep hollow bark, and both were off. Those big eyes seemed to bore right into me, with a sort of trusting but inquisitive look, and made a deep impression upon me. Roe have frequently enchanted me with their daintiness of movement, particularly when viewed from a high seat, where, concealed, I have been able to watch them very close, often almost beneath me, unaware of my presence and going about their business of feeding or nursing their kids. I have always regarded roe as being the most dainty of animals, more delicate than the graceful impala antelopes or the elegant gerenuk that stands on its hind legs to feed on thorn bush shoots. I was recently reminded of gerenuks, which I have watched browsing in East Africa in the past, when I saw our tame red deer hind standing up on her back legs to reach the leaves of a gean tree, the lower branches of which she had already stripped. I marvelled at the way that she stood completely vertically on her hind hooves to reach a remarkable height. The hunter who seeks out his quarry with trophy or meat in mind tends to miss the opportunity of enjoying the enchantment of deer feeding undisturbed or resting peacefully that can be relished by the patient watcher.

Antlers denote more than merely supposed glory accorded to the killer of the bearer of a fine pair of these. As a general rule fine impressive antlers denote the quality of the animal growing them, in the same way that horns usually indicate a good quality beast with sheep or antelope. This is not always the case though. Famous in recent deer history is the story of the rigorous pursuit of the Muckle Hart of Benmore by the author Charles St John. I have seen a replica of the antlers of this famous stag, and when I did so I was surprised to find that they were not in fact impressive at all, despite the legendary size of the beast, nor the description of impressive antlers in the narrative. There are plenty of records of very heavy stags with not especially impressive antlers, and similarly some very fine antlers have been borne by stags that were not remarkable in body.

There can be little doubt that food supply and habitat are of major importance in the forming of both good quality deer and fine antlers, and this has been shown worldwide. Habitat describes the living conditions of the animal, which includes both the availability of shelter from adverse weather conditions and from predators and predatory parasites, and absence of disturbance both from competitors as well as from humans and other causes. Genetics are also clearly of importance, but this factor can be overshadowed by the influence of feed and conditions. When a deer is subjected to inadequate food supply or poor conditions, and continual disturbance, its genetic potential is unlikely to be achieved. It would seem that shape of antler is the most readily observable inherited trait in deer of all species. Certainly roe bucks in differing parts of the country have a tendency to similar localised shape, and certain lines of stags raised in parks, where cast antlers can be collected and retained as records, show recognisable shapes or other characteristics of antler that can be identified in related animals.

Nevertheless the most important of all ingredients in the development of a deer, male or female, is the contribution of its dam. This contribution consists on the one part of the influence over the genetic make up of the young deer, and on the other part of the vital food supply and mothering attention provided. In the case of park or farmed deer the parental contribution is readily noted, particularly with the latter where records will be more assiduously kept, and where limited stag numbers enable both parents of a calf to be known. Such records will undoubtedly reveal that certain hinds consistently produce above average calves, and do so regularly without becoming yeld for a season. Where such stag calves are retained, the records will be able to show, over a sufficient period, which combinations of stags and hinds consistently result in offspring with fine antlers. As is the case with all animals, it is by no means certain that a sire with good antlers will father similarly endowed offspring. Unfortunately in practice few such records will be available, since deer farms do not keep stag calves to full antler potential, other than a few for stock stags, and even in New Zealand, on farms producing velvet antlers, these will be removed before proper comparison can be made. In the wild it is impossible to know for certain which hinds were successfully served by which stag, or to identify later those stags thought to originate from particular sires.

Whatever the effect of genes inherited from the dam might have, the most demonstrable influence on calf growth must be the supply of initially colostrum and then milk. As any stockman, or more particularly any shepherd, knows, an adequate supply of this for a newborn offspring is by no means certain, for a variety of causes. In the case of wild deer, and especially amongst red deer on the open hill in adverse country, a major cause of inadequate milk, and thus calf mortality, must be the condition of the dam as a result of poor feeding or bad weather. A hind in poor condition will not provide sufficient milk for the calf, if any. A weak dam may produce a weak calf that is unable to rise quickly or suckle properly. There can be little doubt that hypothermia resulting from inadequate milk intake, either because the mother has insufficient or because the newborn is too weak to get it, or perhaps because the dam will not co-operate with its young to enable it to suckle for some reason, is a major cause of death amongst red deer calves, just as it is in lambing flocks of sheep. The importance of milk to the young is recognised by the breeders of some pedigree beef cattle. Where some cows may be thought to give insufficient milk to encourage maximum growth potential, the young bull calves are removed from their dam and fostered on to high yielding dairy breed cows for rearing. A hind with insufficient milk cannot raise a good calf.

The factor that governs antler growth is light. This is not surprising when one considers that the whole cycle of life depends upon light. It is the lengthening day that causes plants to grow, birds to nest and lay eggs, and even produces a psychological effect upon humans. No matter how early a season may seem from the point of view of grass or crops growing in a warm spring, it is the daylight factor that principally controls the growth and in practice measurement shows little actual mean resultant difference in grass growth in most years on given dates. Experiments with light have demonstrated all sorts of strange happenings, and upon male deer there is no exception. It has been shown that deer kept in artificial light circumstances can be made to grow two, and even three, sets of antlers in a calendar year by accelerating the cycle so that instead of one period of day length growing and then reducing in a year, the timing is altered to give two and three cycles. In fact, beyond this number of artificial manipulations the deer no longer respond because the cycles are not long enough for growth. Similarly artificially extending the cycle has effect, but only to a certain degree. The scientific term for this influence is photoperiod.

What researchers have learned is that the photoperiod governs the body's production of hormones, and these in turn govern the bodily functions. In the case of deer it is the production of testosterone that principally controls antler growth and cycles. This hormone is mainly produced by the testes, but also by the adrenal gland. If a male calf or kid is castrated young enough it fails to produce sufficient testosterone, and this results in a failure of pedicle growth. Not being a chemist or veterinarian I am unable to understand the full processes of hormonal activity, or of antler growth, in detail, but I believe that other hormones such as oestrogen and stilboestrol can also affect

177

activities such as velvet shedding. The actual levels of testosterone are apparently critical, for though there can be no antler growth without this hormone, too much can have an adverse effect. For instance, a hind given testosterone grows pedicles, but too high a dose and she becomes sterile. Low levels of testosterone promote antler growth, and high levels stop it by mineralisation or ossification, as in the bone growth of young humans. Thus it can be seen that castration of a male deer at a later stage of growth may have a different effect than that upon a young calf, especially if a low level of hormone might be produced elsewhere in the body. A red deer calf castrated early in life, say at six weeks, fails to develop male characteristics, such as mane, antlers, signs of rutting, and so on, and can easily be mistaken for a hind throughout life. We know of a tame deer often seen in a field in front of a farm house not far from here that initially we presumed to be a hind as we drove past. However, we had been told that he is actually a castrated stag, and closer examination confirmed this. I gather that this beast may now be 23 or 24 years old. Seemingly the change of appetite cycles of stags, which are probably influenced by photoperiod, are maintained in castrates, though to a lesser degree.

As I understand it all the foetuses of both sexes of red, fallow and roe deer have indications of pedicle tissue in their skulls. However, subsequent skull growth masks this and pedicles are not evident in newborn young. Testosterone in the male, during its first months of life, induces pedicle growth. This hormone activity then reduces, after the formation of the pedicle, and this encourages a little antler growth, which is hardened by further hormone rise, and this first antler is cast when the hormone levels decrease again. The first little antler has no, or little, coronet. For example, roe deer have peak levels of testosterone in spring, when this causes mineralisation or ossification of the antlers, which harden and lead to velvet shedding, and then again in July, when the sexual activity and rut start. Once this is over and

178

hormone levels decrease, the antlers are shed, and the low levels of testosterone once again promote antler growth and the annual cycle starts again. The timing of the growth of red deer antlers is different of course, since these grow and are in velvet through summer, whereas those of roe bucks grow during the winter and become clean of velvet in spring. Thus it is clear that the photoperiod has a slightly different effect upon roe than upon red deer. In the case of the latter the antler hardening and sexual activity promoted by high testosterone levels coincide.

Contrary to unsubstantiated tradition and the beliefs of many old stalkers, hummels are completely fertile. All sorts of false traditions have been propagated about hummels in Scotland entirely due to misunderstandings about their cause and condition. In fact hummels are rare in continental Europe, and in woodland deer. An occasional hummel has been reported in roe. In poorer country in north and west Scotland hummels occur more frequently. I have read a suggestion that these might represent one per cent amongst stags. Certainly research was carried out on one large deer forest to see whether hummels were any bigger, or different in weight, than normal stags, and a significant number of hummels and half-hummels (stags with only one antler) were measured. It was found that there was no difference at all in mean weights. This suggests that the idea that growing a large set of antlers imposes a burden upon stags in summer, in the same way that raising a calf puts pressure upon a hind, is quite unsubstantiated. Not only has it been proven that hummels are fully fertile, but it has been demonstrated that it is not a genetic factor and that hummels breed perfectly normal stags. If it was genetic, then hummels might well be valuable as stock stags on deer farms, removing the added danger of their antlers. On Glensaugh, the first deer farm, as an experiment by the Rowett Research Institute and the Hill Farming Research Organisation, which I understand ran around 400 hinds at one time, one of the stock stags used for a couple of years, chosen because of his conformation, was a hummel. It is of interest that the hind that was the mother of that hummel stag was 19 years old when she produced him, for if her great age indicated a reduced milk supply it could indicate the reason for his being a hummel.

Photoperiod, or day length, controls testosterone production, and this in turn promotes pedicle growth. However, experiments have indicated that pedicle growth commences at a set level of weight in red deer. Thus it would seem that if a calf failed to reach that set weight before testosterone production decreases, its ability to grow pedicles would be inhibited. There seems to be little doubt that pedicle growth, and therefore future ability to grow antlers, is dependent upon nutrition level in that early period of life. Consequently if a hind has a poor milk supply, through age, lack of body condition, worm burden, mastitis, or other problems, the calf may not develop sufficiently to grow pedicles. Though many young animals that have a poor start in life never really thrive and remain poor specimens throughout life, or more probably die, some do manage to regain ground. Compensatory growth is a familiar happening to the stock farmer. Indeed many utilise this to make young stock mark time in growth over a winter period when feed is expensive, in the knowledge that compensatory growth on new summer grass will enable the stock to catch up on cheap feed. So it may be that a red deer calf with a mother with a poor milk supply, but otherwise good mothering ability, has a slow start and fails to grow pedicles, but subsequently, when it can benefit from herbage consumption, it may then grow well on the solid food and become a perfectly good young beast or yearling, but without the ability to grow antlers. The calf may grow partial pedicles that are apparently incapable of further antler growth at times of future appropriate hormone levels.

There is much tradition and almost folklore surrounding hummels. Until about twenty years or so ago our knowledge of deer was really very limited. The pioneering of deer farming, especially at the Rowett Research Institute in Aberdeen, and then at the Glensaugh deer farm, almost just over the hill from where I live now, has resulted in a tremendous amount of research which has increased our knowledge of red deer greatly. Hummels are now fairly well understood. At one time most stalkers believed and I suspect that a great many still do that hummels are infertile and incapable of breeding properly or that they do breed but the trait of being bare-headed is hereditary. I would guess that a lot of stalkers and people interested in deer will be astonished to know that a hummel has actually been used as a stock breeding stag at Glensaugh experimental deer farm with success.

A hummel is an antlerless stag. One can also get half-hummels or stags with only one antler. The name derives simply from the word humble, being the opposite of a royal, as a twelve-pointed set of antlers is called, or an imperial, with fourteen points. Of course many park and deer farm stags that are well fed have points on their antlers far exceeding these numbers, but such multi-pointed deer are rare in the wild in Britain. The failure to grow antlers resulted in the denigration of the animal, hence the idea that it should be shot. The other tradition surrounding hummels is that since they do not have to go through the annual process of growing antlers, the energy is diverted instead to growing large strong bodies. Thus the idea that large hummels, with superior strength, can beat up antlered stags despite their lack of armament, and take over their hinds, and so either spoil their breeding or procreate a generation of future hummels.

A great deal is now known about antler growth, particularly in red deer. As we know, the Sun is a major influence upon all life. Seasons and weather all originate from this influence, and these in turn affect the growth and behaviour of all living things. This is most obvious in the annual growth of plants, where this depends upon daylight length as a major factor in promoting growth. Deer too are affected directly by daylight length, or photoperiod. In red deer their coat shedding, the periods of appetite reduction, sexual behaviour, and antler growth are all directly connected to daylight length.

As I understand it, as foetuses, both male and female deer have the potentiality of growing pedicles, but this requires the effect of the male sex hormone testosterone to precipitate development. The secretion of this hormone is stimulated by the production of melatonin in the brain, which is influenced by light. The first stage of antler growth is the production of a pedicle from which the bone growth will subsequently form. The young male calf has a flush of testosterone that causes the growth of pedicles, and then this reduces again, before the next stage of growing an antler. Simplifying the explanation, without going into technical details, the supply of testosterone, which is

mostly, but not entirely, produced in the testicles, fluctuates seasonally, with the first flush early in the life of a red deer calf giving rise to
pedicles, and subsequent rises and falls in testosterone levels causing
growth of antlers, ossification and velvet shedding, and casting. There
are various other aspects, including research showing that deer
castrated before pedicle growth may not grow these, but those
castrated after pedicles have formed may fail to grow antlers,
although damage to the testicles, and thus damage to the testosterone
supply, especially when antler growth has commenced, may produce
continued growth as a consequence of no rise in the level of the
hormone to cause ossification. This results in the rare freak peruque
heads. Where pedicles are formed but no further growth of antler
materialises, growth can be induced by causing a wound on the
pedicle. Thus a hummel showing signs of pedicles can be made to
grow antlers by wounding the pedicles, and once this has happened the
cycle of antler growth and casting may well revert to normal. In other
words the failure to grow pedicles, or to complete the process of antler
growth after pedicle formation, possibly resulting from poor nutrition
and low condition of the young animal, does not result in permanent
inability to produce testosterone and otherwise act normally such as
castration would cause.

However, it would seem clear that the origin of a hummel is based
upon its condition as a very young calf in the first few months of life.
As anyone that has reared young animals knows, a number of facts
influence the well-being of a creature in the early weeks of life, and
these include shelter, motherly attention, and in the case of mammals
the vital ingredient is milk. Most of us can think of rather weedy
children that suddenly shoot up in their teens and become robust
adults. The early lack of growth may have many causes in humans,
and possibly in deer too, but with the latter the milk supply is the most
likely. It is quite conceivable that a good strong hind capable of
producing a good calf develops mastitis, or some other illness, and
the potentially good calf suffers a set-back in its first two or three
months. This in turn prohibits satisfactory testosterone production,
and that calf then fails to develop pedicles. This young stag then
becomes a hummel. If there is plentiful solid food, and good grazing
and browsing, the young deer may then exhibit what cattle rearers call
compensatory growth, and catch up with its siblings and develop into
a good beast, except that it has no antlers. In all other respects it is a
normal stag.

A further factor may govern the size and dominance of a hummel,
as already suggested. Flies on growing velvet-covered antlers appear

182

to torment stags, and indicate the sensitivity of these growths at such a time, hence the retreat of these animals to the cooler breezy hill tops, or into sheltered woodlands. The hummel does not have this aggravation in summer and thus can avail himself of prime feeding opportunity. Furthermore, without the sensitive antler growth, he is well able to use his head as a weapon and establish dominance, and there is little doubt that such establishment of pecking order is of material importance in all animal society, and that the display of a fine pair of antlers alone is not sufficient to vanquish opposition.

The extraordinary bone growth on the head of a male deer has many surprises for those interested in deer. For instance, it is now known, as already mentioned, that if the pedicle, or that area, of a hummel is wounded, or traumatised as the scientist might say, the stag will grow an antler, and thereafter continue to do so annually. Presumably this explains half-hummels or one-antlered stags. If both pedicles are damaged, then both antlers will grow, and cast and regrow normally in future. Moreover, once a pedicle has grown on a stag, surgical removal of this will cause an antler to grow in that place. Research has discovered that the crucial tissue on which antler growth depends is the periosteum, which is the membrane round the bone that carries what one might describe as the ingredients for bone growth that are laid down by it to form the bone. Transplanted periosteum will cause antler to grow. One experiment grafted some periosteum to the foreleg of a roe buck! From this a small piece of antler grew, was subsequently cast, and then another piece re-grew! Even more bizarre was the grafting of a piece of periosteum to the cartilage of an ear, on which some antler formed. Apparently it is recorded that in 1894 a roe doe, which I presume must have been a captive or tame animal, was damaged by a piece of window glass that pierced its scalp and irritated the periosteum. This led to the growth of an antler 9.8 cms long. It is reported that in New Zealand deer farmers have cut off the first growth of antler, and this has led to the production of eight-point antlers in just over a year. Therefore it is shown that cranial periosteum is vital to the growth of antler, but that initial pedicle growth is also important for the normal antler growth cycle to proceed naturally.

Freak antlers are always noticeable and the subject of comment. Perhaps the most bizarre of these are what are called peruke or perruque heads. Peruke means wig, and the antlers, if one can describe the growth thus, are so-called because the mass of velvet growth covers the head. Sometimes this happens to such an extent as to virtually blind the unfortunate beast, and often the growth becomes

infected with maggots. The cause of this is the failure of the animal to produce sufficient androgens to cause the antler growth to mineralise and the velvet covering to shed. Consequently the mass simply goes on growing. I have never seen a roe peruke in reality, though I have seen the antlers of a buck that seem to be not fully or properly ossified and with dried velvet still adhering, perhaps due to a malfunction of hormone production, but not in the extreme. I have seen a peruke red deer head, which was lying with some other trophies at the end of a stalker's garden in the far north. The growth was not particularly large, but it was probably a young beast when shot.

Freak antler growths are not uncommon amongst deer, and some of these are perpetuated from year to year. Sometimes antlers are malformed as a result of bodily damage, and this often occurs asymmetrically for some reason. For instance, a roe buck that lost its left leg in an accident developed a deformed short right antler. Another roe, of which I saw the skull, had a very deformed right antler, which looked almost as one might imagine it would have done had the antler melted and flowed down to near the head and re-solidified. This buck had been shot with bird shot and two pellets at least were embedded in its face, and it also had a hernia. One of the most remarkable deformed roe heads that I have seen was shown to me recently by a keeper on the north coast of Scotland. This had a pair of good, nicely-shaped six-point antlers, except one of these was growing horizontally instead of vertically and the brow point must almost have touched the animal's head. The pedicle had apparently been pushed forward, or rather the top of it bent over, perhaps as a result of an accident with a wire fence or some such when the buck was young. The keeper told me that he had known that deer for at least five years: with a head so deformed a similar beast was highly unlikely.

Some research has suggested that big bucks and stags shed their antlers earliest as a result of their greater expenditure of energy during rutting, or perhaps their earlier rutting, so resulting in lost condition and earlier reduction in hormone level. It is also thought that those beasts that cast antlers early in the year grow bigger antlers, and that a stag casting in March is likely to have significantly larger antlers than a beast that casts in June. Whether the antlers grow bigger because there is more time available during the summer for these to develop, or whether the bigger beast with better antlers sheds early anyway, the result would appear to be the logical outcome.

The growth sequence of antlers, and the factors governing optimum growth, are points much discussed by those interested in deer. One prominent researcher has suggested that a young stag that has a poor switch head initially is never likely to produce a good head. On the other hand Henry Evans, in his *Some Account of Jura Red Deer*, refers to a three-year-old stag with six points. This beast and his mother were both very tame, and he had the top of his ear cut off to render him bulletproof. He passed two years as a knobber instead of one year, and then threw out six points. "A somewhat awkward fact for the cock-sure division of observers!"

The pattern of growth of roe antlers over a period of years is not so easy to judge as with red deer because these animals are not readily kept in captivity for study, though a great deal of work has been done on marked roe at Kalo Research Station in Denmark. I can remember many years ago going to a talk given by Helmuth Strandgaard, who was in charge of Kalo at that time, in which he said they had recorded a gold medal-antlered roe buck that was known to be only a yearling. My impression was that many of his audience, ignorant of the degree of work done at Kalo, disbelieved him. There is much talk bandied about concerning the management of roe to improve antler quality, a lot of this based upon age judgement and the idea of progression in antler quality on an annual basis, and with genetic benefit. Whilst genetics may well influence roe antler shape or type in some degree, the demonstrable failure of continental areas to improve the quality of

185

roe antlers despite rigid rules and selection over very many years indicates that environment is of paramount importance. That is to say, both food supply and shelter, from weather and disturbance. Not only is it difficult to demonstrate successive roe heads in wild deer without extraneous factors involved because of an insufficient number of marked animals to study, but ageing roe is fraught with difficulty, and one is sceptical of those pedants who maintain that they can age dead roe, let alone live ones, accurately to the nearest year. What seems logical and likely is that antler size increases with body condition and size, which is dependent in turn upon the animal living in an optimum environment. Factors such as a bad winter (roe grow antlers during winter) or illness, or stress, may well affect antler growth from year to year and disrupt progressive improvement to a substantially greater degree than that of deer whose antlers grow in the easier period of summer.

For all his close observation of deer, and his considerable interest in the subject, Henry Evans writes "I do not think it always easy to judge the age of a mean-headed stag after he has reached five years old, that is to say an ordinary hill stag, of no merit. There are many stags that never grow larger than a fairly good five-year-old animal. Armchair judgement is much easier than hill-judgement." This wise assertion I endorse heartily. Similarly the ageing of mature deer by tooth wear is equally difficult and subjective, and whatever the pedants may endeavour to maintain, the verification of a stag's age remains somewhat arbitrary. I refer to wild stags of course. A great deal of information is known about the progression of annual antler growth in fallow deer and red deer as a result of these having been kept in parks for very many years where individual animals are known. In many parks successive cast antlers have been collected over the years, and not only can progression, and ultimate regression, be seen readily, but also the similarities in blood lines are often discernible. The difference lies in the environment and habitat of course. Park deer are usually adequately fed and not subjected to the rigours and traumas of wild deer. The transformation of antler growth in hill red deer transferred to deer farms is well known. High quality feed can transform mediocre antlers into massive multi-pointed structures in a matter of a season or two, in line with dramatic increase in body weights. As a general rule it would seem correct to assume that antler mass would increase annually for at least several years, with regression occurring when body condition begins to decline. There seems little doubt that antlers can become stunted by illness or poor condition to upset progressive growth however, and Henry Evans points out that monarchs, as he describes really fine-antlered stags, can have bad years and then recover again. Not long ago I was speaking to a young man who rents a deer forest and feeds stags for six months in the year for the specific objective of producing beasts with good quality antlers to sell as high-valued trophies to those choosing to stalk them in the season. He was convinced that he knew a number of these regularly fed stags by appearance and not merely by antler shape, so that he was able to recognise them when they had cast their antlers and were growing the new ones. He was definite in his views that a good royal, for instance, might suddenly become a poor eight-pointer one year, perhaps losing condition because of tooth problems, or some other cause, and then the year after it might revert to being a royal twelve-pointer once again. If this is the case, which seems logical and likely, it poses problems for stalkers and deer managers purporting to practise selectivity in the hope of improving breeding stock with a view to enhancing antler quality.

For all the debate about antler quality and the management of deer, there can be little dispute that attempts to influence antler growth in wild deer over very long periods have shown dismal failure in most species. On most large estates, where records and antlers have been kept for a century and more, there is no evidence of improvement in mean body weights or antler development. Then, as now, occasional large stags appeared, usually beasts that had availed themselves of advantageous habitat such as woodland or crops. Attempts to introduce park deer blood into wild hill herds have had negligible or indiscernible lasting effect. On the other hand, with red deer in certain parks in this country and favoured hunting reserves on the continent, where the animals have been deliberately well fed and looked after in optimum conditions, the comparative body weights and antler formation are impressive, with also an improved quality and fecundity in the hinds, noticeably favourable compared to wild herds in difficult conditions.

We are able to watch deer from our windows throughout the season

of growing antlers, though the ground is largely favoured by hinds mostly we also see young stags during summer, with only the occasional appearance of beasts with larger antlers. It is possible that some of the stags with growth that promises particularly impressive antlers are actually young beasts, since we know that one ten-pointer was carrying only his second head, aged just over two years old, and animals of this age still remain with their maternal groups to some degree. We have watched two stags in velvet, showing then good heads with at least eight points, feeding with hinds in early August one season. Presumably they were two-year-olds, being still with their mother in summer. So we are able to watch the development of the antlers through the summer. The stags start to clean their antlers, or shed their velvet coverings and expose hard horn in August. One summer I recorded on 19 August that we noticed a young stag with quite a nice head of eight points with clean antlers. He was with a group of hinds, which may or may not have been his maternal group, and I noted that he was bothering the hinds, though these were not greatly impressed by him. That season I recorded a yearling stag was still in velvet on 21 August but what I thought was the same animal was starting to clean his antlers, with the velvet beginning to peel off, on 23 August. On the 22 of the month I spotted a single stag with prominent mane and clean antlers, and on 27 August the eight-pointer seemed to be almost rutting from the way that he was running around after the hinds in his group, and again on 30 August, though none of the hinds seemed to be in season and attracting special interest from him, and he was just generally trying to round them up. One small yearling stag was still in velvet in early September.

There has been quite a lot written about the purpose of antlers. That is to say discussion as to whether they are purely weapons, or if they are perhaps items of display to impress other stags and establish a hierarchy. Some people might wonder the purpose of debating such questions, and regard them as akin to pondering upon why a cock blackbird is black and not white, or green, or why a robin has a red breast rather than a blue one. Does it matter? Are there other more interesting questions concerning deer to explore where answers are as yet unknown? I related that a researcher carried out an experiment to examine the possibility of antlers as a status symbol denoting rank, with five young stags that were kept separate from other stags. Then, when antlers were developed, a mature stag with a fine set of antlers was introduced into their enclosure. The researcher concluded that other stags failed to recognise dominance or higher ranking in the pecking order as a result of larger antlers. If one takes a cow from a herd for a while, for some reason, and then reintroduces her again later, some of the others in the herd will generally try her out, and often several of them together, and chivvy her around until they settle down into a recognised pecking order of dominance. There is little doubt in my mind that prominence in pecking order, or dominance, is influenced by several factors, of which body size is important, and antler size too perhaps, but probably also some psychological aspect, or however one should describe this in animals. In human groups the leader is not necessarily the biggest, nor the most handsome, and other factors, such as a strong will, are involved. So I imagine it to be with animals too. However, since the biggest antlers are generally borne by the stag, or buck, in best condition, the selection for dominance is more obvious.

# Chapter 11
# The Hills Turn Purple

Traditionally the heather starts to bloom around the date known to those that walk the hills in search of grouse as the glorious, 12 August. However, although this is often the time that the heather flowers emerge, a warm summer can bring a purple tinge to the moorlands at the beginning of the month, and a cold wet summer can result in the onset of the blooming being delayed for as long as a couple of weeks. We have a little heather on our ground, but the top of the hill in front of the house, over the march, and our horizon, is heather hill, and we look forward to the few weeks when the dark hill tops become that familiar shade of purple. At this time of year we notice signs of wallowing by red deer in the edges of our ponds, and several favoured wet patches of hill where springs emerge in peaty or muddy places. The red deer visit the ponds to eat the reedmace too. I did not plant these roots for the deer originally, but did so because I admire the tall seed heads and like to have a few in a vase in the house for a short time in season. I did not realise how vigorously the reedmace would spread when I planted half a dozen roots in the 1970s. That original pond has now disappeared in a tangle of these tall plants, commonly, but incorrectly, known as bulrushes. In late summer they seem to be favoured by the red deer, perhaps as they are succulent at a time when other plants are ripening, and I notice that patches of the leaves, and occasionally the flowering heads, are eaten off. One summer I tried to lessen what had become an infestation of reedmace in the original pond, since the open water was by then reduced to only a small area. We pulled out large quantities of the roots and cleared quite an area, but to no avail, for within a couple of years the effect of our work was indiscernible. At that time I took several roots and transplanted these to another larger and deeper pond that we had made on the hill. I realised the risk of infestation when the plants took hold and spread, but hoped that much of the centre of the pond would

190

be too deep for it. Thus far this has been the case, but all those roots that I put in the shallow end of the pond were eaten completely by the deer and none now remain at that end. At the deeper end the plants took well but each year the red deer wade out as far as they can and browse the leaves right down wherever they can reach. I am glad that they enjoy them.

Whether the deer come deliberately to feed on the reedmace, or merely do so in passing, I do not know. However, I am constantly astonished at the awareness and sensibilities of wild creatures and their ability to find specific food attractions. Birds, for instance, must have amazing ability to smell. Our farmyard geese are well able to smell sacks of food that they fancy, and peck away at these until they make a hole, if given the opportunity. Ducks seem to be able to find barley thrown into a pond or stream, and somehow know when it is there and when it is not. One afternoon I spent some time watching pigeons feeding in the long grass in the field outside our kitchen window. They did not come in a flock, but in singles, and twos and threes, feeding here and there, almost hidden in the grass, and then flying up to sit on the fence for a while. I was at a loss to know what it was that could attract them specifically to this field, and I went upstairs to observe more closely with a powerful telescope. Eventually I was able to pinpoint what they were eating, and went out to the field to confirm and identify the plant. I discovered that they were eating the seeds of mouse-eared chickweed at a certain stage of ripeness. I was astounded that they could locate these tiny plants and seed heads in the long grass, and seemingly fly in from afar to feed upon them. I wonder if they were able to detect the ripe seeds by smell? I cannot think that they could have seen them from the air. Perhaps they came by chance, with the long grass seeming to be a likely site.

Do deer locate attractive food plants by smell, or by association somehow, or merely by chance? Turnip crops they obviously can smell, for such is evident even to the poorly developed human olfactory sense. I wonder whether deer can smell sweet grass in the fields. I suspect that they can do so, and that roe can quite well scent choice food plants in a garden, tempting them to climb through or jump over inadequate fencing to risk proximity to humans.

At this time of year areas of the lower open hill ground are knee-high in rushes and tall grasses. Several gorse bushes dot the area in front of the house, and I must look at these a thousand times a year, thinking that there is an extra shape there. Sometimes there is, and I see a deer. Sometimes, as I am about to put down the glasses, cursing my inability to remember precisely the minute detail of the hill in the

hundred different lighting conditions, I see an ear twitch in the rushes beyond. Looking more closely I may find another ear, and then another. I have learned by experience over the years that when one spots an uncertain gorse bush and fails to check up on it with binoculars, one then sees it walk or run away! If one wants to see and watch deer one needs to check constantly. How very often one can see a group of deer feeding contentedly, and then a few moments later they vanish as they move into dead ground or behind some bushes. At that point somebody looking for deer would think that there were none within miles. A patient watch and they reappear. A roe deer feeding can vanish completely, as if by magic, as it steps behind a thistle or a small clump of bracken.

Last summer we had a couple of black rabbits on the lower part of the hill. They stood out absurdly against the green grass. They were there all summer, until presumably myxomatosis laid them low in September during its annual eruption. We have black rabbits in several places on the farm, but these two were especially conspicuous from the house. A ginger rabbit was born in the dyke bordering the garden, and we saw it frequently in the field beyond, and watched it grow from the small bunny, which we could see only a short distance in front of Diana's studio, into a three-quarters grown rabbit. One day in autumn the dogs caught it, but we found that it was thin and emaciated and clearly suffering from the annual epidemic of hepatic coccidiosis, or liver rot, which has controlled rabbit populations for centuries by infecting and killing off large numbers of young rabbits, particularly in damp autumn weather. We generally have occasional white rabbits, and odd ginger or piebald ones, somewhere on the farm each summer, but black ones, often called Ministers, are the most common colour variation from the normal.

I doubt whether buzzards take full-grown healthy rabbits often, though the uncommon visiting rough-legged buzzard is supposed to

hunt bigger prey than the common buzzard. Weak rabbits suffering from coccidiosis and myxomatosis are easy prey for them in the autumn, as are young rabbits in the spring. In late summer the buzzards are continuously around the fields. One day I watched one with fascination through the telescope in my study as it sat on the top branch of a dead rowan peering around with watchful eye. What fascinated me was its ability to turn its head, for its neck seemed to twist more than 180 degrees in each direction. Not only could the bird, facing away from me, turn to look directly behind it, but it appeared to be able to turn its head even further, turning round to the right see over to its left side too, as it were behind its left shoulder. Diana and I were going out in the car one day when I saw a buzzard in a field at the far end of the farm and stopped to watch it. This bird, which I presume was a young one, swooped three times on rabbits sitting outside their burrows as we watched; each time it was seemingly clumsily unsuccessful. Whether its attempts to stoop on a rabbit were serious or in fun I could not tell, but from their rapid reappearance the rabbits did not apparently take it as an oppressive threat.

The more one watches deer the more one appreciates that on the one hand a significant part of their behaviour has much similarity to that of other animals, but on the other hand there is much activity that one never sees let alone understands. The difficulties of those endeavouring to do research into deer behaviour are clear. After all it is difficult enough trying to understand that of humans, even if it is well documented, and with animals there can be a danger of anthropomorphising as well as failing to perceive similarity. Moreover, most research on deer has been done in unrepresentative environments and circumstances: one might justly say that any research done on the west coast, for example, cannot necessarily be extrapolated to apply to deer in Grampian, nor could information gathered on a highly stocked flat area of Sutherland or Caithness territory be assumed to be applicable to deer on high Perthshire heather-clad areas. Roe in Surrey have many differences from those in Aberdeenshire, for instance in size, coloration, and behaviour. The roe deer rut in the north-east starts later and goes on well into the last part of August, not surprisingly, with the seasons generally later though summer is shorter. There seems to be a significantly higher ratio of females to males, or perhaps a lower ratio of bucks to does, which may also affect the rut. Whether this is due to heavy commercial shooting of bucks with a lower doe cull, or because of higher male mortality in winter, especially of kids, is a matter of speculation. However, the roe rut is somewhat unobtrusive compared to that of the red deer. One may glimpse a buck chasing a doe across the hill, or see a buck following a doe across the fields, but little more unless one looks for the activity. The red deer rut is unmistakable, however, because on a still night one can hear stags roaring. The autumn equinox, 22 September, is the day of the roaring in Gaelic. The days shorten and the nights lengthen from then onwards as autumn turns to winter and the season changes again.

In this part of Scotland, on the lower ground, with the deer in good condition, the rut starts earlier than higher on the hill or further north. It is a gradual thing. One day one sees a big stag with hinds, or one evening one hears a roar far up the hill in the woods. We listen for roaring and look for signs of stags and rutting activity generally in mid-September, perhaps about the 16th, though the earliest rutting activity that we have seen was on 3 September in a dry, warm year. On that occasion I was looking out of the bedroom window one evening when I spotted some hinds crossing the hill, and then I saw a big stag close behind them. I felt sure that he was rutting for he had that eager determined look about the way he seemed to chivvy the group, though not actually trying to herd them. I heard no roaring. The following evening I saw them again: what appeared to be the same group of half-a-dozen hinds and calves, with the stag behind them. This time, as I spied them through binoculars, I saw him lift his head and roar. I opened the window to hear, in case he did so again, and he did. It was a feeble, hardly audible noise, but it was definitely a roar. The hinds did not seem to be very interested, and it looked as though he was searching for one that might be in oestrus, but he was early and unsuccessful.

The big stags have changed to darker winter coat by late September, and have grown thick impressive manes and enlarged neck muscles. The stags that have been wallowing are almost black. The hinds have

194

grown their winter coats too, and no longer have that sleek reddish summer look in sunlight. Their change is more imperceptible than that of roe deer, whose colour contrast between summer and winter coat is much more marked. On 21 September last year I saw a roe doe in full winter coat, with brilliant white target and prominent anal tush, and on the same day I saw a nice buck still quite red, and as I drove across to check my cows on the far side of the farm I saw a young roe buck with just two small spikes as antlers who was half-changed, with grey flanks and red front, and in fact generally looking rather moth-eaten as they do at time of coat change in spring.

This is the time for the geese to move south too. We hear them long before we see them. Then, searching the sky, we pick out the skein, dots high up, wavering in the wind and getting closer, and then passing overhead on their way south to winter in sheltered lochs or on the sea coast and feed on stubble fields and the remnants left after the potato harvest. The wild geese and the stags seem to go together somehow, both with an enchanting lure. When we hear them we like to go and stand outside the house and listen to them. Perhaps it is the thought of their nesting in remote uninhabited northern lands and then migrating huge distances to their wintering grounds that creates an aura of wildness and freedom, and makes our hearts beat a little faster with a sense of excitement when we hear the geese going over. The distant roar of a stag in the gloaming has the same mystical fascination for us, somehow embodying a true wildness with primeval challenge and mystery. What stag is out there in the darkness in the midst of the woods? Does he have hinds? Is he seeking hinds or challenging a rival? We speculate, but never know.

I often wonder about roaring and its purpose or reason. That is to say, I believe that stags roar in different circumstances, perhaps with different meanings or purpose, and possibly the actual intonation or types of roar signify different meanings were one able to judge these. Very often the first roars of the rutting season that we hear seem to be

from travelling stags, by the apparent rapid movement of the animal, or rather of the sound. I have no idea where our big stags come from, nor whence they depart once the rut is finished. From the size and quality I presume them to be woodland beasts and not ones that have come in from the open hill country. However, stags can and do travel considerable distances in search of hinds. Twenty miles over the hill is little distance to a stag, and this can be easily covered in a night. Sometimes stags seem to travel alone and occasionally a big stag is accompanied by a smaller beast, often referred to as his fag. Out on the hill one can frequently see and hear such stags, especially early in the season, clearly on the move in a determined manner, but stopping occasionally to give a roar and then apparently listen. It would seem that he is calling to locate other deer. Perhaps he is trying to attract a hind in season but unaccompanied by a suitor, or more likely he is roaring a challenge to stags already with hinds, hopeful of hearing an answering roar by which to locate a rival, with the possibility of acquiring his hinds. Another intriguing aspect of roaring is how on some occasions the sound seems to carry great distances, and yet at other times it seems to carry little distance at all. The wind can carry the sound, of course, and the acoustics of the place where the stag is roaring affects the noise, but somehow these do not always seem to be the complete explanation.

One tends to think of a stag standing amongst his hinds, or on the edge of the harem threatened by a rival, roaring defiance or telling him to clear off, but not all roaring takes place in those circumstances. It is not unusual to come across stags on their own roaring. Sometimes one sees a beast that looks clearly run and worn out, almost certainly vanquished and deposed and chased away from his hinds, lying roaring, perhaps rather feebly. One afternoon I heard consistent roaring on our hill and decided to walk up and see what stag was making all the noise. I discovered a quite large stag, with a not particularly good set of antlers, an eight-pointer I think he was, the top half of one side of which had snapped off. He had clearly been rutting and was rather black-coloured. He was standing out in the open in the middle of an old field roaring at frequent intervals with no other deer in sight. After I had watched him for a few minutes I heard another roar from the woods several hundred yards off, and the stag that I was spying turned and stared in that direction, and then roared again. The other stag roared once more, and then remained silent, whilst the one that I was watching continued to roar several times and then finally moved off into the trees, roaring from time to time. I formed the view that he had been beaten up and chased off by the unseen stag and was shouting abuse at him.

On another occasion I saw a fine stag on our hill early one morning, when I glanced out of the window in the midst of carrying out the early morning chores. I focused the telescope on him and saw he was a fine royal. I could see no other deer. He roared a couple of times, and a cloud of breath exhaled as he did so in the frosty morning air. He then pawed the ground and lay down. After lying for a minute or two, he suddenly put his head back and raked the ground behind him, almost as if he had been bitten by an insect, and then quickly got up. He stood for a few moments looking around, and then turned and thrashed the ground with his antlers, and lay down again, rolled, got up again and stood looking downhill. I wondered if he had seen deer down below him, out of my sight, and when he suddenly ran downhill I felt sure that this was so. However, he ran only fifty yards or so and then stood under a small birch tree looking about him. He then proceeded to graze, apparently unconcernedly. As I continued to watch him, admiring the splendid beast, and hoping that he would not get shot by any of my neighbours, he stopped feeding, stood chewing the cud for a few moments, and then roared a couple of times, the cloud of warm breath making a splendid picture as he apparently surveyed the scene below him. However, it appeared that this was a solo performance, since he then proceeded to wander off, nibbling at grass here and there, without any indication that there were other deer attracting his attention. I did not see that stag again. I hope that he survived to another season. One of the unfortunate aspects of the commercialisation of deer stalking in recent years is the attachment of very high values for trophy heads with large antlers. Twenty or thirty years ago a day's stalking was just that, usually with better stags left to breed, but nowadays trophy class red and roe deer antlers fetch enormous sums of money for the privilege of shooting them. Locally I believe that up to £250 is charged for shooting a good stag, but I have heard of up to £900 being charged for shooting a royal. I find this mercenary approach to deer invidious. Clearly some have to be cropped or culled annually, but to differentiate financially in this manner, and to associate some kind of degree of glory in the act of squeezing a trigger towards a royal rather than a spiker, with the former available only to someone rich enough to afford it, in my opinion demeans the whole subject, and the atavistic motives involved.

When one watches a stag guarding his harem of hinds, perhaps herding them away from the approach of a rival, or running to chase off young outliers waiting for an opportunity to move in and to try to grab a few hinds, then the roaring is clearly a defiant warning to

intruders. It is quite possible that the louder or fiercer the roar the greater indication of a dominant stag, and perhaps someone has studied roars, with the ability to differentiate various voices, and discovered some indicative degree. The larger and more powerful stag may well be able to express this in his voice. Certainly the continental Europeans reckon to be able to call and attract stags by roaring, perhaps trying to indicate a lesser stag to entice the bigger beast to investigate and chase him off. I believe that some research has been done with horses that indicates the stallion with the loudest and longest squeal or scream shows the best lungs and the dominant male!

When one appreciates the possible ratio of stags to hinds in much of Scotland, which might be somewhere between two hinds to one stag and even parity, one can have little surprise that the stags controlling different parcels of hinds are constantly changing, with beasts being chased off by fresher rivals when they have been weakened by constant rutting activity harassed by interlopers. Researchers on the island of Rhum have concluded that few stags actually get to breed successfully, and only very few hinds are ever served by the same stag in a following year. So it can be seen that breeding is both varied and haphazard. A big stag may hold a significant herd of hinds for some time, but in practice he may only serve a few of those hinds successfully: others being served by rivals splitting off hinds, or taking over the dominance for a while, or even by outliers sneaking in at night or taking advantage of opportunities. With this situation in mind, and remembering that half of the genetics are passed on through the dam anyway, it can be seen that the supposed management of the breeding success of wild deer by preserving good stags, despite the merit of the attempt, is in actuality purely a matter of chance. Occasionally the mating of a certain stag with a particular hind results in a successful marrying of genes to produce a fine specimen of offspring, though this may be more obvious in a young stag than a hind calf. Whether this breeding strain is ever followed through and later identified is another matter. In the case of hinds it is likely to be easier to identify a strain, because the females probably tend to form loose familial groups; but since these are probably fathered by different stags, and very likely unknown ones at that, little useful information could be acquired other than the judgement that one hind may be seen to produce offspring that develop into good hinds, whoever their father might be. In the case of stag offspring, these will either be chased off, or take themselves off, as yearlings or two-year-olds, and so unless specifically identifiable somehow they will simply mingle with the other stags as of parentage unknown.

At rutting time most of the yearling stags will be chased off from the hind groups by the big stags, but some of these may hang around in the area and rejoin the hinds again later. It is quite usual to see a few spikers and young stags amongst herds of hinds again after the rut has apparently finished. Judging the ages of live stags often presents problems with a considerable variation in body size and antler growth depending upon habitat and individual animal capabilities. In 1890 Henry Evans wrote that armchair judgement is a good deal easier than reality on the ground, and rightly pointed out that many stags never grow larger than a good five-year-old. In optimum habitat two-year-old stags may carry antlers that would be regarded as a sign of stag being three times that age on the open hill or in exposed parts of the north and west. At the research deer farm of Glensaugh almost all second heads carry four to eight points, and a well-fed stag at the Rowett Institute had twelve-point antlers in his second season. This indicates the capabilities of most stags given good conditions in which to grow, and also suggests that in many poor quality hill areas of Scotland the importance of habitat and pressure of deer numbers far exceeds the influence of genetics and breeding over stag growth. In many deer forests occasional large stags appear each season. Whilst it is possible that some are able to thrive better than their peers and make better use of available feed, or benefited from an exceptionally good dam, or marrying of chance genetics, most of these unusually large beasts will have come in from elsewhere to the hinds, or will have benefited from living for much of the year in woodland or sheltered areas with plentiful food, such as agricultural crops, available.

The gestation period of hinds is about 232 days, which compares with 283 days for cows and 150 days for sheep. It might seem to be difficult to ascertain the proportion of wild hinds that come into oestrus. The fact that hinds may be yeld the following year does not necessarily mean that they failed to come into season or conceive, for they may well have done so but subsequently lost the calf, either through abortion or after parturition at some stage. A hind that is in poor condition may well not come into season, or do so late, and one that is still suckling a calf may not have been able to recover sufficiently from this effort to be in rising condition at the end of the summer to ensure oestrus and conception. Research has suggested that in fact most mature hinds do eventually come into season and conceive. Yeld hinds, or females that are not milking and suckling a calf, are by no means necessarily barren. Indeed a cow or ewe that is barren and quite unable to breed is comparatively unusual, and so there is no reason to suppose deer to be any different. It is more than likely that a yeld hind that has not had to support a calf all summer will be in good condition and thus more likely to breed successfully the following year, and that her summer without a calf at foot was due to a mishap to the offspring. I am told that on the Glensaugh deer farm, where they ran in the region of four hundred hinds, the inevitable few yeld ones are given a second chance and the opportunity to breed the following year. The few of those that fail to do so are subsequently culled. Some hinds seem to be able to produce calves annually for a long period of years in the wild, but in most cases where this is recorded the hinds will be known as a result of frequenting areas near habitation and so become familiar, and in these places the feeding may well be better and enable her to maintain good condition. Although food and condition affect the ability of a hind to come into season and conceive, there is no doubt that the factor that initiates this is the photoperiod that governs so many of the aspects of the lives of the deer. Cows come into season all-year-round, and this is because their long domestication has bred the influence of the seasonal rhythm out of them, but sheep, and the majority of animals, including most deer species, have their breeding seasons, and thus their lives, governed by the seasons and daylight length, in much the same way as this controls the growth of plant life too. Recent research has discovered that shortening days cause a substance called melatonin to be produced by the pineal gland in the brain at night. This substance, which sometimes causes lightening of skin in some animals, somehow affects the sexual cycles of deer and sheep, after periods of long light, and artificial application under certain conditions can produce earlier breeding activity in both stags and hinds.

The red deer stag shooting season (in Scotland) runs until 20 October. What is so special about this date? Was there perhaps more point to the choice of this particular date than most stalkers and estate owners appreciate? After all it could have been simpler to let the season run until the end of the month when legislation was drafted. I do not suppose that the thought behind the date was actually as critically based as the figures below seem to show, but I do not know what was in the minds of those who suggested the legislation at the time.

One of the problems with what is euphemistically called deer management, whether in woodland or upon the open hill, is that many of the ideas are based upon tradition and not upon careful thought in the light of what knowledge is now available. In the case of red deer on the open hill this is especially the case, and it seems to me that many of the problems and criticisms arising now, often causing controversy about deer populations, result from the situation where neither deer forest owners nor their stalkers really have adapted tradition to conform to current ideas and deer populations. For instance, we are told that the Scottish red deer population has doubled over the past twenty years, although figures published by the Red Deer Commission do not bear this out and different base dates give different results, rendering differing interpretations as with many statistics, whilst the recorded figures are themselves highly suspect. It would be interesting to extrapolate this guestimate over all deer forests and compare the population trends of individual estate deer, and then compare these figures with those of stags and hinds killed over the period. I suspect that on many estates the traditional figures for stags and hinds taken in a season have not increased greatly, perhaps until the last few years when commercialisation of the shooting has become much more important.

The outcry against the large population of red deer has largely ignored the fact that an increase has occurred in all deer species throughout the country, and in many other countries in the northern hemisphere as well. It has also had the effect of concentrating the efforts to reduce numbers by culling hinds, which are the sex that do the breeding. The problem that arises from this is that little attention is paid to the management of stags on a logical basis. Many people seem to think that a 1:1 stag/hind ratio is acceptable, or even ideal. Except in cases where the objective is unashamedly to have as many stags as possible to shoot in the stalking season, such a view cannot have any logical basis. Such an idea seems to me to be a very short-term one that is fraught with danger, and flies in the face of any attempt to control numbers. Moreover it is mostly the stags that maraud and do damage in winter.

Many attempts have been made to improve the quality of stags over the years. Some estates have fed these in winter. Others have had rigid policies of preserving good heads and large beasts. Yet others have tried to select what they regard as promising young stags for preservation. Some estates claim to be able to demonstrate that their policies have produced improvement. However, when one starts to compare current figures with those recorded over the past hundred years and more it is difficult to detect significant results from such policies. What is dramatically significant is the metamorphosis that takes place when a wild caught red deer is placed in a deer farm or park and given good feeding and shelter. Under such circumstances it can be demonstrated clearly that these two factors are by far the most influential in producing good quality deer.

Many other interesting facets of deer management have been brought to light by deer farming, some of which have been known for a long time but largely ignored on the hill, and other aspects are new knowledge discovered only quite recently. One point that is well known, and obvious, to stock farmers, and demonstrated on deer farms, is that a requirement of a ratio of one stag to one hind is nonsense for a breeding programme. Indeed such a high number of males are likely to interfere with satisfactory breeding. Some deer farms run as many as sixty hinds with a stock stag, though ratios of one stag to between twenty and forty hinds are more normal, with rather less hinds running with a very young stag. Another point recognised by all stock breeders is the influence of the dam, who not only contributes her genes but also has the responsibility of raising the calf. A hind with desirable genes is not much use if she has insufficient milk or is a poor mother. These factors are extremely difficult to assess on the hill.

The main bias of deer management in the Highlands has always been on the selection of stags. However, perhaps the time has now come to forget tradition and pre-conceived ideas and examine the situation more logically, as has to be done in any captive herd or flock of animals, and try to determine other principles governing the improvement of deer quality apart from the obvious ones of food, shelter and stress. One factor that seems to be worth examination is the breeding success of stags. After all there is not much point in retaining a 22 stone Imperial that is incapable of breeding, other than as an ornament. It is all very well having 600 stags to 600 hinds on a forest, but how many of these stags actually breed, and to what degree do the stags that are not the choice as sires interfere with the successful breeding of the more desirable stags? Research on Rhum already seems to suggest that few stags actually achieve successful mating with a number of hinds, and those that do so do not actually serve many hinds each.

On deer farms, as on sheep and cattle farms, the sires are chosen and so known. They may be changed after a period, as a safeguard against infertility problems or some other reason for lack of mating success. In this case the birth date of offspring will indicate the sire, as a result of the known gestation period of the dam. The actual gestation period of all animals is slightly flexible, and with sheep, for instance, though most ewes lamb about the anticipated date judged from a recorded serving date, on occasion some can vary by about a week either side. The gestation period of red deer is 226 to 238 days. So an average expected date of calving would be around 232 days after being mated.

It is an interesting exercise to examine these statistics more carefully. Most red deer calves are probably born between late May and late June. On low ground late May might see the start of calving but probably early June is more normal. On high ground it might be well into June before calves are born. Examination of the table overleaf throws an interesting light on the situation and raises some pertinent questions.

In considering these figures I have ignored the possibility of variation by a week either side of expected dates, since my experience is that this is not sufficiently common to affect the general consideration. What seems clear to me is that calves born after the middle of June are unlikely to have been fathered by those stags rutting during the stag

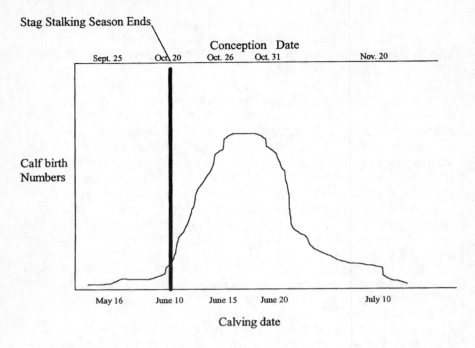

Red deer Hind Gestation Period 232 days (+/- 6 days)

stalking season, which may well be most of the bigger stags. Even calves born at the beginning of June must have resulted from hinds served at the very end of the stalking season, and stags that have mated successfully in early October are likely to result in calves born in the middle of May, the survival of which must be severely in doubt in hill country.

Most people would accept that a stag does not maintain control of a harem on the hill for a long period, particularly where there are other stags present in large quantity. Even then it is a completely unknown factor as to how many other stags manage to get in amongst the hinds in darkness and serve some whilst the master stag of the moment is otherwise occupied.

Is 20 October, the last day of the shooting season for stags, thus highly relevant as being the date before which rutting stags are unlikely to be of much relevance to calving, thus indicating that they might as well be shot since, whatever their quality, they are unlikely to make much contribution to the breeding of the calves born in the following year?

204

The red deer rutting season is an exciting and interesting time for Diana and myself, watching from the windows of the house and studio, or walking on the hill. Diana also takes what she calls her mobile studio on the hill. Many of the deer are used to seeing the ponies feeding quite near them throughout the year and so are not greatly disturbed when Diana rides close to them. Often she has opportunities to sketch deer only a hundred yards or less away from her, whilst her mount stands, and she finds that the ponies can locate deer by sight or scent as quickly as any dog, so that she is often warned in advance of the presence of deer by the pony looking with ears pricked. There seems to be more movement of deer in the rutting time, and the hinds often seem to split up into smaller groups, perhaps as a result of chivvying by stags. It is always interesting to us to see the different stags that come in, which we have never seen before, and these change throughout the season as the dominant stag with the group of hinds tires from rutting activity and is driven out by a fresher beast. At this time of year the mature stag eats little and his weight drops considerably as a result by the end of the rut. Although this is largely due to his rutting activity, seeking out hinds in oestrus, skirmishing with other stags, guarding hinds that he acquires, and so on, as well as wallowing, thrashing and fraying trees in a display of strength to impress would-be challengers, it has been recorded that in October and November captive stags even without the presence of hinds and rutting activities tend to lose their appetite. This too is

probably governed by the daylight factor, though clearly the drop in appetite may be part of the design to enable the stags to concentrate on the rut and procreation activity without being diverted by the urge to feed. Similarly it has been noted that stags also undergo a fall in appetite, even amongst animals in captivity with ad lib good quality feed, in July. Hinds do not show this behaviour, and it would seem reasonable to deduce that stags undergo this period of reduced appetite, after a spell of ability to regain condition in spring, to enable them to seek shelter in dark woods or on high breezy hills, both with poorer feeding, to gain respite from the headflies that torment them by settling upon their growing velvet-covered antlers when the animals are not in a situation to evade these pestilential irritations. On the other hand the hinds are under pressure to feed continuously and as well as they can, either to enable them to supply milk to a dependent calf, or to regain condition well enough to come into season in the autumn and conceive.

Just as strong young stags, and even yearlings, are quite mature and able to breed in optimum conditions with the benefit of good feeding, so also yearling hinds can become pregnant under such circumstances. Not all yearlings may be fully mature, but in sheltered woodland conditions a number of yearling hinds can conceive and produce calves as two-year-olds. Whereas in hill situations they may take a year longer, or more, before coming into breeding condition as a result of slower growth and consequent later maturity, and probably few hill hinds will breed before they are three years old. Without being able to identify hinds with certainty one cannot record other than an impression, but it would seem to us that amongst the red deer that we see on our hill most hinds have calves at foot by mid-summer, and that includes two-year-olds, since the only adults without calves are generally the yearlings also running near their dams. We do not often see yeld hinds, a situation that is quite the reverse to that on the hills only a few miles away, and which emphasises the difference between deer living in good habitat and maintaining good condition, and those on poorer ground, subjected to disturbance and stress from weather, and with lower quality feeding, often made worse by competition from other deer.

One morning early in the rut I took an artist friend to see if we could find and watch some deer. We left the house at first light, and walked up the hill skirting through the edge of the wood and through tall bracken, down wind of an old field, now over-run by thistles and rushes, where I hoped that we might find some hinds, perhaps with a stag. We heard no roaring, but as we approached we spotted a single hind feeding on an open patch of short grass beneath some birch trees slightly below us, and then her calf lying a short way from her. Further down a young staggie, perhaps her yearling son, was grazing. As we got close to the edge of the old field we saw a small group of hinds, accompanied by two staggies, feeding out on some flat rushy ground to our left. Clearly there was no large stag present. We crouched in front of a willow bush by the fence at the edge of the old field, largely concealed by rushes, hoping that the deer might feed closer to us. After a few minutes a young stag, an eight-pointer, suddenly appeared from below us and jumped the dyke into the field and trotted diagonally across it away from us, through the thistles. The two staggies with the hinds left the group and wandered in our direction, jumping the fence and coming level with us about a hundred yards below, stopping to pause and listen, before disappearing into the bracken. Looking back to the field in front of us we suddenly saw a hind racing across the field towards us, pursued by the young stag that we had see a minute or two earlier. They came at full gallop, and the hind leaped a ditch across the field perhaps a hundred yards away from us and bounded up to within twenty or thirty yards of where we crouched. The stag had halted at the other side of the ditch and stood looking at the hind. She had not seen us, and for a moment we thought that she was going to jump the fence straight on top of us. Instead she decided to turn and jump the dyke and head down hill in the direction of where we had seen the staggies. Her pursuer, seeing her jump the stone wall and head down hill jumped the dyke too and headed towards where she had disappeared. We did not see them again.

On another evening I took a friend up to the same spot to look for deer. This time we heard some distant roars in the wood behind us. As we approached the edge of the old field through a damp area of thin birches and willows we caught sight of the silhouette of a hind standing at the edge staring at us. We froze, and after a few moments she turned and slipped away, fortunately without raising alarm. At the edge of the field was another hind feeding, with her calf and yearling hind close by. They gradually moved off to the far edge, and we moved closed to the fence. Out in the field, amongst the growth of tall thistles, we could see the backs of three or four deer. Two of these turned out to be young stags. They moved together into an open patch and started to spar with each other. It was not serious fighting but more a clashing off antlers without serious pushing or attempts to wound the rival. They were fine looking young stags, both eight-pointers, and probably only two or three years old and not yet rutting seriously. A big stag had not yet moved in to claim the hinds. After sparring rather half-heartedly for some minutes they both jumped the dyke into the open flat grassland below us, leaving the couple of hinds still amongst the thistles.

Really serious long fights are not common, at least to witness. Broken antlers seen on stags indicate that they have taken place and also the strength and ferocity of the encounter. It takes some force to break the antler of a big stag. We watched such a serious fight one frosty morning in early October in our top fields. We had walked up the hill to see what deer activity there was in a section of the ground that we cannot see from the house, but which is frequented by both red and roe deer at times. When we stopped to spy and check the top fields for deer amongst the bracken patches, we spotted three or four hinds and calves straggling up the hill with a large stag in their wake. It appeared that they had been feeding on the flatter ground below and were returning to the shelter of the trees where they would spend the day. The front hinds had disappeared out of sight and the stag was rather lingering behind, when all of a sudden another big stag appeared, moving fast and purposefully in the same direction. The first stag turned to meet the rival, and without any of the parallel walking, summing each other up, or threatening gestures, which one often sees amongst rutting stags and probably assists in averting serious fights to some degree, these two beasts rushed at each other. We watched, fascinated, as the stags fought. I thought that we must have watched them for nearly quarter of an hour: my companion timed the display as twenty minutes. The clash of their antlers was impressive and the sound must have been audible for some distance on the still, frosty morning. Clouds of hot breath blew from their nostrils and a mist of steam rose from their bodies as the fight wore on. At first we thought that the blacker, and perhaps slightly smaller, challenger was winning, as he pushed the other in the direction of the now vanished hinds, but the struggle ebbed and flowed as they pushed each other backwards and forwards across the short turf.

A younger stag appeared from somewhere, and ran about just below them as if he was encouraging the two contestants to bash each other up. He grabbed an occasional mouthful of grass, stood

watching the two big stags, and trotted a few yards this way and that. As we watched a spiker also appeared from somewhere too, and joined the audience, trotting around as though cheering the fighters on, himself caught up in the excitement and the adrenaline flowing. The first young stag then moved off, in the direction taken by the hinds. Perhaps he had kleptogamy on his mind! The yearling spiker, perhaps sensing the end of the fight finally trotted off to the right and stood watching from afar. Maybe he was the companion, or fag, of the challenger? Who knows! The fight ended abruptly with the challenger turning tail and running off in the direction that the spiker had taken. The victor stood and roared in his direction, and then slowly, and menacingly, moved towards the vanquished beast which was standing two hundred yards away panting. The latter did not wait for further demonstration of strength, and as the victor moved closer he, and the yearling, cleared off into the trees. Whether the dominant stag regained his hinds we could never know.

Occasionally we see a familiar stag with hinds quite regularly for some days, but often we notice unfamiliar stags that we may not see again. Whether the hinds that we see are regulars in the areas, and the stags constantly changing, or whether a particular stag and his hinds have moved off and their place taken by another different group we do not know, but the former seems likely. Though the stag in charge of a harem appears to have control of those hinds, herding them and keeping them in some place of advantage to him in being able to retain them, the hinds are surely motivated by the wish for food and shelter. A change in the wind or weather certainly dictates their movement and if the whole group decides to move the stag has to follow. When we see deer moving onto the grassy part of the hill in front of the house to feed in the evenings, invariably the hinds appear, intent upon grazing or browsing, with the stag bringing up the rear. The lead hinds dictate the general movement. The stag will round up odd hinds that seem to break away, or chivvy on stragglers at the rear, but he does not stop the lead hinds that have decided to move to a different area. A change in the wind may encourage the whole band to shift to a better sheltered spot, and in the course of this opportunities arise for outlying stags to move in and steal some hinds, or for a rival to challenge the stag, whose attention may be partially diverted by the movement of his harem. Such movement and interchange of stags may be more evident in conditions of adequate feeding and shelter. Out on the open hills choice, or even adequate, feeding areas may not be abundant, nor sheltered places, and so the deer may well be obliged to concentrate upon these, and the temporarily dominant stag may have a better chance of holding his group of hinds together where visibility is better and he can move quickly to round up and return females that wander too far, or to intercept interlopers.

As in the summer we can look out of the window and see odd deer appear at all times of day, with hinds feeding or lying chewing the cud, so in later September and October we can see stags occasionally crossing the ground clearly searching for hinds. One afternoon I was looking out of my study window when I was fascinated to see a stag crossing the open hill in front of the house, nose to the ground like a spaniel after a rabbit. He did not just smell the ground occasionally but walked along nose to the trail, of presumably a hind, all across the open hill, and then disappeared into the trees. I watched a stag similarly following the ground scent of hinds on another occasion. This time I had been watching a group of hinds feeding on the slope of the hill just above our farm track. They were attended by a stag, who was not especially active. The hinds gradually moved off out of sight into the trees, and the stag followed. A few minutes later I saw the hinds sauntering off heading for shelter further up the hill, having crossed a burn and jumped a fence in the trees, and then swung up the hill and back in the direction where I could see them. Suddenly, as I watched them, the stag re-appeared from the trees where they hinds had first disappeared, looking about him rather agitatedly. He put his nose to the ground and quartered where the hinds had been. He ran further up the hill in the open and then, quartering rather like a pointer, must have caught their scent from further up and set off at the gallop in the direction that they were taking. I can only assume that either he had not jumped the fence, or had stopped for a drink in the burn, or to fray a tree, or some such, and had lost his hinds in the trees.

Sometimes going about the farm we can see stags in odd places at this time of the year. I remember that one morning I was checking the cattle at the far end of the farm and decided to shift the cows and calves into another field, through the fenced off end of a piece of wood. As I opened the gate into the field where the cows were I thought that I heard a stag roar, and was intrigued, because I had never heard one in that piece of woodland previously. Anyway, I wondered if maybe my imagination was playing tricks and that I had deer too much on my mind. I opened the gate and moved across the few yards of the end of the wood, outside of which, on the road, my Land-Rover was parked, and opened the gate to the field on the other side. I went into the field and called the cows, and as I turned and looked across the field again I was astonished to see a stag standing stock still against some willow bushes at the far end staring at me. By this time the cows and calves were pouring into the field. After standing for a moment or two the stag slowly walked to the corner and disappeared into the wood. I walked across the field to the corner to look into a cleared area in the wood in case I could see him, but there was nothing. As I walked back across the field I saw the large cattle lorry owned by the proprietor of the local petrol station coming down the hill and waved to him. A day or two later I was in at the garage getting petrol when the proprietor told me that as he had come down the hill that morning, just after he had seen me, and as he was almost up to my Land-Rover parked at the side, a stag had jumped out into the middle of the road within feet of the Land-Rover bonnet. His son, who was driving, got a great fright, and thought initially that it was one of my cattle jumped out over the gate!

As the autumn advances into winter the colours on the hill change. The autumn tints are always lovely, but some seasons they are more spectacular than others. In very dry autumns the birch and other leaves often seem to turn brown and shed early, and sometimes this occurs in particularly wet years too, but in a normal year, when we have sharp frosts in October, the birch leaves turn to yellow and gold, the geans to deep red, the aspens to pale yellow, and the ash trees to lovely shades of pale olive green, all contrasting with the dark greens of the conifers. The heather on the hill has faded to a sombre dark coloured background, and the bracken turns to a variety of browns and yellows, amongst which the deer are sometimes difficult to spot in certain lights. The coats of the deer seem to change as the light catches them. Wet deer sometimes seem to have shiny coats, and at other times look quite black. I find myself constantly picking up binoculars to examine rocks and clumps of rushes which I should know well, having looked at them a hundred times before, but fooled by tricks of light when the dark objects shine in sunlight after rain or glisten on frosty mornings. As the winter comes the habits of deer change. Both red and roe deer become much more nocturnal. Deer are unsettled in windy or stormy weather anyway, and no doubt the reduced shelter of the now

leafless hardwood trees make the warmer conifer plantations seem more attractive. Their cousins on the hills do not have the luxury of such shelter.

At this time of year the number of raptors seems to increase, perhaps attracted by the carcasses of the last rabbits dying of myxomatosis and coccidiosis. Buzzards seem to be everywhere on the farm. Twenty years ago we generally used to see a pair over the fields in autumn; these days it is not at all unusual to see four or six circling about. Eight buzzards together is not uncommon and ten of these raptors circling overhead at once is our record. Often by November a buzzard has started to appear regularly standing in the front field, looking continually around and from time to time running a few yards to peck at a worm or insect in the grass. The flocks of fieldfares and redwings from northern Europe have also appeared and we see them daily dotted evenly over the field outside the kitchen window, hopping about pecking for a brief time before the flock takes off and wheels across the valley to settle in some trees or a different field. I always wonder at the energy that these birds must consume, restlessly moving from one spot to another. In fruitful years when the rowan berries are plentiful the mixed flocks of fieldfares and redwings soon strip the trees that bear the sweeter berries, leaving a litter of orange-coloured skins on the ground below.

# Chapter 12
# Dark Nights and White Days

We often hear foxes at night, in winter, when we put the dogs out last thing before retiring to bed. Occasionally we hear a vixen screaming, around the turn of the year, but mostly it is dog foxes barking up on the hill, moving rapidly by the sound of it. Sometimes we can hear two, and even three, in different directions, giving three little barks before hurrying on. We do not see foxes often, but their sign is everywhere on the farm. Fox droppings are evident at the entrance to rabbit burrows in the fields, indicating nightly prowling, and we see their footprints in the snow. I often wonder what prompts the fox to defecate beside a rabbit hole, and if it is in disgust at failing to catch the occupant, or to terrorise the inhabitants by the evil smell, or perhaps they leave a calling card to indicate that they will be back later!

Except on nights when the thermometer shows the temperature dropped to below minus 10° or 12° Centigrade, or on foul, stormy nights, to give an illusion of cosiness and warmth in the house, we never draw our curtains shut. So sometimes when we glance out of the north-facing landing window, on our way to bed, we are greeted with one of Nature's more spectacular and awe-inspiring displays, the Northern Lights or aurora borealis. Often when I put the dogs out on a clear, starry night I look up uncomprehendingly at the millions of tiny lights dotting the sky and feel humbled by the vastness of space. However, the aurora borealis is undoubtedly one of the most astonishing and awe-inspiring of natural phenomena. Here in the north-east of Scotland, depending upon the clarity of night skies, we may see the Northern Lights a number of times during the winter, but in the far north of the country it is evident more often, and I believe that the occurrence is quite frequent as far north as the Arctic Circle. However, the really spectacular and enthralling displays are rare, and memorable. Usually what we see is what appears to be a series of car headlights coming over the horizon above the hill to the north, flickering high into the sky and then disappearing. Only there is no road there, nor vehicle or man-made lights. The most spectacular display of the Northern Lights that we have witnessed occurred one night on the Ides (15th) of March some years ago. From early evening to well after midnight the whole sky was lit up with a brightness by which reading was possible, more intense than that of the full moon. The light emanated from all the horizons, not just from the north, and varied to include reds and greens and yellows. It was as if there were searchlights all around us in a circle, all focusing their beams on a point directly overhead, creating the illusion of a huge tent over us formed of light. On another night we stood for a long time with friends watching the extraordinary display of streaks and beams of red light emanating from the west, lighting the sky above us, constantly moving and changing. It was once thought that the aurora borealis was caused by moonlight reflecting from Arctic ice, but it is now believed that the origins are connected with sun spots and an eleven-year cycle, due to electrons and protons from the sun entering the Earth's atmosphere at immense speed into the Ionosphere, 100 and more miles above us. These particles apparently disturb the oxygen and nitrogen in the atmosphere and cause light to be emitted, the magnetic fields of the Poles attracting these; hence the display being more visible farther north.

These fantastic displays are rarely seen by urban or suburban dwellers, for the few that are not mesmerised into wasting the limited time allotted to their lives by the artificially provided entertainment of television have their night skies masked by street lights and buildings. Neither do they have the opportunity to savour the magnificent sunrises and sunsets that we see so often, with the skies lit in the east and west respectively by reds and pinks and golds as the ever-changing rays of the sun reflect from clouds. To be able to stand and watch a spectacularly colourful sunset and listen to a stag roaring is an experience beyond price.

Winter is a time when the presence of deer become more evident to many people in the countryside, especially to farmers and foresters. Hungry deer can do much damage. In many turnip crops in this area roe deer can be seen feeding throughout the day, and the depredations of red deer amongst unprotected root crops can be significant. Our late neighbour to the north, across the burn, grew turnips each year to feed his cows. More often than not these turnips became frozen into the ground for long periods, or covered in snow, and provided an attractive food supply for rabbits and roe deer, especially when all else

214

was buried. We could see roe out in these fields at all times of day, sometimes single animals, often two or three and probably a family group, though never the large winter bands that are familiar on fields of oil-seed rape and other crops in northern Europe. I think that probably the formation of roe into large groups in winter is a characteristic of deer living in open country rather than of those in woodland or semi-woodland habitat. The red deer in such environment, however, seem to band up together again after rather fragmenting or scattering at the time of the rut. Possibly this is due to their concentrating on feeding areas, especially if nightly raiding crops or agricultural land. My impression is that at this time of year the deer, particularly red deer, tend to become rather more regular in habit too, as well as being more nocturnal, quite possibly for the same reason. Though we see red deer occasionally in winter during the day when they emerge briefly from the woods, especially in fine weather, mostly they are resting in the shelter of thick woods, when these are available. The roe also move into the conifer plantations in winter, and though we see animals that come out to forage, or glimpse white targets disappearing when we are walking the dogs on the hill, our opportunities to watch deer in winter are more limited. Moreover we winter cattle on part of the hill and this undoubtedly disturbs deer that might otherwise feed there.

When we see deer in winter, especially in snow, we are always impressed by how plump and sleek they look, as a result of their winter coats with the thick hollow insulating hairs making the animals look substantially fatter than they would do if still in summer pelage. I presume that deer have some sort of mechanism for fluffing up their outer hairs of the winter coats, in the same way that birds fluff out their feathers to better insulate their bodies from the cold. In winter our bird tables, well supplied with seeds, peanuts, fat and bones, become active, with a constant stream of birds of several species

215

coming and going, snatching food or pecking away. As they sit in the bushes waiting to flutter onto the tables or hanging baskets, in cold weather some of them seem so fluffed up as to appear almost circular. One morning after a fall of perhaps a foot of snow I spotted some red deer on the hill. At first glance I thought they were roe, my judgement of size and distance perhaps confused by the fresh unfamiliar snow, and the first animal that I looked at was a calf, but as soon as I saw them move I realised by their mode of movement that they were red deer; for roe and red deer walk and run quite differently. There were five hinds with their calves, and a minute or two later, when he appeared from behind some trees, I saw a young stag was with them too. When I first looked at them two of the hinds were lying down, and as dark patches in the snow were not easily spotted. Other animals partially disappeared as they move behind snow-covered clumps of bracken, so that one could only see odd black shapes of their exposed parts against the snow. One hind seemed to be especially belligerent, for I watched her approach another and paw at her with a foreleg. The molested hind turned, and they both reared up on their hind legs and boxed; but the aggressive beast seemed to be dominant and the other ran off a few yards and continued to forage in the snow. The first hind went over to her again a minute or two later and the same thing happened. The aggressive hind then moved downhill and pawed at one of the animals lying down, causing it to rise quickly, and they both boxed briefly before the disturbed beast moved off. An aggressive hind can look quite formidable with ears laid back and hooves flailing. I have read that in some areas examination of hind carcasses has revealed quite a number with bruises and broken ribs and so on, presumably as a result of fighting, though I imagine that some damage is caused by aggression by possessive stags during the rut.

In late summer, when young stags still have antlers covered in sensitive velvet, one often sees them rearing up on their hind legs boxing each other. This sparring is probably partly boisterous play, and partly establishment of a pecking order, and is usually not apparently as aggressive as some of the conflict between hinds. Although I have not heard angry stags myself, for one is unlikely to be near enough wild deer to hear this, I am told that enraged and aggressive stags in the rut can make a variety of quite frightening noises. Those involved with penned deer or animals on deer farms may be familiar with such aggressive sounds as a result of close contact through the protection of fences. A friend told me that he was looking at a massive stag through the fence on a deer farm at rutting time, and he was astonished to hear the stag grinding his teeth, and making

hissing and clicking noises at him and apparently extremely aggressive. Not convinced that the deer fence was adequate protection he decided to use his discretion and retire from the scene. The owner of the deer farm told him that previously that stag had made similar noises immediately before attacking him! I am familiar with sheep grinding their teeth, a rather unattractive sound, but this usually is a sign that the animal is in pain or discomfort. A friend who worked on a deer farm told me they had two stags in a paddock with hinds. One stag, however, was very much the dominant beast and stayed with the hinds, while the other retired to a far corner on his own. For some reason they decided to cull the dominant stag and my friend went in with his Land-Rover and shot it, and dragged the animal into the back of the vehicle. He got back into the Land-Rover just in time, for the subordinate stag realised that there was no more roaring and that his competitor had gone, and seemingly smelled him in the vehicle, whereupon he started to attack it. My friend departed rapidly.

Prolonged spells of hard weather can cause debilitating conditions for deer. Although deep snow is clearly difficult for them, since they have to scrape and dig down to find food, less deep snow is nowhere near so bad for them as cold, driving rain, unless it lies for a long time, or starts to thaw and then freezes, forming a layer of ice over every-

217

thing. Rain on the coats of animals causes evaporation and consequent heat loss, and it is this loss of valuable heat that heavily drains the resources of the deer. We quite often see roe scraping about in a field when snow lies. I do not know whether this applies to roe deer, but observations at the Rowett Research Institute have shown that red deer, even those with plenty of feed and no need to vary their diet, go through a period of appetite reduction and weight loss in January and February. It would seem that they have been designed with this mechanism, again apparently controlled by daylight length, to assist their survival in the worst of winter, perhaps to enable them to shelter longer when the weather is usually at its worst, and so save on energy use. This appetite loss occurs in both hinds and stags, though hinds do not share similar behaviour in October with stags, when the latter are busy concentrating on the rut, or in July when they have a natural instinct to go and shelter from the torment of headflies on growing antlers on high, breezy ground or thick dark woods.

In winter, when food is scarce, red deer will travel quite long distances to feed. Deer can travel several miles quite easily and quickly, except in deep snow of course, and the stags that we used to watch coming off the hills to feed around our little house in the far north travelled a minimum of two or three miles, and probably a lot more, each evening to feed on the fields and grassy areas beside the river. Obviously they are governed by the two necessary requirements of food and shelter. In other words, if the food supply available is close to good cover, such as heather and grass, and sedges and so on outside an accessible conifer plantation, the deer will not travel far. On the other hand if the deer are at risk in open ground and have to travel far back into the hills to find a sheltered spot free from danger they may have to travel a long way each evening to foray down to low ground in search of food. In many countries in Europe it is common to have feeding areas for deer on hunting estates, but these are mostly for woodland deer with shelter close at hand, and little problem with the presence of the deer in mature woods that might cause damage to trees. In this country the feeding of deer in woodland has not been widely tried or successful, but a number of estates in Scotland now feed wild deer on the hill, with a variety of food, including commercially produced pellets of compound feedstuffs. A few estates have also appreciated the need for shelter as well and have opened up commercial conifer plantations to the deer where these are deemed to be beyond danger of damage to timber by the animals.

Providing wild deer with a winter food supply or supplement would seem to have advantage, as well as perhaps a humanitarian aspect in feeding hungry creatures. Heavy feeding may well maintain or even improve the body condition and weights of both stags and hinds, and may result in an improvement of the antler growth of the former. It may also permit more deer to be carried through the winter than the ground would naturally support, for, of course, the population carrying capacity of an area is the level at which it can thrive adequately through the most difficult period of food shortage. In other words the governing factor, or the lowest common denominator, is the food availability during the worst part of the winter. Supplying deer artificially with food may raise this level. However, it seems to me that feeding deer artificially in this way has disadvantages that in many cases may well outweigh the advantages, especially if the degree of feeding is not sufficiently high to make a noticeable difference to the condition of the deer, and not maintained throughout the long period when adequate food may be scarce. Attracting deer to congregate unnaturally to artificial feed places has the disadvantage that many of these animals rely upon the free hand-out and hang about waiting for the food. Deer may be attracted in from a wide area to feed places, but then not disperse widely again. The result then is the same as that which applies to all intensively congregated livestock, as was soon discovered when allegedly healthy deer started to be farmed, and that is the inevitable increase in the burden of parasites and disease amongst those animals. A further disadvantage is that in most places the amount of food supplied is not sufficient a diet in itself for the deer, and as they tend to hang about the area instead of foraging naturally, the net benefit may be less than assumed. A more obvious disadvantage is that the deer congregating in the vicinity of feeding areas may over-graze that ground and degrade the immediate habitat disproportionally.

Unfortunately the result of the artificial attraction of deer to certain areas, and the obvious evidence of their presence, has attracted adverse comment from people with alternative interests in the countryside and without enthusiasm for deer. Because deer are large and

219

obvious, and historically associated with an elite form of hunting, they have been blamed for destruction of habitat and failure of natural tree regeneration with scarcely a mention of the equally, or more, ravenous mouths of sheep, and blue or mountain hares, not to mention the ubiquitous rabbits, which exist in huge numbers on the hilltops but are rarely seen in quantity by passers-by. At night and in hard weather hares descend from hilltops in great numbers in search of food. Moreover, whilst all deer have increased in number quite substantially in the past forty years, over the same period the increase in the rabbit population has been comparatively phenomenal, recovering from the dramatic effect of myxomatosis, which wiped out over 90 per cent of the rabbit population, to a level that must now equal or even exceed pre-myxomatosis levels in some areas, yet without the control by the level of human predation that existed prior to the 1950s when rabbits were a saleable crop for many countrymen and a welcome addition to the table. Little attempt has been made to research properly the impact of rabbits and blue hares on the habitat in comparison to that of deer, or of the impact of deer numbers and population increase on the deer themselves. However, research at the Glensaugh experimental deer farm years ago showed that heather was damaged when there was a density of more than two hinds per hectare, but the heather was maintained when at a level of one hind per hectare. The conclusion was that, in a situation where heather is important as a food ingredient for deer, as on that farm, a stocking level of say one hind and her calf per one and a half hectares was appropriate. The comparison of the deer that we see here on our ground with those on the hills leaves little doubt about the consequence of adequate food and shelter, or about the suitability of habitat for deer. On our hill the natural regeneration of birch is obvious in many places where cattle and sheep are excluded, but these destroy all seedlings within their reach in winter, and in hard weather rabbits do considerable damage to rowan trees and even to quite large birches in some places near burrows in especially severe conditions of snow and ice. By comparison the deer do no damage. That is not to say that deer do not eat trees. Quite often, especially in spring, when undoubtedly the buds are tastier, we see hinds feeding on the lower branches of birch trees, and even standing on their hind legs to reach these. They sometimes come down off the slightly higher ground, along the hill track, and through the gateway onto the rough road that runs across the farm. It is amusing to see how often the deer hesitate in gateways rather like sheep, peering to see if there is some danger, like small boys with some naughty prank in mind. Once the

leader is through, the others are reassured.

When we have watched deer and then visited the place where we have seen them feeding for some time, or resting, or whatever, it has always astonished us as to how little sign we have found that deer have been present. On a number of occasions we have watched deer for some hours, and indeed a whole afternoon, in a particular comparatively small spot, and next day been astonished at how little evidence of their presence has been left in the form of footprints or droppings, or signs of feeding.

Somehow the markings of deer in winter coat seem to be more uniform than those of summer pelage. Perhaps it is that we do not get such good views of red deer in winter or have the opportunity to study them for such long periods as we do in summer, and thus notice how the coloration of rump patches and dark markings vary so much from animal to animal. In summer I often comment upon how white the inside of the hinds ears look when they are facing straight towards one, and how fluffy are their ears, but the contrast with the generally plumper and sometimes glossy appearance of the winter coat is not so noticeable perhaps. Ears can be a sign of the well-being of red deer and both stags and hinds in poor condition often have grey-coloured bare ears with very little or no hair on them, especially in spring or early summer.

Although mortality in both red deer and roe occurs in winter in hard weather, undoubtedly the critical time for both species is in late winter or early spring, which is April and early May in this area. The roe deaths are less obvious, since the remains of corpses are usually hidden in woods or cover, and probably scattered by foxes and other scavengers, but in some parts of the Highlands the red deer mortality can be quite apparent when a winter of hard, cold weather and snow is followed by a wet spring. The toll then on animals low in condition from undernourishment over the winter can be severe. This may be more noticeable amongst stags that have been unable to recover sufficiently their condition after the loss of weight during the rutting period, and amongst calves whose mothers, low in condition themselves, have been unable to provide sufficient milk to ensure that the calf has been strong enough to survive the rigours of winter. Calves infected by liver fluke and worm burdens may not be fit enough to combat the deleterious effect of these parasites which commonly affect red deer, and it seems likely that the first flush of lush green spring

221

growth may well render deer as liable to Staggers, or Hypomagne-saemia (Magnesium deficiency) as it can do, with fatal consequences, to farm livestock. So, at the time when the countryside is full of optimism and excitement in expectation of new growth and easier seasons of warmer weather and lengthening days, this can also be a period of trauma to the deer.

There is an aphorism that simple pleasures are the last refuge of the sophisticated. In my wildest dreams I could not conceive a claim to being thus, but I recognise the clear truth of that concept. The best things in life are certainly free, if one is so fortunate to perceive these and seek to benefit from them, Nature's wonders far exceed man-made ones. However often we see and watch deer, they still have a magnetism, a fascination, which enthrals us. There are so many questions unanswered, and so much to learn. Each time we see deer we seem to see something new, however tiny or trivial. In trying to learn about the behaviour of these animals there is always the danger of an anthropomorphic conclusion. On the other hand we should recognise that there is a great deal of similarity between the behaviour of mammals. A friend, whose experience of deer must exceed in years most of those still present, told me recently that years ago he advised his son, who was becoming a psychologist, in his early years to watch the behaviour of animals and note similarities. How perceptive and apt was this advice. We may know a great deal now about antler growth, and the influence on this by photoperiod, or daylight length, and hormonal production in the body, but understanding why male deer should annually grow and cast this mass of deciduous bone, a trait unique in the animal world, can only be a matter of speculation. More readily understood is the habit, which may seem strange to many people, of the deer re-consuming antlers when given the oppor-tunity. Indeed many animals will chew antlers and bones. In the woods in the south it is unusual in some areas to find cast antlers of roe, or other species of deer, that have not been gnawed or chewed. Much of this will be by squirrels, but undoubtedly many mice and voles, and perhaps even rabbits will chew antlers and bones as a ready source of calcium. Red deer in the hills may well be short of many minerals, and cast antlers and old bones are a convenient source. Henry Evans, in his splendid little book *Some Account of Jura Red Deer*, mentioned that he had seen deer eating carcasses of other deer that had not completely rotted and still were stinking, and that he had found bits of skin inside the stomachs of beasts that had been shot. This apparent trend to cannibalism is not difficult to appreciate if one understands the demand for protein by the deer in bleak moorland

country, and when one has watched frequently ewes and cows gobbling up their afterbirths soon after parturition in a way that somehow appears unlikely and unseemly in a herbivore. However, many animals chew strange, or smelly, objects out of curiosity, and the apparent predilection of deer for chewing antlers and bones may be influenced thus rather than by a craving for minerals.

A few feet outside our living-room window stand a pair of bird tables, with containers of peanuts and baskets of fat and bones hanging from them. Diana replenishes the food supply daily, and often makes bird cakes from a mixture of fat and crumbs and so on to put on the tables amongst the seeds or with which to fill the tit bells and half coconut shells. The result is that throughout daylight hours in winter there is a constant stream of birds of several varieties to and from the adjacent bushes feeding upon the tables. The proximity of suitable bushes, for cover, near a bird table frequented by sparrowhawks, as ours are, is a necessity of course! Many people come into our living-room and are instantly captivated by the flurry of bird activity outside and the proximity of these. So many people express astonishment at the number of birds and their activity, not merely the townies that come and who probably rarely see, or notice, more than an occasional pigeon or sparrow, but many friends who live in the country and have gardens and plenty of opportunity to derive similar entertainment and fascination from the wildlife outside, but do not bother, and perhaps even are unaware of these wonders of Nature. To us our windows are indeed windows on the world outside, from which we can watch in comfort the activity of many wonderful creatures, not least the deer, without disturbing them from the daily going about of their lives, of seeking food and raising young. We are fortunate to be able to watch deer from our windows, and treasure the opportunity; but this opportunity was not entirely gained by good fortune alone and is rather the result of a goal that we sought to achieve.

# Index